THE FILMS of PAUL NEWMAN

The Films of
PAUL NEWMAN

BY LAWRENCE J. QUIRK

THE CITADEL PRESS   SECAUCUS, NEW JERSEY

First revised edition
Copyright © 1971 by Lawrence J. Quirk
Revised edition copyright © 1981 by Citadel Press
All rights reserved
Published by Citadel Press
A division of Lyle Stuart Inc.
120 Enterprise Ave., Secaucus, N.J. 07094

In Canada: Musson Book Company
A division of General Publishing Co. Limited
Don Mills, Ontario

Manufactured in the United States of America by
Halliday Lithograph, West Hanover, Mass.

Library of Congress Cataloging in Publication Data

Quirk, Lawrence J.
    The films of Paul Newman.

    1. Newman, Paul, 1925-   I. Title.
PN2287.N44Q5   1981   791.43′028′0924   81-38541
  ISBN 0-8065--0783-7   AACR2

To
JAMES E. RUNYAN
The Best Friend I Have Ever Had

ACKNOWLEDGMENTS

With special thanks to Allan J. Wilson for his consistent kindness and moral support through a dozen of my Citadel Press books since 1968; to Arthur Smith for his unfailing efficiency, courtesy and gentlemanliness; and to Florence Washington for many helpful kindnesses over the years; also to Mark Ricci and The Memory Shop, New York; Ernest D. Burns and Cinemabilia, New York; Movie Star News, New York; Kenneth G. Lawrence and the Movie Memorabilia Shop of Hollywood; the staff of the New York Public Library's Theatre & Film Collection, Library and Museum of Performing Arts, Lincoln Center, New York; Academy of Motion Picture Arts & Sciences, Hollywood; Pete Sansone and United Press International, New York; Marty Monroe and Wide World Photos, New York; Warner Bros., Paramount, Columbia, 20th Century-Fox, Universal, Metro-Goldwyn-Mayer, National General-Cinerama, United Artists, ABC, NBC, CBS, and James E. Runyan, Michael Ritzer, Arthur Tower, William Schoell, Douglas Whitney, John Cocchi, Don Koll, Wynn Loewenthal, Stephen Sally, Albert B. Manski, the late Frank Leyendecker, Ray Gain, Robert Burns Gable, John and Lem Amero, Warren Garland, Richard W. Callahan, Fred Trebel, and to various friends, associates and observers of Mr. Paul Newman who prefer not to be named.

Contents

Early in his career.

PAUL NEWMAN:
The Actor And The Man

Paul Newman turns fifty-seven on January 26, 1982. He has been a film actor for twenty-seven years and has appeared in forty-six movies. He is gray now, and lined, but he is still slim and lithe, and his legendary blue eyes glow as fiercely and charismatically as ever. He remains preeminent on the American entertainment scene, as both actor and director, despite the large chunks of time he has reserved for racing cars—an avocation some of his friends and associates consider obsessive.

He calls the shots on his career and makes films when and how he wants, choosing subjects that appeal to him—though the bulk of his choices over the past decade have proved unwise.

For almost twenty-four years, he has remained married to a highly talented actress, Joanne Woodward, who is a legend in her own right but who, for the most part, has displayed the balance and unselfishness to complement rather than combat him, both in his work and in his personal life.

Newman has fathered six children from two marriages. His only son, Scott, died tragically of an accidental overdose of drugs and alcohol in 1978, at twenty-eight. Newman's daughters range in age from thirty to fifteen.

Newman has been tendered a number of Academy Award nominations and has won numerous acting awards. As of the early 1980s he is highly respected for his scandal-free private life and his genuine and sincere concern for liberal political aims and humanitarian ideals. He lives a commonsense, disciplined personal life and in his own nonsentimental, practical way cares deeply about people.

Newman started off as an actor of comparatively narrow range and through quiet persistence and channeled energy has expanded the horizons of his talent to the point where the mannered, gimmicky style of his early years has given way to a mellow, balanced, underplayed acting technique that surpasses in essential eloquence the image of his more flamboyant years.

When he originally came to widespread public notice in his first film, *The Silver Chalice*, in 1954, the twenty-nine-year-old actor was dismissed as a Brando lookalike, another also-ran Actors Studio product from TV and the theatre. He then undertook a slew of film roles that won him increasing respect in Hollywood and with the movie public: the character actor of *Somebody Up There Likes Me*, the tormented introvert of *The Rack*, the glamorous gangster of *The Helen Morgan Story*, the matinee idol of *Until They Sail* and *The Long Hot Summer*, and the young man on the make for love and success of *The Young Philadelphians* and *From the Terrace*.

He tended to get lost in splashy epics like *Exodus*, but when handed an intimate story about an obsessed pool shark, as in *The Hustler*, or a sensitive man probing his own complex inner depths, as in *Cat on a Hot Tin Roof*, or a beach boy mourning the passage of youth as in *Sweet Bird of Youth*, he proved his creative mettle, in spades. Always at his weakest in comedy, he did develop, with patient efforts through the years, a reasonable facility in this genre, though neither Newman nor anyone else expected he would ever catch up with Cary Grant.

Up to a decade ago, he sought out truly creative people—producers, directors, writers, other gifted actors—and spurred them on to solid accomplishment in partnerships that led to fine pictures like *Hud, Cool Hand Luke, Rachel, Rachel,* and *Butch Cassidy and the Sundance Kid,* all produced in the 1960s. In *Hud* he gave a classic portrayal of a thoroughly amoral man. In *Cool Hand Luke,* he delineated with telling impact the anguished but stubborn defiance of a prison-camp loner. In *Rachel, Rachel* he spread his wings as a director for the first time and guided Joanne Woodward through a sensitive study of the buried life in a heart-hungry woman. Even after major stardom had arrived, Newman did not hesitate to take small parts (as, for instance, the battler in Hemingway's *Adventures of a Young Man*), if he thought the role had depth and dimension and offered a challenge.

During the sixties, even his career mistakes were committed with the best of intentions. Going beyond his range at the time, he overreached himself as the bravura-style bandit of *The Outrage* or the 1905 French anarchist of *Lady L*; and in Hitchcock's 1966 *Torn Curtain* he missed the fey nuances and tongue-in-cheek implications of a spy part that Cary Grant in his prime could have waltzed through. But then, with characteristic resilience, Newman would turn around and deliver a marvelously adept delineation of a

Circa 1955.

PAUL NEWMAN:
The Actor And The Man

cool, antihero private eye in *Harper* or underplay with mellow self-assurance the playful and humorous outlaw of *Butch Cassidy and the Sundance Kid* (1969).

Over the years he acquired a reputation as the male sex image par excellence for millions of American women fans, beginning with 1957's *The Helen Morgan Story,* in which, as Larry Maddux, the love-'em-and-leave-'em gangster-bootlegger to whom Ann Blyth passionately sang "The Man I Love," he projected the most potent masculine chemistry and romantic *sangfroid* since Clark Gable. He sustained this image, with variations, through such films as *The Long Hot Summer, The Young Philadelphians, From the Terrace, Sweet Bird of Youth,* and *The Prize,*

though in the 1970s he increasingly went in for character parts as in *Pocket Money, The Life and Times of Judge Roy Bean,* and *Buffalo Bill and the Indians,* possibly in deference to his advancing years.

Yet even now, with age fifty-seven looming up, he is still a sex symbol to millions. Once, years ago, he said of this persistent sex-boat image, "To think that after *Hud* and *Cool Hand Luke* and all the parts I've dug into, I come off as the guy women would most like to go to bed with—it's frightening." He snorts with wry amusement when told that Rachel Ticotin, who played his nurse love-interest in the police drama *Fort Apache, the Bronx,* reportedly said, "It's hard to keep calm before the camera when Paul Newman

With Joanne Woodward

kisses you."

Newman has always prepared for each role with great care, aiming usually to get in two weeks of solid rehearsals before a camera turns. He has advocated plenty of rehearsing because "it gave me a chance not to just sit and intellectualize about a part but to get up on my feet and run through it. If you can rehearse a dozen key scenes with the other actors and get the style and progressison of the character, you've got the part licked."

He usually goes in for on-the-spot research. Back in 1964, for instance, before *The Outrage,* in which he played a Mexican bandit, he lived in Mexico for several weeks, observing the people and the locales and saturating himself in the atmosphere. Before *Hud,* in which he played a young Texas rancher, he visited Texas and lived for a while among ranchers of the type he would portray, trying to catch all the surface nuances and the inner essentials. For *The Long Hot Summer* he went to Clinton, Mississippi, and loafed around beer joints and pool halls, getting the ambience he wanted. He has said, "If I feel that a character is close to me, my homework is minimal. I write voluminous notes to myself on the back of a script. It all breaks down to the way the character walks or uses his hands, his motions

and his movements. I think that once you get the physical quality of a character, the inner person comes by itself."

Nonetheless, even in his mid-fifties, his acting range, despite twenty-seven years of efforts to expand it, remains limited. He accepts this philosophically. "I tried for classics and fell on my face. Let's face it—there are few actors who can avoid limitations. Only the great, great actors have an inexhaustible source of variety. Brando, when he is really on, when he is interested, when he is involved, can do it; so can Olivier, Gielgud, Richardson, Guinness. My wife, Joanne, can do it. But not me."

Oddly enough, Newman has shown himself more truly the artist he has always aspired to be in his directorial stints, most notably when guiding his gifted wife, Joanne Woodward, through admirable films like *The Effect of Gamma Rays on Man-in-the-Moon Marigolds* (1972) and *The Shadow Box,* a television film shown to critical raves in late 1980. "He feels less inhibited behind the camera," a friend has commented. "The deep, sensitive, creative, delicate side of him comes out as a director; as an actor up front, he seems almost ashamed to show it; it makes for an odd personality split, artistically."

Paul Newman was born in Cleveland, Ohio, on

January 26, 1925, the son of Arthur Newman, a prosperous sporting-goods-store owner. His uncle Joe Newman was a well-known Ohio journalist and poet. Paul seems to have had a happy, normal childhood and adolescence, free of physical or psychic traumas. He attended the local elementary schools and Shaker Heights High School, from which he graduated in 1942. Newman then went on to Kenyon College in Gambier, Ohio, but left in 1944 to enlist in the navy. He was then nineteen. Assigned to the V-12 program (a college officer-training program) at Yale, he was eliminated a few months later because of color blindness. For the following two years he served as a radioman, third class, on naval torpedo planes in the Pacific.

Discharged in 1946, he went back to Kenyon, graduating in 1949 with a bachelor of arts degree in English. Relaxed, happy-go-lucky, with a jauntily magnetic personality that appealed to both sexes, he seems to have had (unlike so many artists) a nerve-sound, smooth-flowing youth, untrammeled by feelings of negative uniqueness or melancholy alienation. In college he managed to be in the center of the good times, did his share of girl chasing, cultivated a taste for beer that has never left him, and claims he was graduated "magna cum lager."

The slick masculine charm that was to put millions of women under his spell in, say, *The Young Philadelphians* has its fountainhead in those college years, in which his masculine identity and self-image seem to have been rendered permanently wholesome and positive because of the immediate acceptance he commanded from fellows and girls alike. It is all the more remarkable, then, that living as he did in this atmosphere of wholesome extroversion, and very much a part of it in soul and spirit, he managed, somehow (known to the heart of Paul Newman alone), to distill the insights and sensitivities to the human condition that gave the world the introspective delicacies of *Cat on a Hot Tin Roof* and *The Rack* and the strengthful compassion for humankind that radiates from *The Hustler* and *Cool Hand Luke* and appears in the admirable dramas he has directed for movies and TV. Strange are the ways of the individual artist's development.

In college he was on the football team but was not good at the sport. After participating with his teammates in a barroom brawl, he was kicked off the team and placed on probation. Almost by default he drifted then into campus dramatics, and while running a student laundry, he managed to get into a dozen undergraduate plays. The personal attractiveness that he enjoyed projecting, to win attention and admiration, doubtless provided his original motivation for joining the drama group.

In the summer of 1949, now thoroughly sold on acting, the twenty-four-year-old Newman went to Williams Bay, Wisconsin, where he cut his teeth on such plays as *The Glass Menagerie* and *The Candlestick Maker*. That autumn he joined the Woodstock Players in Woodstock, Illinois, where he appeared in sixteen plays. About this time he met an attractive young actress named Jackie Witte, fell in love, and married. His first child, Scott, was born in 1950.

In 1950, Newman's father died, and Paul found himself obliged to return to Cleveland, where he was soon in charge of the family sporting-goods store. The next year was perhaps the unhappiest of his life. Years later, he told a reporter, "When I decided to go into acting, I wasn't 'searching for my identity.' I didn't have grease paint in my blood. I was just running away from the family retail business—and from merchandising. I just couldn't find any romance in it. Acting was a happy alternative to a way of life that meant nothing to me." On another occasion he said of this period, "I was very successful at being something that I was not, and that is the worst thing that can happen to a man."

In 1951 he cut out of the business, took his share and savings and his wife and small son and went off to New Haven, to the Yale School of Drama. He remained a year, winning a master's degree in drama. He appeared in various plays while there, winning the attention of New York agents and scouts. He also won the respect and approbation of his instructors, who advised him, in 1952, to go to New York and seek a career without delay. Thanks to his independent income, he was able to shortcircuit the usual harsh struggle that often comes at this point in an actor's life.

In New York, his evident talent and personal aplomb, along with his solid background and good connections, soon got him into several tele-

A 1969 appearance on television as Guide for "From Here to the Seventies."

vision shows. By September 1952, he had a running part in *The Aldrich Family,* and soon TV executives were taking increasing note of him. Like other young TV actors, he ran the gauntlet of Philco, U.S. Steel, *Playhouse 90,* etc.

Parts in "The Web," "The Mask,"· and "You Are There" were followed by substantial TV leads, and the critics grew increasingly kind. In the musical version of *Our Town* he co-starred with Eva Marie Saint and Frank Sinatra. In "The Battler," an adaptation for TV of an Ernest Hemingway story, he gave a first-class portrayal of a punch-drunk old pug. Newman's rendition followed the pug's regression, via flashbacks, from a cocky and unbeatable young champion of twenty to the untamable prison tough of thirty to the panhandler of forty and the bum of fifty-

five whose mind and body have deteriorated to the point where he is little more than a vegetable. It was a tour de force. J. P. Shanley in *The New York Times* said of it: "Paul Newman had to surmount grotesque makeup but was quite effective."

Critic Harriet Van Horne said of his live one-hour performance in *Kaiser Aluminium Hour's* "The Army Game": "Acting and production were excellent with special honors going to Paul Newman as the distraught private." His reviews for *U.S. Steel Hour's* Theatre Guild presentation, "Bang the Drum Slowly," in which he played a baseball player, were also good. In *U.S. Steel Hour's* "Five Fathers of Pepi," about an orphan boy who is cared for by five Italian merchants, Newman had a chance to deliver an Italian char-

14

acterization. *The New York Times*'s Jack Gould said of him: "Mr. Newman was very pensive and has great big eyes."

Later he did "The Eighty-yard Run" for *Playhouse 90,* with Joanne Woodward and Darryl Hickman. David Shaw had made a ninety-minute script from a short story by his brother Irwin Shaw. The plot dealt with a man unhappy in his career and his marriage who recalls the greatest moment of his life—his eighty-yard run in a college football game. *The New York Times* termed it "absorbing" and Newman's and Woodward's performances "excellent."

Newman worked most intensively in television in the early and mid-fifties—before the era of taped and filmed shows.

Newman later said, "TV was exciting because it was live. Men like Tad Mosel and Paddy Chayefsky and Max Shulman were writing for television, and they made it an inventive era. Call it kitchen sink, inner search, what have you—it was great." He added, "The trouble was, as it turned out, that what could have been good Broadway plays were burned out in a single night on *Robert Montgomery Presents, Philco Playhouse, Studio One,* and the rest of them. That whole glorious period of television has disappeared." (By the 1960's Newman was rarely, if ever, seen on TV, except in his movies, but in 1963 he did narrate a USIA film, *Bridge to the Barrios,* and in 1969 he served as narrator for *From Here to the Seventies,* an NBC News two-

At time of arrest in Mineola, Long Island, on charges of leaving the scene of an accident and passing a red light. This was in 1956, during a time of great personal unhappiness

and-a-half-hour special exploring the United States then and in the coming decade).

Also in the early and mid-fifties, Newman studied intensively at the Actors Studio. In 1956 he said, "If I've shown any development as an actor, it's mostly to be credited to the Actors Studio and my work there under Lee Strasberg. In fact, I still consider myself a student, and whenever I am in New York, I attend classes twice a week."

Toward the close of 1952, Newman was signed by the Theatre Guild for his first Broadway play, William Inge's *Picnic*. He opened on Broadway on February 19, 1953, and, under Joshua Logan's taut, sharp direction, gave an excellent supporting performance as Alan Seymour, the well-meaning but unimaginative rich boy who loses his girl (Janice Rule) to a physically magnetic ex-classmate (Ralph Meeker) who upsets the lives of those around him in a small Kansas town. The critics responded well to Newman, and his performance garnered such accolades as "well played" and "excellent."

During the run of this play, he met and formed a friendship with Joanne Woodward, who was understudying both Janice Rule's and Kim Stanley's roles. The camaraderie of co-workers progressed into a sterling friendship, which in turn evolved into a passionate romance that was to endure through five years under trying circumstances.

During this period, Newman and Woodward made every effort to keep their growing mutual love dignified and decent. Newman was anxious about the possible effect of divorce on his three children, and he wanted to spare his wife's feelings as much as possible and to spare Joanne any unnecessary hurt. There is reason to believe that this was Paul Newman's first major encounter with genuine unhappiness, and nothing in his hitherto upbeat life had prepared him for dealing with it. Of his breakup with his first wife he once said, "I feel guilty as hell about it, and I will carry that guilt for the rest of my life."

Under such stresses, Newman did not always use the wisest self-control. On the night of July 7, 1956, he was picked up by the Mineola, Long Island, police for passing a red light and leaving the scene of an accident in which he destroyed some shrubbery and a fire hydrant. He reportedly gave the police a hard time and was brought handcuffed to the station and jailed. His picture *Somebody Up There Likes Me,* in which he portrayed fighter Rocky Graziano, had just opened. The story is that he told patrolman Rocco Caggiano, "I'm acting for Rocky Graziano. What do you want?" and Caggiano snapped, "I'm Rocky, too, and you're under arrest for leaving the scene of an accident."

His treatment by the press during these years left him hostile and defensive, and he tended to guard his private life zealously, sometimes to the point of paranoia. In fairness, it should be noted that in the years since, neither he nor Woodward has garnered the slightest bit of sensational publicity of any kind. Whatever dark night of the soul he knew at that time, it was, in comparative terms, mercifully brief.

Joanne Woodward was born in Thomasville, Georgia, on February 27, 1930, the daughter of wealthy book-publishing executive Wade Woodward, who later became a vice-president of Charles Scribner's Sons. Her parents had been divorced, and years later she told a reporter of the emotional suffering this had brought upon her, adding, "Because of this, I have been more than careful about getting married."

When she was fifteen her family settled in Greenville, South Carolina. In high school she became intensely interested in amateur theatricals. Despite her reticence on the subject, there is reason to believe that her early life was lonely and unhappy in some ways. Encouraged by her high school dramatic coach, who sensed in her the depths of feeling and the instincts of a true actress, she studied for two years at Louisiana State University and then returned to Greenville, where she appeared in a little-theatre production of *The Glass Menagerie.* She then persuaded her parents to let her go to New York. For two years she studied at the Neighborhood Playhouse, then at the Actors Studio (where Newman also studied). Then she began accepting TV engagements, along with the understudy spot in *Picnic.*

During the run of *Picnic,* Newman was offered a long-term Warner Bros. contract at $1,000 a week, and he accepted it. He went to Hollywood in early 1954, and Woodward followed later in the year, having obtained a contract with 20th Century-Fox. Newman made his debut in Warners' *The Silver Chalice* under Victor Saville's direction. A turgid costume drama, in which he played a Greek slave with sculpturing talent transported to ancient Rome, he found himself awash in a complicated plot dealing with Pagan-Christian conflicts. *The Silver Chalice* was, in Newman's opinion, one of the worst pictures of its decade, and it embarrassed him so much that about ten years later, when they put it on TV in Los Angeles, he took out ads in the newspapers apologizing for it. This only served at the time to call added attention to the rerun of his maiden film effort, and that night it ran up a very high rating. Newman recalls that when he saw the film for the first time, "I was horrified, traumatized."

During this period everyone began noting *ad nauseam* how much like Marlon Brando he looked. He once declared in exasperation to an interviewer, "Someday, dammit, they're going to say that Marlon Brando looks like *me!*" Typical of the less charitable reviews for his first film was

the one by *The New Yorker*'s John McCarten, who wrote waspishly, "Paul Newman delivers his lines with the emotional fervor of a Putnam Division conductor announcing local stops."

The film was released in late 1954. Early 1955 found Newman, presumably still in a state of trauma, back in New York, this time on Broadway in a substantial part as the demented gangster in Joseph Hayes's exciting and fast-paced *The Desperate Hours,* with Karl Malden, Nancy Coleman, and George Grizzard. Under Robert Montgomery's capable directorial guidance, Newman offered an excellent performance as one of three escaped convicts who invade the home of a respectable couple with two children and terrorize them while awaiting get-away money. Newman, as Glenn Griffin, the gangster who hated his father and transferred his hate to Malden, his hapless victim, received his best reviews yet, typical among them that of John Chapman,

Training with former middleweight champ Tony Zale for Rocky Graziano role in *Somebody Up There Likes Me.*

With Joanne Woodward on their wedding day in 1958.

who styled his performance "splendid; tensely maniacal." This solid triumph helped take the bad taste of *The Silver Chalice* out of his mouth.

Newman continued to busy himself with Actors Studio work and TV projects he considered worthwhile. However, the Warner Bros. contract had to be fulfilled, and he reluctantly resumed film work. Warners, with nothing tailored to his measure on hand, decided on a temporary loan-out policy for him. In the best tradition of those stormy Warner rebels of yore, Bette Davis and James Cagney, Newman soon developed a prime set of beefs against the studio, which paid him only his standard $1,000 per week while renting him out for $75,000 each film.

A plum then fell into his hands—the role of Rocky Graziano, the boxer who rose from the depths to success. The film was *Somebody Up There Likes Me,* under Robert Wise's direction for Metro-Goldwyn-Mayer. In typical preparatory style, Newman spent two weeks with Graziano, studying his every mannerism and absorbing and incorporating into his own creative scheme

the primary personality facets of the man. When the film was released in the summer of 1956, his performance was hailed for its characterizational integrity and raw power, and it turned him overnight into the year's brightest new star.

Again on a loan-out deal to Metro-Goldwyn-Mayer, he did *The Rack,* in which he was affecting and powerful as a sensitive young Army captain, on trial for treason, whose will was broken by subtle Communist brainwashing that exposed his secret weaknesses. Still another film at Metro, in 1957, under Wise's direction, was *Until They Sail,* with Jean Simmons. In this he played a young U.S. Marine captain, rendered cynical by a broken marriage, who finds love with a lonely war widow. The distaff audience began to sit up and take notice of Newman in this, for his role— and the way he fit it—was cut from matinee-idol cloth. Then it was back to his home studio, Warner Bros., for *The Helen Morgan Story,* in which he projected so much male magnetism and taut authority as Larry, a gangster and bootlegger who did his gal, Ann Blyth's Helen Morgan, dirt while periodically bedding her, that he had become by the end of 1957 a matinee idol as well as an increasingly respected actor.

Meanwhile, Woodward was with Newman constantly in Hollywood. His divorce was final, and the gossip columnists insisted (rightly) that their marriage was imminent. Woodward had appeared on Broadway briefly in 1956 in *The Lovers* and had made a so-so start in films with *Count Three and Pray* and *A Kiss Before Dying* and *No Down Payment,* but suddenly she was handed a superb role, as a woman afflicted with three personalities, in *Three Faces of Eve.* This won her the 1957 Academy Award, thus assuring her career in Hollywood.

On January 29, 1958, Newman married Woodward at Hotel El Rancho Vegas, in Las Vegas, after which they left immediately for New York and a European honeymoon. Just prior to marrying, they had starred together for the first time on the screen in Jerry Wald's production of *The Long Hot Summer,* based on some of William Faulkner's fiction. When the film was released in early 1958, the reviews were quite good, with *Time* describing Newman's performance in it as "keen as a crackle-edged scythe," in his role of Ben Quick, the pushy young redneck who woos and wins Clara Varner (Woodward), the daughter of Southern oligarch Will Varner, played in his usually grandiose and arresting style by Orson Welles. This was Newman's first film, incidentally, with director Martin Ritt, with whom he was to have a rewarding creative relationship.

Again back at Warners, and with the Cannes Film Festival Prize as Best Actor of 1958 for *Long Hot Summer* on his shelf (he was the only American honored that year), Newman worked with producer Fred Coe and director Arthur Penn, both from TV, on *The Left-Handed Gun,* a screen adaptation of Gore Vidal's teleplay *The Death of Billy the Kid.* Though it opened to mixed reviews and did poor business at the time of its first release, *The Left-Handed Gun* has found its own cult audience since. The film, which was in some ways ahead of its time, attempted to break new ground in its delineation of Billy the Kid's character as that of a mixed-up adolescent with basically good instincts. Newman's performance was a complex, mannered

one, subtly conceived.

For his next picture, at Metro-Goldwyn-Mayer, Newman won his first Academy Award nomination. As Brick, the inwardly tormented young heir to a Southern estate who is at loggerheads with his wife and his father and is blocked by guilts connected with the suicide of a cherished friend, Newman turned in a delicately shaded performance of varying moods. Elizabeth Taylor, who starred with him as his neglected young wife, won a nomination for this also, her performance being especially hailed because her husband, Mike Todd the producer, had died in a plane crash while the film was in production. There was criticism of director-writer Richard Brooks's elimination of the homosexual theme and other Williams elements that had made the Broadway play so piercing and true, but for Taylor and Newman, the film represented a decisive step forward in their careers.

From Metro-Goldwyn-Mayer, Newman went again on loan-out to 20th Century-Fox, this time for *Rally 'Round the Flag, Boys!* a comedy, again with Joanne Woodward, in which he was guided by Leo McCarey. This spoof of suburban living, from the Max Shulman novel, in which Newman is forced to contend with his wife's disregard of her marital duties and the temptations seductive neighbor Joan Collins offers, indicated rather pointedly that Newman's gifts for comical satire were distinctly limited.

Then it was back to Warners again for the last picture he ever made there under his original contract. This was the film version of the Richard Powell novel *The Philadelphian.* As *The Young Philadelphians,* it attractively show-cased Newman in one of the roles with which he was to become strongly identified, the sleek, slick young man on the make for success and women who always seemed to land on his feet like a cat and waded through all obstacles with brazen insouciance. Vincent Sherman guided the fast-paced script, and though it was commercially oriented, the film did have its moments.

In 1959, Newman arranged to buy up his Warner Bros. contract for $500,000, a radical, but in his view necessary, decision that set him back financially for some years. Recalling this, years later, he referred again to the niggardly $17,500 he got for his last Warner picture, while the

Studying a script with Joanne Woodward in 1958.

studio had loaned him out at $75,000, thus exploiting his talent for profit. When Warners reneged on an outside picture they had promised to let him do, he told Jack Warner off, in no uncertain terms. "And this," Newman recalled, "was early in the game, when I really couldn't afford to tell him off. But I really didn't give a damn."

At this time (early 1959) he had returned again to Broadway in Tennessee Williams's *Sweet Bird of Youth,* opposite Geraldine Page, under Elia Kazan's direction. Reviewers wrote that he played the beach boy Chance Wayne (to Miss Page's fading movie star, Alexandra del Lago) for all it was worth, and the play was an enormous hit both critically and with the public.

While he was still appearing in the play, he was moonlighting days in 20th Century-Fox's film version of John O'Hara's *From the Terrace,* once more with Joanne Woodward. As Alfred Eaton, he was again a young man on the make who eventually becomes disillusioned with the success rat race and leaves his rich wife (Miss Woodward) for a simple, affectionate girl (Ina Balin). The picture did not do well, being regarded as flimsy and poorly motivated and not true-blue O'Hara.

With this, their third picture together, the young Newmans were becoming increasingly known as another Spencer Tracy–Katharine Hepburn combine. Certainly their respective chemistries blended tellingly, on as well as off screen, and their acting together had a naturalness and a reality that were very attractive. Woodward obviously understands Newman's temperament and creative genie better than anyone he has ever known, and vice versa. He has styled her "the last of the great broads." They

Joanne Woodward on the night she
won the Oscar in 1958.

had become parents of a daughter, Eleanor, in
1959, and Woodward, though she continued to
be a working actress *(The Sound and the Fury,
The Fugitive Kind),* shrewdly subordinated her
own career to her husband's and functioned as
his chief booster.

In 1960, Newman, Woodward, and their baby
girl went to Israel, where Newman began work
on Leon Uris's *Exodus* for Otto Preminger. This
bestselling property concerned the Israeli fight
for independence in 1947, with Newman playing
the Hagannah leader Ari Ben Canaan. Eva Marie
Saint, Peter Lawford, Jill Haworth, and Sal Mineo
were also in the picture. Despite its large cast
and lavish production, *Exodus* did not do well,
and Newman's critics said he had failed to exude
heroic stature and hadn't put sufficient depth and
humanity into his role.

Exodus proved only a temporary setback, for
next Newman joined forces with producer-direc-
tor Robert Rossen for *The Hustler* at 20th Century-Fox. Filmed in New York, the picture
displayed Newman as a drifting pool shark who
is temporarily redeemed by love. Piper Laurie
gave an effective performance opposite him, and
George C. Scott was impressively sinister as his
bête noire. This time he won enthusiastic critical
approval, and his portrait of a man obsessed with
pool, but self-destructive in love, won him another
Academy Award nomination.

Later in 1961, Newman teamed again with
Joanne Woodward and director Martin Ritt for
Paris Blues, with Sidney Poitier and Diahann
Carroll co-starring. Despite his creative affinity
with Ritt, both came a cropper this time, the
problem being a weak story. It was a paper-thin
tale of two jazz musicians in Paris who must
choose between love for their American girl-

friends or the pursuit of their careers. Newman elects for the career, Poitier for his girl. Louis Armstrong and Duke Ellington provided some memorable musical moments, but the critics shrugged off the picture as insubstantial fluff.

Next, Newman went back to Metro-Goldwyn-Mayer for the film version of his hit 1959 play *Sweet Bird of Youth,* again with Geraldine Page, and with Rip Torn and Madeleine Sherwood repeating their Broadway roles. Again Richard Brooks was assigned to tackle a film rendition of a Williams theme (as he had with *Cat on a Hot Tin Roof),* and once more Brooks fell afoul of the critics for emasculating Williams's conceptions in deference to the Production Code and the then woefully immature standards of Hollywood producers, who felt that tacked-on happy endings and roseate divorcement from reality (especially Williams reality) were what audiences wanted. Though Page managed to deter Brooks from tampering too much with her role of the fading film star who has sought refuge in alcohol, hashish, and kept boys, Newman's role suffered somewhat in the general watering down.

Still, he garnered such adjectives as "excellent" and "very good," though his chronic mannerisms were commented upon and the total effect was not what he had hoped. Significantly, Newman did not receive an Oscar nomination for this film. His defenders feel that if the picture had been done as it was on the stage, he might have won a nomination *and* an Oscar.

Next, at 20th Century-Fox, Newman repeated his TV role of the battler in *Hemingway's Adventures of a Young Man.* As the punch-drunk old fighter who has descended to the status of a dim-brained bum, he and his faithful sidekick (Juano Hernandez) encounter Richard Beymer during Beymer's episodic wanderings as the young Hemingway. The critics commended Newman's sterling character performance, which called for an authentic submergence of his own personality, and also praised him for undertaking a brief but meaty part even though he was a ranking star.

Newman then went over to Paramount for *Hud* with director Martin Ritt. The highly creative and galvanic collaboration of the two led this time to a smash hit with both critics and public and another Oscar nomination for New-

man as the amoral young Texas rancher who essentially cares only for himself. In *Hud* Newman was right as rain in a film that refused any compromise with truth. Patricia Neal went on to win the Academy Award for her wise and womanly performance as the housekeeper who is attracted to Hud but understands him only too well and resists him. The critics and the public began to wonder at this point if Newman weren't being passed over for the Oscar with suspicious frequency, and the rumor gained credence that Hollywood politics was doing him wrong. Since his clash with Jack Warner, Newman had always been classified as a rebel and loner who called the shots as he saw them, and he had also frankly and publicly stated his preference for the East as a domicile. Reportedly all this did not go well with the denizens of the studios, and voter blocs from various studios reportedly combined to defeat him at times when his performance was better than that of the year's winners.

Newman has said of his always-a-best-man-never-the-groom relationship with the Oscar: "I'd like to win about sixty-nine nominations—I think that's an interesting number—and at the age of ninety, crawl on my hands and knees, ridden with arthritis, to pick up an Oscar. That would be kind of stylish. It's nice to be nominated, but I don't think my life will be incomplete if I never win an Oscar."

Certainly his next picture after *Hud* wasn't calculated to win him one. Again he went from a sterling winner to an abject loser. And again Woodward shared in a turkey (she had not had a *good* picture with her husband since *The Long Hot Summer).* The picture was 1963's *A New Kind of Love,* directed and written by Melville Shavelson, a silly and inconsequential comedy laid in Paris, having to do with a woman-chasing journalist and a drab ugly duckling who goes glamorous and lassoes him. The picture was long on comedy gags and photographic gimmicks and short on genuine wit or substantial story, and once again the critics called attention to Newman's inability to master comedy. No Rock Hudson and Doris Day, let alone Cary Grant and Irene Dunne, were they, though Woodward came over as more of a comedy "natural" than did her husband.

Nor did Newman's final 1963 picture, *The*

Prize, fare any better. An inane and insubstantial blend of adventure and romance, laid against a background of Nobel Prize awards in Stockholm and based on a somewhat fustian novel by Irving Wallace, the film showcased Newman as a tippling, womanizing novelist who sets out to solve the kidnapping of one of his fellow prizewinners, a physicist, by the Russians. Again Newman was called upon to do comedy scenes, and Mark Robson proved no more adept at guiding Newman through the intricacies of Cary Grant–style farce than McCarey or Shavelson had been. One hopefully amusing scene featured a half-nude Newman in a nudist colony, and, as usual, critical attention was called to the grim heavy-handedness with which Newman went about a situation of which David Niven could have made capital. The adventure stuff in the film was shrugged off by the reviewers as silly and poorly motivated.

His next was *What a Way to Go!* an episodic farce about a millionairess (Shirley MacLaine) who keeps losing her husbands via inane situations and bizarre deaths. Playing the second of MacLaine's five husbands, Newman appeared as a Paris painter who invents a machine that converts music into paintings. Though he becomes a successful and lionized artist, he eventually gets himself caught in the mechanism of the machine and is killed. For this stint neither he nor Mac-Laine garnered particularly enthusiastic reviews, nor did the picture, which the reviewers fobbed off as forced in humor and an overblown production. Some critics, however, noted a slight improvement in Newman's comedy style.

That same year, 1964, Newman and Woodward went back to the New York stage, in the off-Broadway James Costigan play *Baby Want a Kiss.* In this they essayed the roles of a phony Hollywood married couple, famed movie stars, who visit a less successful writer friend (played by Costigan) and disillusion him with their garish insincerities and sexual rapacity. For this play Newman garnered the best comedic reviews he had ever known, thanks, it was rumored, to director Frank Corsaro's shrewd guidance as well as his own hard work. Woodward was also well received, but the play, which they did on a limited run to benefit their beloved Actors Studio,

With Shirley MacLaine in 1967, when both were presented with "Best Actor-Actress of the year" awards from the National Association of Theatre Owners.

23

With actor Claude Dauphin and director Peter Ustinov during his fortieth birthday celebration (1965) on the set of *Lady L* in Paris.

fared less well.

In the early sixties the Newmans had settled down permanently in the New York area, living at various times in their New York apartment, their converted carriage house in Westport, Connecticut, and their California home, used on trips to Hollywood. Newman's three oldest children, Scott, Susan, and Stephanie (by his first wife), spent much time with them on visits, and by 1965 Newman and Woodward had three daughters, Eleanor. Melissa, and Cara.

Once again, Newman and Martin Ritt teamed for the picture in which Newman feels he gave his best performance, *The Outrage*. Based on the Japanese movie *Rashomon* and the stage vehicle of the same name, it dealt with the differing tales told by assorted witnesses concerning an alleged murder of a nineteenth-century Western traveler and the rape of his wife. Both crimes were allegedly perpetrated by a bandit, played by Newman. The film purported to present, in heightened form, the many aspects of truth. Though the role was a bravura one and afforded Newman many mood changes and a range of approaches, and though he had researched it thoroughly in his usual manner, studying assorted Mexican types and living among them, the critics opined that he played it much too broadly and with too many gimmicks, one reviewer even comparing him to the late Leo Carrillo, who in the thirties specialized in garishly played Mexican types.

Talk continued about Newman's limited range and his insistence on undertaking roles beyond his proper sphere of appeal, and once again he did it in *Lady L,* made early in 1965 but not released until 1966, after *Harper,* reportedly to take tail-end advantage of the latter picture's phenomenal success. *Lady L,* from the Romain Gary novel, displayed Newman as an anarchist and revolutionary in 1905 Paris who robs the rich, Robin Hood style, to help the poor. He becomes involved with a laundress (Sophia

Loren), who later becomes the wife of a British nobleman, retaining Newman as her lover for the next fifty years. Consensus of the critics' reaction to this was *The New Yorker*'s observation that Newman's performance seemed "about as far from Paris and anarchism as, say, Akron and the Young Republicans are." Newman and David Niven were, moveover, by the nature of their roles overshadowed by Loren, whose part was the centerpiece. But even she did not escape criticism.

Newman had a stroke of luck in having *Harper,* his next picture, released before *Lady L,* for at this point he badly needed a smash hit. Newman showed himself surprisingly adept in a role perfectly tailored to his measure. As the antihero private eye who is no better than he should be but has a thorough understanding of life and people, he wanders through Los Angeles' lower depths seeking the kidnapper of a millionaire. His performance was compared favorably to those Humphrey Bogart had done in the genre, and for good measure, the former Mrs. Bogart, Lauren Bacall, was on hand as the millionaire's wife who hates him and hopes he has been killed. Janet Leigh, Robert Wagner, Julie Harris, and a particularly strong cast (highlighted by Shelley Winters's performance as a boozing ex-

star) delivered sterling performances in a taut, entertaining thriller that perfectly blended excitement, comedy, and suspense.

This was Newman's first picture at Warners in seven years. But he had come back in different circumstances, as a superstar in a relatively independent position and with a percentage of the film's profits. His old adversary Jack Warner came down during rehearsals, and photos were taken of the two smiling together. Later, Newman used one of the photos on Christmas cards, with the line "Peace on Earth—Good Will Toward Men," and sent one to Warner. In later years he referred to Warner as a vulgarian, mentioning that Warner referred to Joanne Woodward as Joan.

Next Newman co-starred with Julie Andrews, under Alfred Hitchcock's direction, in *Torn Curtain,* which proved conclusively that the Hitchcock and Newman talents did not blend. Hitchcock had obviously expected another Cary Grant–Ingrid Bergman team in the Newman-Andrews combination, but both stars lacked the tongue-in-cheek, gossamer-spirited approach needed to lift this turgid story of behind-the-iron-curtain intrigue off the ground. The reviewers complained that Newman and Andrews played the leads too literally, as if they really intended

Named with Natalie Wood the world's favorite actor and actress at the 23rd Annual Golden Globe Awards Banquet in 1966.

25

With director Alfred Hitchcock and Julie Andrews on the set of *Torn Curtain.*

20th Century-Fox. The two had evolved a loose collaborative arrangement in which they worked together in projects that particularly excited them. Screenwriters Irving Ravetch and Harriet Frank, Jr., who had collaborated on a number of Newman pictures by now, joined them for this. The cast was strong: Fredric March, Richard Boone, Diane Cilento, Cameron Mitchell, Barbara Rush, and Martin Balsam. Newman was colorful if taciturn in his role of John Russell, a white man who had been kidnapped in childhood by the Indians and raised as one of them and who proves himself the only resourceful and courageous passenger on a stage coach held up by bandits. The story implied the need for tolerance, but reviews were mixed, some calling Newman's performance "versatile" and others "implausible." Around this time the jokes became more frequent regarding Newman's penchant for films with titles beginning with the letter *H* (*The Hustler, Hud,* and *Harper* among them).

Newman then went on to a film that many consider his high-water mark as an actor. Based on a hard-hitting novel by Donn Pearce, who had personally known the horrors of Southern prison camps, and directed in taut, tough style by Stuart Rosenberg, *Cool Hand Luke* presents Newman as a convict loner who wins the men's respect by his defiance of the guards and who eventually pays with his life for his independence of spirit. Bosley Crowther of *The New York Times* was in the vanguard of critical approbation, calling Newman "superb" in this. Again it was noted that when properly cast, Newman could deliver in superior style, and he had never been in better form than in this role in which, as a critic noted, he was called upon to be "funny, stalwart, submissive, defiant, pathetic and eventually tragic." Donn Pearce acted a bit as one of the convicts and, by serving as technical advisor, helped lend a unique authenticity.

Newman unwisely chose, in his next film, *The Secret War of Harry Frigg,* to return to the type of comedy role in which he was not at his best. The film was a slight and silly affair about a kooky private in World War II whose ability to escape from stockades results in his being drafted by the army to rescue four Allied generals from Axis imprisonment. When he falls in love with the attractive countess (Sylva Koscina) in whose

to extract a missile secret from an East German scientist, nor was Hitchcock regarded in this, his fiftieth picture, as being at the top of his form. Newman, perhaps defensively, professes utter disdain for the film.

Ever restless for challenging and unique parts, Newman next did *Hombre* with Martin Ritt for castle they are waylaid, the rescue operation slows down. The double-g in the surname of the title character was castigated as a vulgar box-office ploy, and the Newman tendency to be grim when he should have been fey was, as usual, given its share of comment.

Joanne Woodward had meanwhile been making occasional films without her husband (*A Fine Madness, A Big Hand for the Little Lady,* etc.), and she and writer Stuart Rosenberg came upon a novel, *A Jest of God,* by Margaret Laurence, that she very much wanted to do as a labor of love. It was a simple story about the quiet heroism in an unsung, humble life, in this case the life of a Connecticut schoolteacher who at thirty-five feels that life is passing her by and who reaches out frantically for love, only to know disillusionment. Rosenberg did a screenplay, but he and Woodward experienced tremendous difficulty in securing backing for it, since the story was not considered box office. Newman got interested in the project, secured the necessary financing, and shot it in five weeks in Connecticut.

Of this picture, *Rachel, Rachel,* his first as a director, Newman said: "It singles out the unspectacular heroism of the sort of person you wouldn't even notice if you passed him on the street. The steps the characters take are really the steps that humanity takes—not the Churchills, not the Roosevelts, not the Napoleons, but the little people who cast no shadow and leave no footprints. Maybe it can encourage the people who see it to take those little steps in life that can lead to something bigger. Maybe they *won't,* but the point of the movie is that you've got to take the steps, regardless of the consequences." Newman, of course, understood his wife's nature and potentialities so well that he got an unusually responsive and sensitive performance from her, with the result that she won her first Academy Award nomination since her Oscar-winning year, 1957, and she received the award of the New York film critics, to boot. The New York film critics also honored Newman as best director of 1968 for the film.

Winning, released in the first half of 1969, represented the first joint project of Newman, Joanne Woodward, and John Foreman, under the corporate title The Newman-Foreman Company. (In the years that immediately followed,

Newman's assorted corporate wheelings and dealings proved somewhat confusing to follow, allying himself as he did with 20th Century-Fox, Paramount, and Universal in turn, and adding new partners along the way, with various new names for the associations as they evolved. In June 1969 Newman announced, along with Barbra Streisand and Sidney Poitier, the formation of First Artists Production Company Ltd. This company arranged for the distribution of the films in which all three would appear. For some time, Newman had been in the one-million-dollar-per-picture category [as of 1981 he made as high as three million dollars a picture], with

With Donn Pearce, writer, technical advisor and ex-prison camp inmate, on the set of *Cool Hand Luke,* 1967.

With Joanne Woodward and Henry Fonda on the set of their picture, *A Big Hand for the Little Lady,* 1965.

advantageous profits percentages thrown into the package. Financial and corporate affairs, the bane of all superstars, began to take up much of his time.)

Winning turned out to be a solid, suspenseful racing drama with a deeply human story deftly intertwined. Newman and Woodward portray a racing driver and his wife who have drifted apart because of the preoccupying stresses of his career, resulting in her infidelity with another racer, Robert Wagner. The Newmans, in their seventh picture in eleven years, won favorable reviews from the·critics, who had obviously developed a new respect and admiration for the couple's persistent efforts to increase quality in pictures. One typical review stated, "The driver and his woman come vividly alive, thanks to the Newmans' ability to create flesh-and-blood people."

Universal had released *Winning.* Then, under the auspices of the George Roy Hill–Paul Monash (Campanile) producing group, Newman co-starred for a 20th Century-Fox release with Robert Redford, *Butch Cassidy and the Sundance Kid,* based quite loosely on the legend of two famed Western outlaws of 1905 vintage. The film presented Butch (Newman) and the Kid (Redford) in human—and humorous—terms. A new facet of Newman's acting skills, first manifest to viewers in *Winning,* again made its presence felt: his ability to underplay. In *Butch Cassidy and the Sundance Kid* his style was mellow and light, with many humorous episodes to highlight this zany yet poignant study of two outlaws of individual stamp who had outlived their day. The picture was a signal triumph for both stars, and it was noted that Newman, relaxed and

Arriving with daughter Susan for the 1968 Academy Awards presentations.

mellow as never before, had all but handed the picture to Redford with the subtle understatement of his playing.

Newman next put his production group under Paramount's auspices. Under the banner of Rosenberg-Newman-Foreman productions and with Stuart Rosenberg directing, he did *WUSA*, which dealt with the problems of an itinerant disk jockey who got mixed up in the political activities of a conservative radio station. Joanne Woodward, Anthony Perkins, and Laurence Harvey co-starred. The picture was based on Robert Stone's novel *A Hall of Mirrors,* and the screenplay was written by Stone. A study of neofascism in this country, it was passionately defended by Newman but drew mixed reviews.

Newman went on to *Sometimes a Great Notion,* with John Foreman producing and Richard Colla directing. It was shot on location in Oregon, with Henry Fonda, Lee Remick, and Michael Sarrazin in the cast, and dealt with a colorful logging family. Halfway through the shooting,

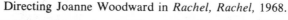

Directing Joanne Woodward in *Rachel, Rachel,* 1968.

Newman broke his ankle in a fall from a motorcycle. This necessitated closing down the project, with five weeks left to go. Later Richard Colla withdrew and Newman took over the direction. This became the second film for Newman as director, and at the time he began making public statements to the effect that as an actor he might be running out of steam and had difficulty finding parts that were not retreads of characterizations he had already given.

Meanwhile the Newman-Foreman Company also completed *They Might Be Giants,* starring Woodward and George C. Scott. (She played a psychiatrist, Scott a problem patient.) At that same time *Sometimes a Great Notion* opened to so-so reviews.

In April 1971 Newman was seen on television as the star of *Once Upon a Wheel,* an ABC-TV network special that explored the excitement and dangers of automobile racing. An ardent racing fan since *Winning* got him interested, Newman served as narrator and participant in this behind-the-scenes analysis of a popular American sport and the men who engage in it. The special was filmed on location at various racetracks in California and North Carolina, the Indianapolis Speedway, the Soap Box Derby in Ohio, and the Nuremberg, Germany, racing track, among others. Various racing champions appeared on the special, and such stars as James Garner, Kirk Douglas, and Glenn Ford did cameo spots as participants in a Pro-Am event at the Ontario Motor Speedway in California.

In the early 1970s, in addition to branching

Receiving the New York Film Critics Award for best director, for *Rachel, Rachel,* 1969. Joanne Woodward, at right, won best actress award for same film.

Awarded the William J. German Human Relations Award of the American Jewish Committee from producer Mike Frankovich, 1969. Award also went to Joanne Woodward, center.

out with corporate and racing activities, Newman took an ever-increasing interest in politics and public service, as well as assorted humanitarian activities. He claimed that he would never run for public office because he understood his limitations of temperament and was satisfied to stay within them. He added, though, that as an American citizen who was interested in, and concerned about, what was going on in this country, he felt it his right and duty to pull his oar. He styled himself politically, as of 1972, a liberal Democrat. As far back as 1963 he had been very much present for the civil rights March on Washington. With fellow actors Marlon Brando, Anthony Franciosa, and Virgil Frye, he went to Gadsden,

Alabama, also in 1963, to help promote racial harmony. In the 1968 presidential campaign he was an enthusiastic supporter of Senator Eugene McCarthy, whom he said he deeply admired for the guts he had displayed in opposing, almost alone, President Johnson's war policies. In early 1968, Newman stumped for the senator, speaking for him on college campuses and helping to spearhead the McCarthy movement in his home state, Connecticut. That year Newman also served as a delegate to the Democratic National Convention.

Newman's movies of the 1970s were, for the most part, a depressingly uneven lot, at times downright mediocre—reflecting Newman's dis-

In Gadsden, Alabama, in 1963, after a conference with Republic Steel Corp. officials on racial problems. He and actors Virgil Frye, Marlon Brando and Anthony Franciosa (left to right) were refused audience with the Mayor, who called them "rabble-rousers."

All lined up on the set of *Towering Inferno,* left to right: Robert Wagner, Fred Astaire, Richard Chamberlain, Newman, William Holden, Faye Dunaway, Steve McQueen, Jennifer Jones, O. J. Simpson and Robert Vaughn.

satisfaction with scripts and his increasing preoccupation with other aspects of life, especially racing.

Oddly contradictory statements began appearing about Newman in the press during this decade—for instance, that his box-office popularity was great though many of his films did poorly. Nonetheless, his going rate straight into the 1980s has been one to three million dollars a film. *Pocket Money,* a 1972 dud co-starring Lee Marvin, got very bad reviews; this was counteracted by the admiration heaped on Newman's sensitive direction of *The Effect of Gamma Rays on Man-in-the-Moon Marigolds,* starring his wife, which premiered later that year. The badly received *Life and Times of Judge Roy Bean* and *The Mackintosh Man,* the latter a tediously convoluted spy drama, were followed by a major hit, *The Sting,* a Chicago crime caper in which Newman was reunited with Robert Redford for smash results at the box office and with the critics. *The Sting* won an Oscar as best film of the year.

1974's *The Towering Inferno,* in which New-

man's son, Scott, had a small role, was dismissed as "disaster rubbish," and *The Drowning Pool* in 1975 emerged as a limp attempt to retread Newman's 1966 *Harper* success. A cameo role in Mel Brooks' 1976 *Silent Movie* was followed by a much-criticized spoofing of yet another Western "hero" *(Buffalo Bill and the Indians).* Many in the press opined that the 200th anniversary of the republic was hardly the time for debunking legends so tastelessly. Nor did Newman fare any better in 1977 with *Slap Shot,* which was roundly criticized for its strong language, amoral attitudes, and brutal depictions of hockey infighting.

Meanwhile, Newman had waxed hot and cold on a projected film version of *The Front Runner,* Patricia Nell Warren's poignant homosexual love story about a track coach and a runner. Newman finally decided against it because, he said, he feared the public wouldn't accept him as a middle-aged gay in love with a kid half his age.

Quintet, in 1979, was labeled obscurantist nonsense about a post-glacial era, and in 1980

With Roger Ward, former National Racing Champion and two-time Indianapolis winner while taking lessons and getting pointers for his role in *Winning,* 1969.

the well-intentioned but soundly trounced Irwin Allen disaster film *When Time Ran Out* opened and closed with startling speed.

In early 1981 Newman's cop drama laid in the blighted South Bronx, *Fort Apache, the Bronx,* opened to mixed reviews, with some blacks and Puerto Ricans vigorously protesting that the film unduly denigrated their image and Newman angrily denying that any bigotry was present and pointing to his liberal record over the years as refutation of the charges.

In *Absence of Malice,* released later in 1981, Newman portrayed a warehouse owner connected with the disappearance of a Hoffa-type union boss and up against a zealous press investigation by reporter Sally Field, with romantic and journalistic intrigue abounding.

Newman's mind obviously hasn't been on filmmaking during his fifties, though he has often claimed that it is difficult to find worthwhile scripts and that on occasion he has to make do with what he can find. But his main interests, as of the early 1980s, seem to be political and humanitarian activity—and, of course, auto racing. He has continued his devotion to liberal causes, serving as an active member of SEA (Seaside Environmental Alliance). He has gone out personally to tramp the beaches seeking anti-oil-company signatures. Recently he was a special ambassador to the U.N. Conference on Nuclear

Edward Asner and Newman, in uniform for their roles, on the location of *Fort Apache, the Bronx,* with the director, Daniel Petrie

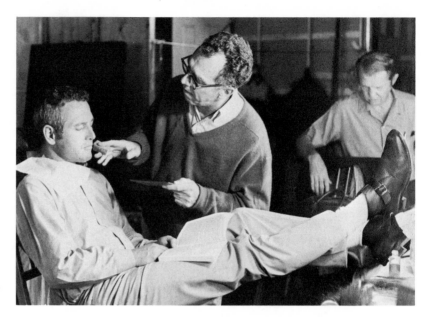

Being made up on the set.

Disarmament, "serving with great distinction and sincerity" as one colleague put it.

Nowadays the Newmans continue to alternate between their Connecticut and California homes; in addition, as has always been true, home is where a film's location happens to be—and that, in the fast-paced 1980s, can be anywhere in the world. The brightest professional note for the Newmans in years was struck with the respectful and highly admiring reception of the TV drama *The Shadow Box,* directed by Newman and starring Woodward and Christopher Plummer. Based on a Pulitzer Prize–winning play, *The Shadow Box* was telecast to great acclaim in December 1980. Again Newman's artistry showed itself more fully as director than as actor.

Newman's daughter Susan, a professional actress, served as co-producer on *The Shadow Box*. She has turned out to be better adjusted than her brother, Scott, a sensitive young man who found being Paul Newman's son a greater psychological burden than he could sustain and who led a

Newman helps his wife, Joanne Woodward, prepare a scene for *The Shadow Box,* the ABC-TV presentation of the Pulitzer Prize–winning play that won Mrs. Newman and Christopher Plummer many accolades when it was telecast in December 1980. That's Plummer with his back to camera.

Newman poses during a break from *Fort Apache, the Bronx* with Pete Tessitore and Tom Mulhearn, the former police officers whose experiences formed the basis of the film's story line.

troubled life until his death in 1978. The Newmans continue to grieve over Scott's death, and Woodward maintained in a recent interview that she and her husband find it hard to live with depictions of them in the press as perfect homemakers and perfect parents. She added that they had made their mistakes just like everyone else.

When Newman was once asked the secret of his successful twenty-three-year marriage to Woodward, he told a reporter, "I know this is going to sound corny, but there's no reason to roam. I have steak at home; why should I go out for a hamburger?" Recently he said that he delighted in presenting Woodward in *The Shadow Box* "just the way she is around the house—kinky and voluptuous."

On other occasions he has said of his marriage, "It's not always fine and dandy—it involves two people with very different approaches and attitudes to things—but I think it has a certain thickness to it. We go through periods where we think we've been bad parents and periods where we think we see each other only as reflections of ourselves—all the usual jazz. But there's affection and respect and a good deal of humor.

Though at times we have had the feeling that we were being tugged and pulled and put upon and existed only for other people and not ourselves."

One of his director friends has said of Newman, "Paul doesn't think of himself as a great actor, so he's always looking for other ways, outside of show business, to prove himself." Joanne Woodward has put a brave public face on Newman's continuing compulsion to race cars, for which he has won a number of top prizes. He races with a manic compulsiveness and many feel that his age (pushing fifty-seven) militates against his continuing for too much longer in a sport so rough and dangerous. At one point he narrowly escaped serious injury when another vehicle landed on his car's roof: his helmet made the difference. He dotes on the Datsun 280 ZX that he had custom built for hard use.

Woodward reportedly accepts all this with rueful humor, even a kind of wry approval, along boys-will-be-boys lines. Newman has said, "I get a charge out of it—it keeps me vibrant." There are a number of theories about the reasons Newman persists in this risky pursuit: the desire to keep young, the need to prove his manhood in

Speaking at a protest meeting against the ABM system.

his fifties, when many men fear that their masculinity is waning and look for dramatic symbols with which to maintain an image. One Newman friend, refuting reports of an unconscious death wish, declared, "Paul loves life, and he will get the last gallon of gas out of it, and to the end."

Newman once said, "I'd like to be remembered as a guy who tried—tried to be a part of his times, tried to help people communicate with one another, tried to find some decency in his own life, tried to extend himself as a human being. Someone who isn't complacent, who doesn't cop out. You've got to try—that's the main thing."

In the early 1980s, Paul Newman and Joanne Woodward seem to have struck a wise and mellow balance in their lifestyle that any couple, in or out of show business, might well envy and attempt to emulate. Even their greatest personal tragedy was turned to positive account when they created the Scott Newman Foundation, named for Paul's late son. The foundation has instituted a program that, over three years, will award $150,000 to writers, producers, and directors of the outstanding prime-time network programs dealing with drug-abuse prevention. Woodward stated poignantly to one reporter that via this foundation, she could feel that Scott's tragically truncated young life had served a good purpose.

One fact has emerged as Paul Newman faces fifty-seven: his mellow creativity, as a person and as an artist, did not come easily but resulted from earnest industry and a persistent struggle toward clearly conceived goals. And now that he has attained those middle, vintage years, his present life is the richer for all that has gone before.

With Cary Grant and Joanne Woodward, 1968.

The Films
of
PAUL NEWMAN

With Pier Angeli

The Silver Chalice

1954   Warner Bros.

CREDITS

A Warner Bros. release of a Victor Saville Production. Directed by Victor Saville. Screenplay by Lester Samuels from the novel by Thomas B. Costain. Edited by George White. Music by Franz Waxman. Photographed in CinemaScope and Warnercolor by William V. Skall. Running time, 142 minutes.

CAST

Virginia Mayo, Pier Angeli, Jack Palance, Paul Newman, Walter Hampden, Joseph Wiseman, Alexander Scourby, Lorne Greene, David J. Stewart, Herbert Rudley, Jacques Aubuchon, E. G. Marshall, Michael Pate, Natalie Wood, Peter Reynolds, Mort Marshall, Booth Colman, Terence de Marney, Robert Middleton, Ian Wolfe, Lawrence Dobkin, Philip Tonge, Albert Dekker, Beryl Machin.

THE FILM

Paul Newman has always felt apologetic about this, his first picture, made when he was twenty-nine and freshly signed to a Warner Bros. contract after television work and one appearance (Picnic) the year before on the Broadway stage. Reportedly, he cringes whenever it is shown on television. To be sure, the film gives only elementary indication of the forceful, confident performer who was to emerge on the nation's screens in the next three years. There is little here to remind one, for instance, of the bold, brassy Larry of 1957's The Helen Morgan Story. It is

With Virginia Mayo

also possible that Victor Saville, talented man that he was in other ventures, was not the best possible director for a novice of Newman's stripe. He was, to be sure, a greenhorn before the movie cameras; there are certain minor awkwardnesses and gaucheries and infelicitous facial expressions marring his projection, but it should be pointed out that the film itself is stilted, overly stylized, ramblingly episodic and confused as to plot and point. A film version of the Thomas B. Costain novel, it lacks the relative clarity and narrative drive of its source, and comes out a hodgepodge of early Christian idealism, Nero's villainous machinations, the intrigues and power plays of such early Christian figures as Peter, Luke, Linus, and Ignatius, all limned in ponderous, statuesque style by usually competent character actors.

The plot, reduced to the simplest common denominator amidst the constantly shifting panoramas and dramatic ebbings-and-flowings, has to do with a talented young Greek sculptor, Basil (Paul Newman) who is sold into slavery through the machinations of a conniving uncle who wants the boy's inheritance. In Rome, where he is subjected to the usual deprivations until he wins rec-

ognition for his bravery and talent, he alternates in romance between his shy and loving and self-effacing young wife, Deborra (Pier Angeli) and the more flamboyant and enticing Helena (Virginia Mayo) who had known him in childhood. In Jerusalem he had become involved with Christian leaders, and is eventually commissioned to create a reliquary, a receptacle for the chalice from which Christ drank at the Last Supper.

He runs afoul, of course, of various pagan villains, is forcd into assorted exhibitions of swordplay, is captured and escapes—and eventually wins freedom and happiness. Newman's embarrassment with this film is entirely understandable; the leading film critics whose smiles and/or frowns he was bucking for the first time were not, for the most part, hospitable to his fledgling talent, and there is also no denying that in this picture he was wooden and tense.

Nevertheless, there are clear glimmerings of the Newman to come—the chemistry was there, even then; the eyes flashed intermittently with the hypnotic gleam that the later Newman patented and made his own, and several scenes that required Newman to rouse himself from the impassivity forced upon him by the nature of his role,

Paul Newman

With Joseph Wiseman, right

With Pier Angeli

showcased his virile magnetism. The charisma that was to make him famous was on distinctly elementary display in *The Silver Chalice* but it was there for anyone who cared to observe closely. Some noticed it, even then, and now anyone sufficiently interested can spot it on its next TV re-run.

REVIEWS

Brog. in *Variety*
The picture serves as an introduction for film newcomer Paul Newman. He's a personable young man who will probably make an impression on the femmes. [He] handles himself well before the cameras. Helping his pic debut is Pier Angeli, and it is their scenes together that add the warmth to what might otherwise have been a cold spectacle.

John McCarten in *The New Yorker*
As the Greek sculptor, Paul Newman, a lad who resembles Marlon Brando, delivers his lines with the emotional fervor of a Putnam Division conductor announcing local steps.

Otis L. Guernsey, Jr. in the *New York Herald Tribune*
[The film] is what might be called a limited epic. It is about early Christians, and Palestinian rebels, and Nero, and all that, in a mammoth-sized con-tinuity running well over two hours. There are none of the trimmings, though—it looks like a little theatre production of *Quo Vadis?* with stylized sets and without lions or other extras of the movie midway. It is left to rely entirely upon its plot, which is, of course, tricky, episodic and overblown.

A. H. Weiler in *The New York Times*
In providing a modicum of excitement and generous portions of extravaganza, they have turned out a cumbersome and sometimes creaking vehicle that takes too long to reach its goal. In spinning the saga of the cup from which Christ drank at the Last Supper, they have employed a largely tested cast that rarely distills emotion or appreciable conviction from their roles. . . . Paul Newman, a recruit from Broadway and video, who is making his film debut in the role of Basil, bears a striking resemblance to Marlon Brando but his contribution is hardly outstanding. As a youth who has been cheated of his inheritance by a covetous uncle, sold into slavery and eventually chosen to create the holy relic, he is given mainly to thoughtful posing and automatic speechmaking. And despite the fact that he is desired by the extremely fetching Helena and the wistful Deborra, his wife, he is rarely better than wooden in his reaction to these fairly spectacular damsels.

With Everett Sloane

Somebody Up There Likes Me

1956   Metro-Goldwyn-Mayer

CREDITS

Produced by Charles Schnee. Directed by Robert Wise. Associate Producer, James E. Newcom. Screenplay by Ernest Lehman, based on the autobiography of Rocky Graziano, written with Rowland Barber. Music by Bronislau Kaper. Song "Somebody Up There Likes Me" sung by Perry Como. Lyrics by Sammy Cahn. Director of Photography, Joseph Ruttenberg, A.S.C. Art Director, Cedric Gibbons and Malcolm Brown. Film Editor, Albert Akst, A.C.E. Assistant Director, Robert Saunders. Perspecta Sound. Running time, 112 minutes.

CAST

Paul Newman, Pier Angeli, Everett Sloane, Eileen Heckart, Sal Mineo, Harold J. Stone, Joseph Buloff, Sammy White, Arch Johnson, Robert Lieb, Theodore Newton, Robert Loggia, Judson Pratt, Matt Crowley, Harry Wismer, Sam Taub, Donna Jo Gribble, Robert Easton, Ray Stricklyn, John Rosser, Frank Campanella, Ralph Vitti.

THE FILM

After the debacle of *The Silver Chalice,* Newman had returned to Broadway, where he scored resoundingly as the half-demented gangster in *The*

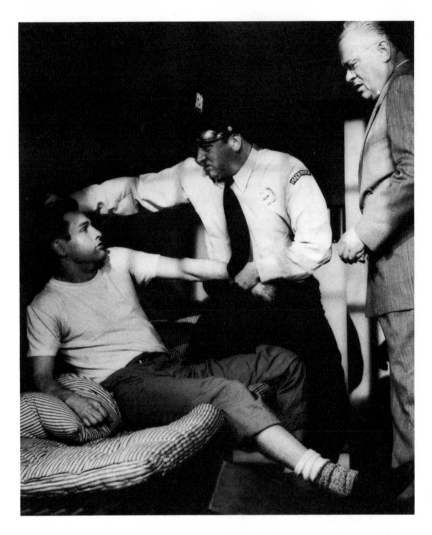

Paul Newman, at left

Desperate Hours. When offered, on loan-out to Metro-Goldwyn-Mayer, the role of Rocky Graziano in the film version of the autobiography the fighter had published with Rowland Barber, Newman decided to accept, as he recognized the fine opportunity for a solid, in-depth characterization.

Before embarking on the film, Newman spent considerable time in New York with Graziano, absorbing his mannerisms, his walk, his vocal tones, speech patterns, boxing stance. The two men talked for long periods of time, and Newman went back to Hollywood with the rudiments of his forthcoming characterization fixed firmly in his mind. Then began the second phase of his painstaking preparation; he worked out constantly in the gym at the Hollywood YMCA, and brushed up on his boxing with top professionals.

In peak condition at thirty-one, Newman reported on the MGM lot in fine fettle, and rarin'

to go. This was his first picture with perspicacious director Robert Wise, who understood how to bring out the best in individual performers according to their special gifts and creative insights, and he guided Newman through this, his second film, with masterly control and tactful understanding. The Actors Studio training that Newman had not been able to successfully apply to his Greek slave role in *The Silver Chalice* lent itself more readily to the Graziano part, and he incorporated what techniques he thought would best serve.

Newman, as everybody around him knew, was anxious to make good this time around, for his Warner film had left a bad taste in his mouth. The screenplay by Ernest Lehman was taut and hard-hitting, and Newman had the benefit of sincere, workmanlike support from Pier Angeli, Everett Sloane, Eileen Heckart, Sal Mineo and

Harold J. Stone. Since his first film Newman had found himself constantly compared to Marlon Brando, whose appearance and general aura were admittedly similar. Newman made no secret of his resentment of this persistent comparison, which he considered a handicap, and a disservice to both actors. Once he reportedly declared, "Maybe they'll say someday that Brando looke like *me!*" In *The Silver Chalice* they had said he looked like Brando did in *Julius Caesar* (both had Roman settings) and in *Somebody Up There Likes Me* they were to say that he looked like Brando in *On the Waterfront.* The Brando look-alike tag was to persist for several years, but it became gradually apparent that Paul Newman was very much himself, with a unique style and quality all his own.

In *Somebody Up There Likes Me,* Ernest Lehman's screenplay followed the broad outlines of the book Graziano had done with Barber. It was all there in the film as in the book—the underprivileged childhood and adolescence, the descent into delinquency and crime, the fixed fights, the dawn of self-respect and the gradual climb to his own brand of human dignity and the channeling of his energies into a constructive career as a boxer. As a champion fighter, operating under principles of fair play and rigid physical fitness, Graziano's fierce animal drives and courageous if crudely projected fighting-heart were to be utilized eventually as an inspiration to America's youth. Citing his own handicaps, his difficult upbringing and early conflicts with the law, Graziano seemed to say to confused, defensive youngsters from environments similar to his own, "If I can come out right, then so can you!" Pier Angeli is affecting in the somewhat romanticized part of Graziano's wife and chief inspiration, Norma, who sticks by him under difficult circumstances. Fumbling, inarticulate and crude, Rocky has his problems courting her as a gentleman should, and the scenes in which he tries to get across his feeling for her are moving and powerful.

Rocky's relations with his manager Irving Cohen (Everett Sloane) and his tortured relations with his parents (Eileen Heckart and Harold J. Stone) are limned convincingly. The climactic fight between Graziano and Tony Zale is one of the most exciting exhibitions ever seen on the screen. Former middleweight champion Zale

With Pier Angeli and Everett Sloane

With Pier Angeli

played himself in this sequence, and he and New-man had trained exhaustively in advance, with the result that the scene rang true.

Newman's reception from the critics in his sec-ond film was excellent, his performance being hailed as convincing, well thought out and char-acterizationally sound. At last he had effected a secure beachhead in Hollywood.

REVIEWS

John Beaufort in the *Christian Science Montor*
Although Paul Newman's shambling, impulsive performance as Rocky has inevitably recalled Marlon Brando's portrayals of Neanderthal types, Mr. Newman nevertheless adds his own insights and vivid portraiture. The writing and acting (of the film) are pungent, racy, and down-to-asphalt.

Brog. in *Variety*
For Paul Newman [the film] is a showcasing that should help remove the Brando look-alike handi-cap. His talent is large and flexible.

Arthur Knight in *The Saturday Review*
Lehman's work is especially effective because it makes its points without preaching, and because his points give a purpose to the picture beyond the representation of a grim, even sordid success story. . . . Paul Newman makes a convincing, somewhat Brandoesque young pug.

Bosley Crowther in *The New York Times*
Let it be said of Mr. Newman that he plays the role of Graziano well, making the pug and Marlon Brando almost indistinguishable. He is funny, tough and pathetic in that slouching, rolling, smirking Brando style, but with a quite apparent simulation of the former middleweight champ. . . . Robert Wise's direction is fast, aggressive and bright, and the picture is edited to give it a tre-mendous crispness and pace. The representation of the big fight of Graziano with Tony Zale is one of the whoppingest slugfests we've ever seen on the screen.

Jesse Zunser in *Cue*
Paul Newman is excellent as Rocky, with his hunched, half-crouch, rolling gait and Italo-New Yorkese accent.

In *Collier's*
In the title role, Paul Newman looks and sounds almost as convincing as Graziano himself. He shuffles and jigs constantly, seeming always alert for a prize-ring bell or an opponent's swing. His marbles-in-the-mouth stammer and sneer are in

With Tony Zale

the neorealistic tradition of Marlon Brando, Rod Steiger and the late James Dean (who, like Newman, were students at New York's Actor Studio). His moments of tenderness with his wife (Pier Angeli) are touching in their inarticulate clumsiness. And his chest and biceps measure up to the brawniest of Hollywood's beefcake actors.

Frank Leyendecker in *Boxoffice*

The picture will be much discussed, especially for Paul Newman's outstanding performance, and should build up favorable word-of-mouth. Newman's remarkable portrayal of the nervous inarticulate delinquent will give his screen career a tremendous boost.

The Rack

1956   Metro-Goldwyn-Mayer

CREDITS

Produced by Arthur M. Loew, Jr. Directed by Arnold Laven. Screenplay by Stewart Stern. Based on the teleplay by Rod Serling. Director of Photography: Paul C. Vogel, A.S.C. Art Directors, Cedric Gibbons and Merrill Pye. Set Decorations, Edwin B. Willis, Fred MacLean. Recording Supervisor, Dr. Wesley C. Milter. Assistant Director, Robert Saunders. Music by Adolph Deutsch. Film Editors, Harold F. Kress, A.C.E. and Marshall Neilan Jr. Makeup by William Tuttle. Technical Advisor, Col. Charles M. Trammel, Jr. USAR. Running time, 100 minutes.

CAST

Paul Newman, Wendell Corey, Walter Pidgeon, Edmond O'Brien, Anne Francis, Lee Marvin, Cloris Leachman, Robert Burton, Robert Simon, Trevor Bardette, Adam Williams, James Best, Fay Roope, Barry Atwater.

With Edmond O'Brien

THE FILM

In this, the second of his two Metro-Goldwyn-Mayer loan-outs from Warners to be released in 1956, Newman came through with a performance that superbly complemented his earlier Rocky Graziano portrayal. In *The Rack* he showed himself a performer of sensitivity and psychological discernment, with a deeper capacity for feeling and a wider range than had been previously credited to him. Any suspicion that *Somebody Up There Likes Me* had been a mere characterizational stunt and that Newman's own true personality would not register with screen audiences, was conclusively dispelled.

Here, for the first time, that special brand of Newman passionateness was on full display. An actor who was obviously not ashamed of his emotions, so long as he judged them sincere and heartfelt, Newman here projected a compelling synthesis of manly decency and emotional susceptibility.

As the young Army captain charged with collaboration during the Korean War, he is subjected to a court-martial, and the depths of his character and personality-makeup are explored relentlessly and, finally, cathartically. Though prior to his defection his war record had been exemplary and he had won a number of citations, Captain Edward W. Hall, Jr. (Paul Newman) stood accused of delivering pro-Communist propaganda lectures to his fellow prisoners in a North Korean camp. It was also proved that he had signed treasonable statements at the behest of his North Korean captors. Former buddies accused him of informing and other reprehensible practices. Lieutenant Colonel Frank Wasnick (Edmond O'Brien) his defense counsel, tries to win acquittal by pointing out to the court that every man has his breaking point, beyond which he has little or no responsibility for his actions.

Wasnick examines the months of mental torture to which Hall's captors subjected him prior to his unorthodox behavior. Then he proceeds to examine Hall's early environmental influences and emotional conditionings. Major Sam Moulton (Wendell Corey) his prosecuting officer, is concerned only with whether Hall committed his misdeeds while under no legally acceptable form of duress. Moulton harps on the "threshold of pain" principle, and declares that other American servicemen had exceeded this, so why couldn't Captain Hall?

49

With Anne Francis and
Walter Pidgeon

Aggie Hall (Anne Francis), Hall's widowed sister-in-law, sticks loyally by him through the proceedings, but his father, the obtuse and insensitive Colonel Edward Hall, Sr., at first misunderstands his son and finds his trial humiliating, but when it is brought out that the young captain's Achilles heel (which his North Korean captors discovered) lay in a childhood marred by his mother's early death and his preoccupied father's cold denial of affection, resulting in a lifelong crippling of Hall's spirit, father apologizes to son, and in one of the film's most moving scenes, finally proffers the affection for which the captain had all his life been starved. Newman and Pidgeon were especially fine in this delicate scene, played side-by-side in the front seat of an automobile, and which the slightest overshading could have made maudlin.

Here and throughout the film, Newman's great capacity for feeling, always filtered through a wholesomely masculine prism, was made manifest. It is brought out that when his captors had

With Anne Francis

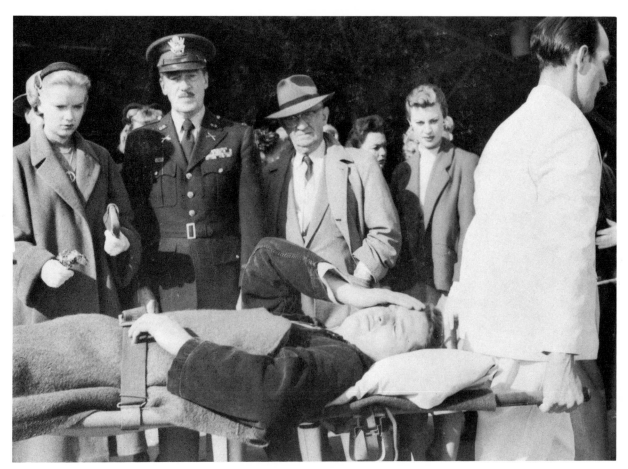

With Anne Francis and Walter Pidgeon

given him the news of his only brother's death in action, he had neared the ultimate breaking point that delivered him as a puppet into their hands. Nevertheless, the court finds Captain Hall guilty, and correctly so, for he admits that he did not quite reach the ultimate breaking point under torture. In a closing statement, the captain expresses deep regret that he had not risen to the occasion and thus known "that moment of magnificence" that hardier American prisoners had experienced. The captain thus emerges as justly sentenced but nonetheless worthy of compassion and understanding.

The Rack sealed the stardom which *Somebody Up There Likes Me* had won for Newman. In the earlier film he had shown a solid grasp of characterization; in *The Rack* he was displayed as expressively feelingful. Two more judiciously chosen assignments for a rising screen personality could not have been brought out in more timely sequence, for together they gave Newman in one year—1956—the rounded cinematic image necessary for major screen success.

REVIEWS

Lawrence J. Quirk in *Motion Picture Herald*

. . . a powerful, moving and adult drama of a young Army officer's court-martial for collaboration with the enemy as a prisoner of war in Korea. Gripping, compassionate in theme, penetrating far below the surface psychologically, avoiding stereotypes for most of the way, replete with superb acting performances from a gifted cast, and directed by Arnold Laven with a tough, taut economy and a sensitive, magically right timing and emphasis in the more dramatic and emotional sequences, *The Rack* is a provocative and creative piece of work . . . intelligent, adult filmgoers will respond warmly to its stimulating intellectual content and sensitive probings into the deep wells of the human heart . . . as the harried

51

With Anne Francis and
Walter Pidgeon

captain, Paul Newman turns in a performance of thorough integrity and shows himself an authentic talent. Well-chosen roles from here on should place Newman on the topmost rung . . . the characters and events are fictional, but the theme is reminiscent of much in the headlines sometime back, and what it has to say about patriotism, the essential integrity of the American spirit and way of life, and the ingredients of the complex human soul has a truth and validity all its own.

Bosley Crowther in *The New York Times*
A brilliantly detailed performance by Paul Newman in the role of an American army captain on trial for collaborating with the enemy while a prisoner during the Korean conflict gives a much more disturbing emotional impact to [the film] than is actually compounded in the drama unfolded. . . . For the job of showing [the captain's] feelings and suggesting the strain and agony he went through in the unseen prelude, Mr. Newman

is finely qualified. He truly achieves in this picture a remarkable tour de force. In his facial expressions, his gestures, his pauses and his use of his voice, he makes apparent in one figure a singular personal tragedy—the whole film is done with smooth dispatch.

Joe Pihodna in the *New York Herald Tribune*
One of the most honest, hard-punching and thoroughly absorbing motion picture productions to be presented here this year . . . a gripping, tightly-wrought and most convincingly-acted movie. The dialogue is terse, straightforward and often bitter. . . . Paul Newman, as Captain Hall, must certainly be mentioned for honors as an actor this season. He is at once a trembling mother's boy and a grimly resolved man and officer. He is so convincing as the boy-man caught in the trap of war that one squirms in his theatre seat as Mr. Newman answers the court-martial attorney.

With Jean Simmons

Until They Sail

1957   Metro-Goldwyn-Mayer

CREDITS

Produced by Charles Schnee. Directed by Robert Wise. Associate Producer, James E. Newcom. Screenplay by Robert Anderson. Based upon a story by James A. Michener. Music by David Raksin. Lyric for song, "Until They Sail" by Sammy Cahn. Sung by Eydie Gorme. Director of Photography, Joseph Ruttenberg, A.S.C. Art Directors, William A. Horning and Paul Groesse. Film Editor, Harold F. Kress, A.C.E. Cinema-Scope. Perspecta Sound. Process lenses by Panavision. Running time, 94 minutes.

CAST

Jean Simmons, Joan Fontaine, Paul Newman, Piper Laurie, Charles Drake, Sandra Dee, Wally Cassell, Alan Napier, Ralph Votrian, John Wilder, Tige Andrews, Adam Kennedy, Mickey Shaughnessy.

With Piper Laurie and Jean Simmons

THE FILM

Newman was reunited with director Robert Wise for his third Metro-Goldwyn-Mayer loan-out from Warners, and whereas Wise had obtained a solid character performance from his star in *Somebody Up There Likes Me,* this time around the able director succeeded in showcasing Newman as a formidable candidate for matinee idol status.

As a tough, crisp, disillusioned U.S. Marine Captain in World War II New Zealand who cynically investigates servicemen's requests to marry New Zealand girls, he is a grim clam indeed and seeks surcease in drinking because of an earlier marriage that didn't pan out. Then he meets Jean Simmons, a young war widow, and soon he is defrosting into moods that permit him and Miss Simmons to express tender feelings of a kind and quality seldom seen on the screen during the 1950's.

This film, of course, was not so much an acting challenge for Newman as an opportunity to prove he could hold his own with the best of them when it came to romanticizing his leading lady. And if that was the point that Newman and Wise consciously set out to make, they succeeded, though the film itself drew somewhat mixed reviews.

The basic story dealt with the four Leslie sisters of Christchurch and their reaction to the tide of boisterous, extroverted American GIs who came to New Zealand during the war on route to assorted battle zones and romanced the local girls "until they sailed." Barbara Leslie Forbes (Jean Simmons) is faithful to the memory of her husband, who was killed after one month of marriage. She is a balanced and civilized person, with her emotions under good control. Anne Leslie (Joan Fontaine) is a prim spinster who masks her fear of men beneath a guise of prissy disapproval. She softens under the romantic ministrations of a gentle captain (Charles Drake) who is later killed in action, leaving her pregnant with his child. The third sister, Delia (Piper Laurie) a passionate, unstable type, marries a local low-life, Phil Friskett (Wally Cassell) who later goes off to the war. The youngest, Evelyn (Sandra Dee) wistfully observes her sister's lives and quietly waits for her one-and-only, who is also at war. The Leslie sisters' parents are dead and their only brother has been killed in the war. Almost all the men of New Zealand are away in the fighting, and the virile GIs present emotional and sexual problems for the love-starved women.

All react individually. Newman, as Captain Jack Harding, is softened and humanized by his love for Barbara, who returns his feeling once her scruples are dispersed. Delia's need for fulfillment drives her into a career of promiscuity with officers, and when her husband returns from the war and discovers what she has become, he murders her. A happier fate is projected for Evelyn, who is reunited with her childhood sweetheart. Miss Simmons was excellent in the film, and contributed her own creative perceptions to her love scenes with Newman, and the feelings their characters project, warring with the desire of both to "do the right thing," despite the abnormal stresses of wartime, come through as right and true.

REVIEWS

William K. Zinsser in the *New York Herald Tribune*

[The film] has moments of genuine tenderness and truth. Robert Anderson's script ponders the tricks that war plays on human emotions . . . all the actors are good, particularly Jean Simmons and Paul Newman as the pair who control their emotions, so as not to make the same mistake as other wartime couples, and therefore find themselves under a cruel stress.

A. W. in *The New York Times*

The terrible loneliness of New Zealand's women whose men were away at war and the aftermaths of their liaisons with GIs are given serious, if unspectacular, consideration. But despite an adult approach to an important facet of World War II, these romances and blighted affairs seem only wistful remembrances of things past. The genuine tugs at the heart are few and far between in this bittersweet but basically restrained chronicle . . . although Mr. Newman's portrayal is sometimes glum and casual, it is, nevertheless, generally effective. . . . Unfortunately, there is a good deal of introspective soul-searching before this narrative arrives at its sad and happy endings. Although this is a disturbing chapter in their history, the women who have the affection of the visiting Yanks only "until they sail" generally react with cultivated emotions.

With Joan Fontaine and Jean Simmons

With Jean Simmons

Whit. in *Variety*
Under Wise's deft and sensitive direction, Anderson's screenplay takes explosive form in following love affairs of four sisters. Clandestine romance is subtly handled. And in touching on loneliness of love-starved years, plot builds dramatic punch. Topflight cast generates often poignant unfoldments which allows both lightness and tragedy. Characters right down line are outstanding, Simmons and Newman as chief protagonists faring best.

Lawrence J. Quirk in *Hollywood Stars*
In *Somebody Up There Likes Me,* Paul Newman revealed himself as a solid character star. In *The Rack,* he showed he could handle the heavy dramatics with the best of them. And now, in *Until They Sail,* he gives every evidence of becoming a matinee idol *par excellence.* When Newman holds Jean Simmons in his arms and starts delivering, the ladies in the audience find him irresistible (from what I could judge from feminine responses all around me) and the men wonder what this guy's got that *they* haven't got. A screen loverboy who can be boyish, aggressive, shyly sensitive and masculinely direct, all at the same time, is someone to be reckoned with. This is not so much a dramatic part for Newman as a chance for him to show what he can do as a romantic lead, and he delivers in fine style.

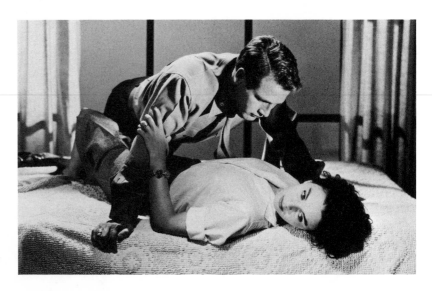

With Jean Simmons

With Ann Blyth

The Helen Morgan Story

1957   Warner Bros.

CREDITS

A Warner Bros. release of a Martin Rackin production. Directed by Michael Curtiz. Screenplay by Oscar Saul, Dean Riesner, Stephen Longstreet and Nelson Gidding. Camera, Ted McCord. Art Director, John Beckman. Musical numbers staged by LeRoy Prinz. Songs sung by Gogi Grant. Editor, Frank Bracht. Running time, 117 minutes.

CAST

Ann Blyth, Paul Newman, Richard Carlson, Gene Evans, Alan King, Cara Williams, Virginia Vincent, Walter Woolf King, Dorothy Green, Ed Platt, Warren Douglas, Sammy White, Peggy De Castro, Cheri De Castro, Babette De Castro, and Jimmy McHugh, with Rudy Vallee and Walter Winchell as themselves.

THE FILM

Warners had held the rights to *The Helen Morgan Story* since 1942, a year after Miss Morgan's death, but due to problems with the casting and screenplay (some twenty writers reportedly worked on it at various times) the studio did not get around to filming it until fifteen years later. Any inner discomfiture Newman might have experienced concerning his yo-yo swings between his home base, Warners, and Metro-Goldwyn-Mayer, where he found himself loaned for three

With Ed Platt and Alan King

films in eighteen months, should have been allayed upon reflection, for he was rapidly establishing himself as a highly versatile actor, veering as he did from Roman-style heroics in *The Silver Chalice* to solid characterization in *Somebody Up There Likes Me* to heavy dramatics in *The Rack* to matinee-idol-style romance in *Until They Sail*.

Between them the MGM-Warner combine were putting the Newman boy on the cinematic map— and he was able to add still another facet to his image with *The Helen Morgan Story*.

For as prohibition-era gangster and bootlegger Larry Maddux, Newman, then thirty-two, demonstrated that he could hold his own with Raft,

With Alan King and Cara Williams

58

Cagney, Bogart, John Garfield or any other tough-boy, love-'em-and-leave-'em type around. Despite the maudlin and melodramatic aspects of the screenplay, which sugarcoated the facts of the famed singer's life and fictionalized where the simple truth would have better served, Newman, complemented ably by Ann Blyth's sincere performance as Helen, projected his masculine charisma as never before. In this he was undoubtedly aided by the shrewd and tough-fibred direction of Michael Curtiz, who had guided Miss Blyth and Joan Crawford through *Mildred Pierce* at Warners twelve years before, and who knew how to isolate the essential quality in a player that impelled audience response.

Curtiz had also guided many a Warner tough-guy through his paces over the years, and Newman also got the benefit of this. Nonsentimental, arrogant in his maleness, crudely opportunistic, toughly insensitive, the character of Larry Maddux, as written, directed and acted, projected its own intrinsic truth, he being just the type a number of spirited, life-hungry women of the Morgan stripe would have found themselves loving and hating at the same time. Newman put across all the chemistry and power and personality force that made Miss Blyth's long-term infatuation with him understandable. It was perhaps the one thing about the picture that *was* understandable, for the plot, so fictionalized and gimmicked-up as to border on the incredible, follows Helen Morgan from her song-dance-and-hula days in a Chicago amusement park, where she meets smooth ladies' man promoter Newman, through her abortive beauty contest triumph in Canada, of which she was robbed because it developed she was not Canadian, to her encounter with distinguished lawyer Russell Wade (Richard Carlson) and her on-again-off-again things with Larry, who periodically makes love to her, then deserts her, leaving her ever more wounded and jaded.

Larry, in off-hand style, compensates for his failure to give Helen emotional security by finding her various singing jobs along the way. But he negates even this when he tips off the police to raid a New York spot in which she is singing because he has quarreled with the owner over the control of bootlegging territory. Languishing in jail, Helen appeals to Wade, who obtains her

release and begins romancing her. The publicity over the raid catapults her into a series of nitery singing engagements which soon make her the toast of Broadway for her piano-top, heart-in-her-voice style. (Such famed Morgan standards as "Can't Help Lovin' That Man" and "My Bill" are dubbed for Miss Blyth by Gogi Grant). Helen's romance with Wade withers when she learns he is married, and Larry comes back into her life, as he always seems to do at crucial times. Though disillusioned with Larry, she cannot resist him. Larry visits Wade and suggests the wealthy attorney purchase a nightclub for Helen with Larry as front man. To give Helen security, Wade agrees.

The opening night of The House of Morgan is a glittering affair, and when Ziegfeld casts her as Julie in *Showboat* in 1927, Helen really becomes the Queen of Broadway. But elation turns to bitterness when she learns that Wade, not Larry, backs her club, and that Larry has been using her name and fame to further his own purposes. Again she breaks with Larry. Wade's wife visits Helen in her dressing room and tells her she will never give him a divorce to marry Helen.

Helen begins to drink heavily. Revenue agents break up her club. She begins losing jobs because of drunkenness, then goes to Europe, scorning Larry's offer to buy her another club. The stock-market crashes, wiping out Helen's savings, and Larry is wounded while hijacking a warehouse and is sent to prison. Helen drinks her way to the gutter. Wade traces her to a Harlem dive and tries to help her but she is too far gone. She winds up in a Bellevue alcoholic ward, where Larry is allowed by the police to visit her. There, for the first time, he tells her he loves her.

One day, her illness cured, Helen finds Larry waiting for her outside the hospital. He takes her under a pretext to her old club where Broadway's elite are waiting to fête her. With tears in her eyes, she sings one of her famed torch songs—to the watching Larry.

As the plot sketched above indicates only too clearly, the screenplay is outrageously sentimental, melodramatic, tortuously forced, and twisted out of all semblance to the actual Morgan life history, which, had it been "told like it was," would have made for a far more solid and true unfoldment. But the picture did expand Anne

With Ann Blyth

Blyth's range as an actress, her Helen Morgan stint being quite creditable, and it took Paul Newman several giant cuts upward toward the top of the 1957 male-film-idol totempole. To millions of American women of that year, he had become the man they would best like to be loved-and-left by, and with the critics he was winning increasing respect as an actor of force and versatility.

REVIEWS

In the *Toronto Globe and Mail*

. . . The minutes between the songs are almost universally soggy, whether dealing with Miss Morgan's love lives (a small-time crook and utter heel and an urbane, kindly, and rising New York lawyer), nostalgic glimpses of the 1923-33 era, or the singer's resounding crash to the pavements of skid row. . . . Paul Newman's grapplings with the role of the gangster lover are generally successful, with the exception of those moments when he is weighed down by foolishly brittle dialogue.

KAP. in *Variety*

[The screenwriters] have taken some of the leg-ends and some of the realities of the Roaring 20's and loosely attributed all of them to La Morgan. The story line sometimes strains credulity and the dialogue and situations occasionally give the production a cornball flavor. Overall plot of a woman in love with a heel (best exemplified by the fade-out shot on the song "Can't Help Loving That Man") will, however, be an asset for distaff audiences eager to use the handkerchiefs. . . . Director Michael Curtiz has done a good job with the material at hand, injecting a pacing and bits of business that help maintain interest. . . . Newman is very good as the rackets guy, giving the part authority and credibility.

William K. Zinsser in the *New York Herald Tribune*

[The film] will not go down as a landmark of originality, but sentimentalists may have a good time and an occasional snuffle. Miss Blyth is appealing as the mournful heroine and Paul Newman is excellent as the selfish promoter, providing the hard crust on a soft meringue.

The Long Hot Summer

1958   20th Century-Fox

CREDITS

Produced by Jerry Wald. Directed by Martin Ritt. Screenplay by Irving Ravetch and Harriet Frank, Jr. Based on two stories, "Barn Burning" and "The Spotted Horses" and a part of the novel *The Hamlet,* all by William Faulkner. Director of Photography, Joseph La Shelle, A.S.C. Art Direction, Lyle R. Wheeler and Maurice Ransford. Music by Alex North, conducted by Lionel Newman. Song "The Long Hot Sumner" by Sammy Cahn and Alex North. Film Editor, Louis R. Loeffler. CinemaScope. Color by Deluxe. Color Consultant, Leonard Doss. Running time, 115 minutes.

CAST

Paul Newman, Joanne Woodward, Anthony Franciosa, Orson Welles, Lee Remick, Angela Lansbury, Richard Anderson, Sarah Marshall, Mabel Albertson, J. Pat O'Malley, William Walker, George Dunn, Jess Kilpatrick, Val Avery, I.

With Lee Remick

Stamford Jolley, Nicholas King, Lee Erickson, Ralph Reed, Terry Range, Steve Widders, Jim Brandt, Helen Wallace, Brian Corcoran, Byron Foulger, Victor Rodman, Eugene Jackson.

THE FILM

This time around, Warners sent their wandering boy over to 20th Century-Fox for Jerry Wald's *The Long Hot Summer,* an ambitious Cinema-Scope-Deluxe Color rendition of several Faulkner works. Here for the first time he was directed by Martin Ritt, with whom Newman was to have a most rewarding future association, artistically. Fox—and Ritt—proved timely aides to Newman's career progress, and in *The Long Hot Summer* he solidified his previous gains and reinforced his image as the New Male Hormone-tickler of the screen.

This film was notable for another "first"— Newman's initial appearance on the screen with Joanne Woodward, who won an Academy Award (for *Three Faces of Eve)* the year the film was released—and married Newman. Made in the months just prior to their marriage, the film crackles with their mutual feelings toward each other, lending an extra crispness and credibility to their scenes together. In fact, so right was their chemistry as starring lovers that they even gave that gargantuan (in more ways than one) talent, Mr. Orson Welles, pause in his scene-stealing attempts.

Thus was inaugurated the Newman-Woodward on-screen team that was in time to rival that of Spencer Tracy and Katharine Hepburn. Director Ritt and Newman quickly established a rapport during the shooting, and the result was his sharp, intelligent portrayal of Ben Quick, the young Mississippi redneck who is rumored to be a "barn-burner"—a varmint who settles his grudges by burning his enemies' property. Quick comes to

With Orson Welles

With Joanne Woodward

work as a sharecropper for Will Varner (Welles) a Deep South-style oligarch who keeps rigid control over his neighborhood, and dominates (but has not broken) his frustrated spinster daughter Clara (Joanne Woodward) and his weakling son Jody (Anthony Franciosa) who has none of his father's will-to-power and seeks surcease with his pretty wife Eula (Lee Remick).

Varner, after several abrasive clashes with Quick, senses that the brash young upstart is his kind of man and a more fit heir to his empire than his own son. Clara meanwhile is getting nowhere with her mother-dominated, tepid-spirited boy-friend, Alan Stewart (Richard Anderson). Varner tries to get Quick into his family by railroading a marriage with Clara. Clara will have none of it, for despite her strong physical attraction to the brash and sardonic Quick, she considers him

With Joanne Woodward

crude and pushy. When Varner brutally informs Jody that he prefers Ben to him and intends to add him to the family despite all odds and make him his heir, Jody becomes enraged and attempts to trap his father in a burning barn, feeling that Quick will get the blame, due to his prior reputation. But at the last minute, the conscience-stricken Jody rescues his father.

By this time, Clara realizes she loves Ben, and that his toughly enterprising nature has a more affirmative cast than she had previously suspected. Will Varner has his way in the matter, after all—but so does his longtime mistress, Minnie (Angela Lansbury) who at last cajoles old Will into making an honest woman of her.

With his characteristic thoroughness, Newman prepared himself for *The Long Hot Summer* by going to the town of Clinton, Mississippi for three days, where he lounged unrecognized in the bars, pool parlors and restaurants of the town in order to correctly reproduce the speech patterns and mannerisms of the inhabitant of a typical Deep South community, similar to the "Frenchman's Bend" of the film.

REVIEWS

In *Time*

Newman's performance is as mean and keen as a crackle-edged scythe.

Bosley Crowther in *The New York Times*

[The scriptwriters] have developed a tight, word-crackling script that lines up the bitter situation in quick scenes and slashing dialogue. Martin Ritt has directed for tension . . . for scornful, sarcastic attitudes on the part of the contenders. And these roles are effectively played. Paul Newman is best

With Joanne Woodward

as the roughneck who moves in with a thinly-veiled sneer to knock down the younger generation and make himself the inheritor of the old man. He has within his plowhand figure and behind his hard blue eyes the deep and ugly deceptions of a neo-Huey Long. He could, if the script would let him, develop a classic character.

Paul V. Beckley in the *New York Herald Tribune*
A beautifully written, well-directed, very tense but yet humorous film with some strong, hard-bitten characterizations and, flashing through it like heat lightning, a seriousness that is not tasteless but has almost the dry lightness of the French style.

Powe. in *Variety*
Newman slips into a cracker slouch with professional ease, never allowing a cornpone and molasses accent to completely disguise his latent energy and native intelligence.

The Left-handed Gun

1958   Warner Bros.

CREDITS

A Warner Bros. release of a Fred Coe production. Directed by Arthur Penn. Screenplay by Leslie Stevens, based on a teleplay, *The Death of Billy the Kid,* by Gore Vidal. Camera, J. Peverell Marley. Music by Alexander Courage. Ballet by William Goyen and Alexander Courage. Set decorations, William J. Kuehl. Costumes, Marjorie Best. Makeup, Gordon Bau. Assistant Director, Russ Saunders. Art Director, Art Loel. Film Editor, Felmar Blangsted. Sound: Earl Crain, Sr. Running time, 105 minutes.

CAST

Paul Newman, Lita Milan, Hurd Hatfield, James

With Lita Milán

Congdon, James Best, Colin Keith-Johnston, John Dierkes, Bob Anderson, Wally Brown, Ainslie Pryor, Martin Carralaga, Denver Pyle, Paul Smith, Nestor Paiva, Jo Summers, Robert Foulk, Anne Barton.

THE FILM

The Left-handed Gun has had a curious history. Based on Gore Vidal's teleplay, "The Death of Billy the Kid," and directed by TV's Arthur Penn as his first motion picture, it received reviews at

With James Congdon (left)

the time of its initial 1958 release that were distinctly polarized, with some reviewers expressing themselves as unable to make head nor tail of it and others lauding it as an interesting if not entirely successful experimental-type Western that attempted to synthesize subtle psychologizing with Western-style action pyrotechnics. This critical dissension has continued over the past thirteen years, and the film has taken on cult elements, with its avid defenders arguing hotly, in and out of print, with its scornful detractors.

Undoubtedly, Newman, Penn and screenwriter Leslie Stevens tried to blaze some new trails, drawing upon the inspirations provided by Newman's good friend Vidal in his original TV script, and in some respects the film was ahead of its time. "Different" Westerns were not exactly in style in 1958, and it is interesting that even at that time, Newman was trying to set new trends and get himself into films that got audiences to thinking and reacting in an individual way.

Unappreciated in its own time, except by a few of the more discerning critics, *The Left-handed Gun* is slowly finding its proper place among the film legends. Certainly, Penn and cameraman J. Peverell Marley tried to expand the film creatively, with original shots and unorthodox characterizational nuances, and Newman's performance in it is fetchingly fey (a sort of ancestor of his equally playful *Butch Cassidy* of 1969), al-

ternating animal cunning with an almost boyish insouciance.

Newman and Penn saw young Billy the Kid as a confused adolescent with good potential, gone wrong because of his self-destructive bents. As played by Newman, Billy is reckless, impulsive, yet capable of spurts of generosity and loyalty. Like his cousin-under-the-skin, the Rocky Graziano of *Somebody Up There Likes Me,* Billy symbolizes raw animal energy with no place to go but whereas Newman's Graziano succeeded in channeling his negative instincts into constructive channels, becoming a famous boxer, his Billy the Kid fails to find a socially acceptable outlet for *his,* thus bringing on his premature destruction.

Newman got Billy's disparate inner elements across very well. A performance that in 1958 might have seemed diffused and obscurantist, by 1971 standards seems subtly improvisational and many-faceted. Stevens' cinematic transcription of Vidal's teleplay is laid in the West of the 1880's. Newman thoughtfully limned the inarticulate fumblings and awkwardnesses of a boy who had been given no education and no love, and who consequently lacked true character balance. When kindness or fairness in any form are shown him, he reacts like a grateful puppy, and when his benefactor, the rancher Turnstall (Colin Keith-Johnston) a philosophical kindly type who goes unarmed, is murdered by a deputy sheriff and

three other men, Billy vows to avenge his death.

He sets out to stalk all four, along with his two buddies, Charlie Boudre (James Congdon) and Tom Folliard (James Best). Billy kills two of the men he is after, then is forced to escape to Mexico. Here he becomes briefly involved with Celsa (Lita Milan) a gunsmith's wife, but the illicit liaison spurs further flight. Boudre and Folliard find and kill the third murderer of Turnstall, and Billy tracks down and kills the fourth during a wedding celebration. He is captured but escapes from jail. He is then tracked down and finally slain by a posse headed by lawman Pat Garrett.

This, then, is the basically simple plot, but Penn and Stevens, with Newman's indispensable contribution, have succeeded in portraying in depth Billy the Kid's complexities and warring instincts, his adolescent outlook, rudimentary sentiment and animal spirits. That blending of con-

tent and style which seemed confusing to 1958 audiences has, as before noted, a more fresh, recognizable look in 1971, and it gives conclusive evidence that at a relatively early point in his film career, Paul Newman was in deadly earnest about bringing something fresh, provocative and meaningful to a cinema that in the 1950's was still too reliant on the pat and predictable. *The Left-handed Gun* is not without its flaws, but it deserves an A for its excellent intentions, some of them surprisingly well realized.

REVIEWS

Howard Thompson in *The New York Times*
The sad thing is that some television people have tried to make a Western that's different. And by golly, it is . . . it takes forever, very little of it makes sense, and the whole thing is so laboriously

arty that it hurts. . . . The picture should have stayed on the home TV screen or settled for plain talk. . . . Poor Mr. Newman seems to be auditioning alternately for the Moscow Art Players and the Grand Old Opry, as he ambles about, brooding, grinning or mumbling endlessly.

Powe. in *Variety*

A smart and exciting Western paced by Paul Newman's intense portrayal of The Kid. . . . Plenty of action and the added value of a psychological story. . . . The best parts of the film are the moments of hysterical excitement as the three young desperadoes rough-house with each other as feckless as any innocent boys and in the next instant turn to deadly killing without flicking a curly eyelash. Although this is Penn's first picture, he shows himself in command of the medium, using motion picture technique and advantages, such as in a wild house-burning, that are not available elsewhere, to their fullest value. Newman dominates the picture.

With Lita Milan

Paul Newman (left)

Cat on a Hot Tin Roof

1958   Metro-Goldwyn-Mayer

CREDITS

An Avon Production for Metro-Goldwyn-Mayer. Produced by Lawrence Weingarten. Directed by Richard Brooks. Screenplay by Richard Brooks and James Poe. Based on the play by Tennessee Williams. Photographed by William Daniels. Art Direction, William A. Horning and Urie McCleary. Set Decoration, Henry Grace and Robert Priestley. Assistant Director, William Shanks. Special effects: Lee Leblanc. Color Consultant, Charles K. Hagedon. Editor, Ferris Webster. Recording Supervisor, Dr. Wesley C. Miller. Miss Taylor's Wardrobe, Helen Rose. Hairstyles, Sydney Guilaroff. Makeup, William Tuttle. In Metrocolor. Running time, 108 minutes.

With Elizabeth Taylor

CAST

Elizabeth Taylor, Paul Newman, Burl Ives, Jack Carson, Judith Anderson, Madeleine Sherwood, Larry Gates, Vaughn Taylor, Deborah Miller, Hugh Corcoran, Brian Corcoran.

THE FILM

Back to Metro-Goldwyn-Mayer went Newman in early 1958 for his first on-screen bout with a Tennessee Williams character—Brick Pollitt of *Cat on a Hot Tin Roof*. Ben Gazzara had originated the role on Broadway in 1955, with Barbara Bel Geddes as his wife Maggie and Burl Ives as Big Daddy. Elizabeth Taylor, fresh from a *Raintree County* Oscar nomination and encouraged by her husband Mike Todd into essaying more ambitious portrayals, played the Maggie role opposite Newman, with Burl Ives as Big Daddy. Guiding the ensemble was director Richard Brooks, who with this and a later film (*Sweet Bird of Youth* also with Newman) would be forced to weather the charge that he had watered-down and emasculated Williams' intentions in the film versions of his plays.

Today, of course, this 1958-style Production Code tampering would be ruled out, but Brooks tried to get across the spirit if not the letter of Williams' frankly morbid intentions, and thus helped along what was perhaps the most delicately-subtle and emotionally-multi-layered performance Newman had yet given on the screen. Miss Taylor also exceeded her previous cinematic work, her sterling performance being all the more admirable because her husband, Mike Todd, was killed while the picture was shooting and she was forced to resume despite her grief, with Newman and Brooks lending all possible moral support.

Newman's performance was beautifully disciplined and modulated, subtly suggestive of the homosexual elements Williams had injected into the stage Brick, and while some critics felt that Newman's actual personality was too strong for the essentially weak and passive character that was Brick's as Williams conceived him, his reviews were for the most part laudatory. Many Newman aficionados consider this one of his top performances; it was obvious that he felt it sincerely, had thought it through, approached it with creative humility and thorough commitment, concentrating on the most minute nuances and plumbing and catharsizing his own depths in the process, resulting in a thoroughly credible Brick.

The well-known story deals, of course, with a rich Southerner, Big Daddy Pollitt (Ives) who is feted by his family on his sixty-fifth birthday. Big Daddy is dying of cancer, but his family (Big

Mama, his wife (Judith Anderson); his older son Gooper (Jack Carson) and Gooper's wife Mae (Madeleine Sherwood) keep the fact concealed from him. Also on hand as houseguests are Big Daddy's younger son, Brick (Newman) and his wife Maggie (Miss Taylor). Brick, who has broken his ankle during a drunken spree on an athletic field, keeps to his room during his visit, drinking heavily and rebuffing the pathetically persistent advances of his passionate young wife, whom Brick suspects of having been unfaithful with his now-dead college friend Skipper, whom he idolized. Despite Brick's coldness, Maggie is protecting his interests against Gooper and Mae, whom she suspects of planning to rook her and Brick out of the family inheritance.

Brick's infatuation with the late Skipper is implied in the film rather than stated overtly, as it was in the play, and as acted by Miss Taylor it is obvious that Maggie is deeply troubled over the Skipper involvement and the memories it evokes. It develops that Skipper had committed suicide after phoning Brick to beg his help—a help Brick had denied him. This purportedly fills Brick with guilt and confusion, which his father forces him to admit. In retaliation Brick tells Big Daddy that he has cancer.

Meanwhile, Gooper and Mae continue their maneuverings, though it is obvious that Brick is his father's favorite. To counter Gooper and Mae, and the grandchildren they flaunt, Maggie tells Big Daddy that she is pregnant—a pathetic lie that her in-laws challenge, adding that they have heard her at night begging the stubbornly-unresponsive Brick for love. The spectacle of Maggie's travail and her stubborn loyalty to him, plus a cathartic conversation with his father that establishes a better communication, finally arouses Brick from his withdrawal and his ancient obsession about Skipper, and he realizes that Maggie really loves him. He then informs her that they will proceed to make good on her brave pretensions to pregnancy.

Richard Brooks continued to insist for years that with this film, as with *Sweet Bird of Youth,* he captured the spirit if not the exact letter of Williams' message, but many disagree with him while granting that he was working against difficult odds, considering the screen conventions of the era. There was, however, much commendation of Miss Taylor's and especially Newman's shrewd and subtle intimations of what was really going on beneath the surface of their characters, and *Cat on a Hot Tin Roof,* when viewed after thirteen years, continues to display them in a most

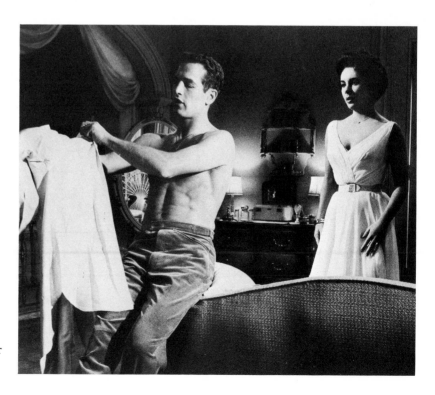

With Elizabeth Taylor

With (left to right) Jack Carson, Madeleine Sherwood,
Burl Ives, Judith Anderson, Elizabeth Taylor

With Elizabeth Taylor

creditable light. Newman received his first Academy Award nomination for this film. Miss Taylor was also nominated.

REVIEWS

Hollis Alpert in *The Saturday Review*
All reference to [homosexuality] has been eliminated . . . but even though the plot has become rudderless, the movie still has some exceedingly well-drawn characters to offer. . . . Paul Newman is adequate as Brick, even though the character is now virtually a static one.

Judith Crist in the *New York Herald Tribune*
The [stage] theme of homosexuality has been dropped. Mr. Newman's Brick is now a weakling who prefers the bottle to his beautiful wife and refuses to undertake adult responsibilities.

Ron. in *Variety*
Newman again proves to be one of the finest actors in films, playing cynical underacting against highly developed action. His command of the articulate, sensitive sequences is unmistakable and the way he mirrors his feelings is basic to every scene.

Penelope Houston in the *London Observer*
Paul Newman, with his look of a sulkier Brando, seems, if anything, a little too strong for Brick.

Bosley Crowther in *The New York Times*
Mr. Newman is perhaps the most resourceful and dramatically restrained of the lot. He gives an ingratiating picture of a tortured and tested young man.

With Burl Ives

With Joan Collins

Rally 'Round the Flag, Boys!

1958   20th Century-Fox

CREDITS

Produced and directed by Leo McCarey. Screenplay by Claude Binyon and Leo McCarey. Based on the novel by Max Shulman. Music by Cyril J. Mockridge. Conducted by Lionel Newman. Orchestrations, Edward B. Powell. Photographed by Leon Shamroy. Art Direction, Lyle R. Wheeler and Leland Fuller. Set decoration, Walter M. Scott and Stuart A. Reiss. Editor, Louis R. Loeffler. Special photographic effects, L. B. Abbott. Wardrobe design, Charles Le Maire. Hairstyles by Helen Turpin. Makeup by Ben Nye. Assistant Director, Jack Gertsman. Sound, Eugene Grossman and Harry M. Leonard. Color consultant, Leonard Doss. CinemaScope. DeLuxe Color. Running time, 106 minutes.

CAST

Paul Newman, Joanne Woodward, Joan Collins, Jack Carson, Dwayne Hickman, Tuesday Weld, Gale Gordon. Tom Gilson, O. Z. Whitehead, Ralph Osborn III, Stanley Livingston, Jon Lormer, Joseph Holland, Burt Mustin, Percy Holton, Nora O'Mahoney, Richard Collier, Murvyn Vye.

THE FILM

When, in late 1958, Paul Newman ventured into

With Joanne Woodward

the first farce-comedy film of his career, he had eight pictures under his belt—none of them comedies. He had appeared as tragedian, lover-boy, character star, Roman slave and Mr. Love 'em and Leave 'em. And what the growing legions of Newman admirers now wanted to know—and went to *Rally 'Round the Flag, Boys!* to find out—was: could Newman Put Over Comedy?

Everything seemed to be going for him in this, his first attempt at the genre. He had doubling as both producer and director the formidable Leo McCarey, who knew comedy backwards and forwards and had been proving it on the screen for over 25 years. He had the moral support of his wife Joanne Woodward, who was co-starring with him for the second time. Max Shulman's novel, on which the film was based, had been amusing enough, and McCarey and Claude Binyon, a proven pro, had co-authored the screenplay. The film boasted top-drawer photography, grade-A musical scoring, last-word production mounting—but the result was strangely disappointing.

For the second time in his screen career Newman drew below-par reviews (the first time had been for *The Silver Chalice*). The consensus: Comedian he was not. He was accused of over-acting, of trying too hard, of being arch when he should have been genial, of being broad when he should have been subtle. It was obvious that Cary Grant, David Niven and Gig Young had nothing to sprout gray hairs about; Newman gave no indication of putting them out of business. Miss Woodward (whom some considered more of an acting "natural" than her hard-working husband) fared somewhat better, and even got herself compared to the late Carole Lombard as a farceuse, exhibiting as she did a relaxed aplomb that her husband seemed unable to quite muster. A certain grimness seemed to come over Newman's aura during even the most bumptiously hilarious scenes, a grimness his subsequent comic ventures (with the possible exception of the stage romp, *Baby Want a Kiss)* never really overcame. He tended to be sardonic when he should have been fey; he would use his entire body, complete with heavy-handed gestures and mannerisms, trying several shades too hard for laughs when a flick of an eyebrow or the gentlest of double-takes would have done the trick. It was, however, conceded that Newman's desire to vary his pace and branch out, was in itself commendable.

Leo McCarey seems to have done his best to defrost and de-grim Newman and encourage him to underplay (Newman partisans declare that McCarey was past his prime and didn't give his star the proper guidance), but whatever the truth, the net result was Grade C Newman, Grade B-plus Woodward—and even the film itself, for all McCarey's inventiveness, did no better than B.

The plot, which in some ways was an ancestor of George Segal's recent *Loving,* had to do with one Harry Bannerman (Newman) a typical Connecticut commuter with a good job in Manhattan, a pretty wife, Grace (Miss Woodward), two fine children and a ranchstyle house complete with mortgage. The problem was one of those standards: Grace is so wrapped up in civic causes that she has little or no time for snuggling with Hubby when he comes home from struggling with the demons at points south. Enter the man-crazy *femme fatale* next door, Angela Hoffa (Joan Collins) who is bored with her husband Oscar (Murvyn Vye) and lights up like a beacon when Newman comes into view across the back yard.

The Army plans to launch a top secret enterprise in Newman's town, Putnam's Landing, and Grace heads a committee to oppose it, sending the reluctant Harry to Washington to apply pressures that will defeat the project. Angela follows and invades Harry's hotel room. Grace also descends on Washington hoping to surprise Harry—and surprise him she does.

Harry, now something of a grass widower, is persuaded by the Army to in turn persuade his fellow townsmen to go along with the secret project. He is also deputized to keep the tactless and buffoonish Captain Hoxie, the Army representative (Jack Carson), from alienating everyone in town. Grace is also back in Putnam's Landing, licking her wounds after the Angela

With Joanne Woodward

With Joan Collins

Washington-hotel-room fiasco, and she is more militant than ever against the government project. She plans, and leads her Indian-costumed committee in, a mock Plymouth Rock pageant. They also attack the military. At length, Colonel Thorwald (Gale Gordon) is given the okay from Washington to spill the beans; Putnam's Landing is to be a missile base site. The people are won over to the government project; Grace and Harry decide that the Angela misunderstanding isn't worth a break and make up. But in their reconciliatory enthusiasm they accidentally push the launching lever and off goes the missile into space —its only passenger a befuddled Captain Hoxie.

REVIEWS

Powe. in *Variety*

Somewhat slow and labored humor . . . a bed-room farce of split-level thinking in split-level housing . . . unmistakably a McCarey picture. Some of the gags are as elaborate and as carefully timed as a dance sequence . . . McCarey handles story so there is never any slightest chance of anything coming to a real conclusion. The situations are real, but what happens within them is so far beyond reality as to preclude genuine belief.

Stan Helleur in the *Toronto Globe and Mail*

Newman and Miss Woodward try hard and this is probably the reason they don't make it. The experienced, successful artists at broad satire or slapstick never seem to be trying too hard.

In *Cue*

Paul Newman and Joanne Woodward, who play the husband and wife around whom most of the action spins, tend to overact (and archly, at that).

With Joan Collins

Bosley Crowther in *The New York Times*
As crazy a lot of sheer farce madness as has been put on the screen in some time pops out in [this film]. And what's more, it's played by two of Hollywood's most formidable young dramatic stars, Joanne Woodward and Paul Newman. How's that for crazy, man! . . . For all the apparent odds against her, Miss Woodward makes a cheerful farceuse, on the order of the late Carole Lombard, and Mr. Newman plays it broadly for howls. [The film] is no epic. But it's good for laughs.

In the *New York Herald Tribune*
It has a certain bumptious charm, although neither Paul Newman or Joanne Woodward seem particularly comfortable in their farcical roles. There are a number of diverse but familiar elements in the story . . . a little too much attention is given to Newman's domestic troubles and one has the feeling that everyone is very much aware of just how funny they are being, but the upshot of it is a merry and colorful package for the holidays.

In *Time*
Max Shulman's comic novel bubbled like an aging chorus girl. McCarey's picture fizzes like an overheated bottle of pop. But chances are the customer who nuzzled the one will guzzle the other. . . . Still, there are moments.

The Young Philadelphians

1959   Warner Bros.

CREDITS

Directed by Vincent Sherman. Screenplay by James Gunn. From the novel *The Philadelphian* by Richard Powell. Director of Photography, Harry Stradling, Sr., A.S.C. Art director, Malcolm Bert. Film Editor, William Ziegler. Music by Ernest Gold. Musical Supervision by Ray Heindorf. Sound by Stanley Jones. Main Title designed by Maurice Binder. Costumes designed by Howard Shoup. Set decorations, John P. Austin. Makeup Supervision, Borden Bau, S.M.A. Assistant director, William Kissel. Running time, 136 minutes.

CAST

Paul Newman, Barbara Rush, Alexis Smith, Brian Keith, Diane Brewster, Billie Burke, John Williams, Robert Vaughn, Otto Kruger, Paul Picerni, Robert Douglas, Frank Conroy, Adam West, Fred Eisley, Richard Deacon.

THE FILM

Here was the quintessence of a Paul Newman film, circa 1959: the shrewd, enterprising, consummately self-seeking young man on the way up. No one could delineate such characters better than Newman; his sleek self-sufficiency was never at a loss, and he always seemed to land on his feet like a cat, whether in pursuit of success or women or both.

In this filmization of Richard Powell's novel about the intrigues and power struggles among Philadelphia's *haute monde,* Newman played Tony Lawrence, a young man with a rather suspect nativity. Tony's mother, Kate (Diane Brewster) had jilted contractor Mike Flanagan (Brian Keith) in 1924 to marry socialite William Lawrence (Adam West) who proved impotent on his honeymoon and promptly killed himself. A shocked Kate that night had given herself to Mike, who thus sired Tony.

Mike resents the fact that he must keep his parental role a secret so that the socially aspiring Kate as a Lawrence widow can raise Tony as a Lawrence scion—albeit without the family money, as Lawrence's mother, suspicious of Tony's parentage, had disinherited both. Tony, unaware of this lurid background, grows to manhood on the Main Line, attends Princeton where he is admired for his looks and brains, and instilled with his mother's fierce ambitions by osmosis, pursues a law career with single-minded intensity. He falls in love with Joan Dickinson (Barbara Rush) daughter of prominent lawyer Gilbert Dickinson (John Williams) but when Dickinson slyly dangles a post-law school spot in his law office if Tony will postpone his marriage to Joan, Tony jumps at it.

Joan, disillusioned and deeply hurt, marries another man, Carter Henry (Fred Eisley) who is later killed in the Korean War. Next Tony mulcts Louis Donetti (Paul Picerni) out of a summer assistantship to bigshot lawyer John Wharton (Otto Kruger) by playing on Wharton's frustrated wife's interest in him. Mrs. Wharton (Alexis Smith) makes a play for Tony, invading his bedroom in the dead of night while her elderly husband lies sleeping down the hall, but Tony shrewdly fends her off (while still saving her pride) by pretending he wants to marry her and coming on too strong. Whereupon the security-conscious lady makes a beeline back to her husband.

Tony's maneuverings in Philadelphia are briefly interrupted by Korean War service, in which his classmate and buddy, Chester Gwynn (Robert Vaughn) loses an arm. Soon Tony is back wheeling-and-dealing in Philadelphia, this time in Whar-

With Barbara Rush

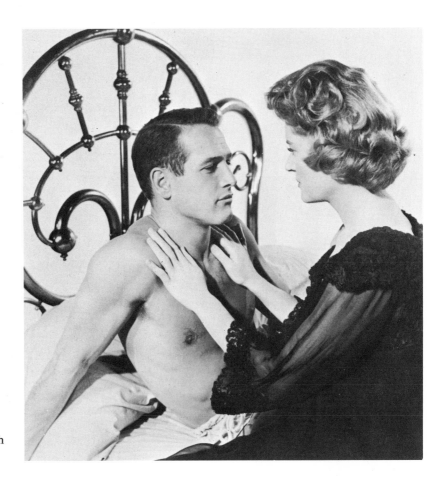

With Alexis Smith

ton's law firm. He also commences re-romancing the sadly cynical but still infatuated Joan, now a widow. He worms his way into the confidence of a superficially addled but basically shrewd multi-millionairess, Mrs. J. Arthur Allen (Billie Burke) by pointing out ways she can save on corporate taxes.

As Tony's success grows, he is urged by Mike Flanagan to enter politics. Then he learns that Chester Gwynn has been accused unjustly of murdering his conniving uncle Morton Stearnes (Robert Douglas) who has been withholding Chester's inheritance for specious reasons. He decides to defend Chester in his murder trial. Doctor Stearnes (Frank Conroy) threatens to reveal what he knows of Tony's parentage if Tony persists in rattling Stearnes' family skeletons while defending Chester. Kate and Mike, pressured by Doctor Stearnes, reveal his true ancestry to Tony. Joan and Tony quarrel again over his opportunism and part, but Tony, characteristically undeterred by these catastrophes, determines to free

Chester at any cost. He pushes the trial to a successful conclusion, getting Chester acquitted with the revelation that his supposedly murdered uncle had actually committed suicide because of ill-health. Joan's faith in Tony's basic integrity is restored, Tony decides that he may be a better person than he thought he was, and Tony and Joan exit the courtroom arm in arm.

Vincent Sherman, who had guided some of Joan Crawford's and Bette Davis's slicker films at Warner Bros., put Newman and Company through their paces in fast-paced, keep-it-percolating style, and the 136-minute movie seems much shorter than it actually is, since audience interest was continuously sustained. There was much that was pat, glib and superficial about the picture, but it was undeniably a package of quick-moving, glossy entertainment, and didn't pretend to be anything more than that, and even though Newman was allegedly discontented at the time and fighting to get out of his Warners' contract, he was never in better form, with his performance

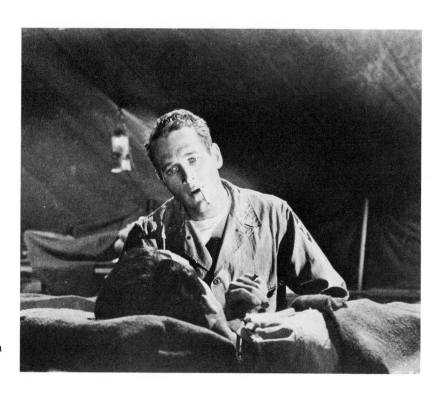

With Robert Vaughn

exuding a ferret-like cynicism that his private problems may have helped him to limn more sharply than usual.

REVIEWS

Lawrence J. Quirk in *Screen Slants*

The Young Philadelphians is about as archetypal a Paul Newman picture as can be devised, at least in so far as it showcases one of his emerging screen incarnations, namely the young-guy-on-the-make. Our boy moves lithely through this slick, sleek picture as its slick, sleek hero—everlastingly enterprising and inventive, smooth as satin with the ladies he romances and the people he aims to use, a young-man-on-the-way-up and may the devil take the hindmost; a male Eve Harrington who at times puts his *All About Eve* female counterpart to shame with his brazen aplomb, endless schemings and tart putdowns of people who prove troublesome.

When lovelorn Alexis Smith leaves the bedroom of her aging husband to "take the longest walk of her life"—down the hall on little cat feet to the roguish, half-nude Mr. Newman's bedroom, he cleverly gets rid of his employer's wife by giving *her* the impression *she* is getting rid of *him*. (There's a tip, fellows; get rid of your unwanted girlfriend Newman-style by pretending to come on so strong she'll recoil).

The picture is well-oiled, deceptively quiet-motored in its mechanics and plot convolutions but cacophonous and raucous enough to make any Bogart or Cagney happy once the somewhat specious melodramatics take over. Director Vincent Sherman keeps it all nicely paced, Mr. Newman is never at a loss no matter what—or who—presents problems, and Barbara Rush as the Philadelphia society girl who is disillusioned by his opportunistic maneuverings gives her best performance to date. Robert Vaughn is excellent as a young heir being rooked out of his inheritance, veteran Billie Burke is delightfully fey as a rich woman Mr. Newman charms and cajoles into giving him her law business, and it is good to see old favorites like Frank Conroy, Robert Douglas, Otto Kruger and John Williams in top form. But it is Mr. Newman's picture, and never has he been more the quintessence of the crass, pragmatic go-getter who lacks the finer subtleties of temperament or sensibility. When a distraught Miss Rush explains her tolerance of his self-seeking monkey-shines by telling Mr. Newman that she doesn't stop loving someone just because he doesn't measure up to her expectations, he walks out on her

84

snarling that *he* does just that. The film could well be subtitled "Why Ladies Love Cads."

Of course it's pat, thin stuff for much of the time, and the courtroom pyrotechnics toward the end are contrived to the point of the outrageous— but who really wants to turn cinematic purist and start splitting hairs on this or that when Paul Newman is engaging us mightily with his entertaining maneuverings onward and upward. And despite the hefty support he gets from a slew of accomplished performers, it's Mr. Newman who succeeds in making this picture look more solid and craftsmanlike than it actually is. Who said films were primarily a *director's* medium?

Frank Leyendecker in *Boxoffice*

Paul Newman's name, coupled with that of Barbara Rush, offers the best hook on which to hang an exploitation campaign. Both are noted for fine acting and Newman, particularly, has proven a favorite with the younger set.

In *Time*

For a moment there, it looks as if the picture is going to make an honest if not very original point. But before anyone can say Fish House Punch, the script gives the hero a splendid opportunity to save his soul without losing any money.

Jesse Zunser in *Cue*

Although some may call Richard Powell's popular novel of contemporary social conflicts in The City of Brotherly Love "soap opera," in film form it makes for a solidly integrated story—interesting, well-written, directed and acted. Under the careful, tasteful direction of Vincent Sherman, a fine cast makes the story seem, perhaps, more reasonable than it is . . . the film has been elaborately produced, extravagantly set and costumed.

With Joanne Woodward

From The Terrace

1960   20th Century-Fox

CREDITS

Produced and directed by Mark Robson. Screenplay by Ernest Lehman. Based on the novel by John O'Hara. Photographed by Leo Tover, A.S.C. Art Directors, Lyle R. Wheeler, Maurice Ransford, Howard Richman. Music by Elmer Bernstein. Set Decorations by Walter M. Scott and Paul S. Fox. Special Photographic Effects, L. B. Abbott, James B. Gordon. Assistant Director, Hal Herman. Film Editor, Dorothy Spencer. Orchestration, Edward B. Powell. Hairstyles by Helen Turpin. Gowns designed by Travilla. Makeup by Ben Nye. Sound by Harry M. Leonard and Alfred Bruzlin. Color by DeLuxe. Color consultant, Leonard Doss. Running time, 144 minutes.

CAST

Paul Newman, Joanne Woodward, Myrna Loy, Ina Balin, Leon Ames, Elixabeth Allen, Barbara Eden, George Grizzard, Patrick O'Neal, Felix Aylmer, Raymond Greenleaf, Malcolm Atterbury, Raymond Bailey, Ted DeCorsia, Howard Caine, Kathryn Givney, Dorothy Adams, Lauren Gilbert, Blossom Rock, Cecil Elliott.

THE FILM

20th Century-Fox decided to cash in on the young-man-on-the-make vogue Newman had set at Warners in his recent *The Young Philadelphians,* and persuaded the star to appear in *From the Terrace,* a rather turgid screenplay concocted

With Ina Balin

from John O'Hara's novel of the same name. O'Hara's Philadelphia and Richard Powell's Philadelphia are brothers-under-the-skin only in the respect that they afforded Paul Newman another chance to demonstrate (this time in O'Hara style) just how an attractive and ruthless young Philadelphian gets wherever he is going.

Though O'Hara is a far more penetrating and perceptive novelist than Powell, the film version of his novel proved inferior to Warners' version of Powell's—primarily because O'Hara's original was watered-down. Even so, the novel was regarded widely as second-rate O'Hara, and the movie version of 1960 must go down in cinematic history as second-rate Newman, in the respect that the rickety screenplay did not sustain the star's efforts at salvage. Even the creative touches of talented director Mark Robson didn't help.

The critics thought it one big cliché and insufficiently motivated characterization-wise, though some praise was accorded Newman for his not-completely-successful attempts to triumph over the script's deficiencies. His competent performance here was all the more remarkable considering that he moonlighted from his stage appearance in *Sweet Bird of Youth* to make the film, and the toll on his creative energies must. have been considerable. The plot of the novel was boiled down and compressed in time to accommo-

date what the screenwriters probably imagined would make a fast-paced, attention-holding movie, but at 144 minutes it seems to go on forever.

This time around, Newman played Alfred Eaton, a young Philadelphian of good family who returns from World War I to find his mother, Martha Eaton (Myrna Loy) bogged down in alcohol and his father, Samuel Eaton (Leon Ames) a wealthy businessman, as unfeeling and autocratic as ever. Alfred is uptight with his father because the elder Eaton continues to idolize his dead older brother, to whose memory Alfred is still playing second fiddle. Next Alfred must cope with the revelation of his mother's adultery, and proceeds to warn her lover to leave her alone, henceforth. All this domestic infelicity proves a bit much, and Alfred scorns employment in the family business to take off for New York, where he joins his friend Lex Porter (George Grizzard) in an aeronautics venture.

On a Long Island weekend, Alfred meets and falls in love with Mary St. John (Joanne Woodward) a wealthy heiress, and they are married. When Alfred saves the life of the grandson (Jimmy Martin) of James Duncan Mac Hardie (Felix Aylmer) the grateful old man takes Alfred into his Wall Street investment house, and soon Alfred is wheeling and dealing away. His exploits on Wall Street are soon monopolizing his time

With Joanne Woodward

and attention, with a consequent neglect of his husbandly duties, and the restless and erotic-natured Mary is soon back romancing with a former flame, psychiatrist James Roper (Patrick O'Neal).

On a business trip to a small Pennsylvania town, Alfred falls in love with Natalie Benziger (Ina Balin) a sweet-natured, unassertive girl who lacks Mary's demanding nature and pampered ego. The two fight their growing love at first, but eventually succumb after much soul-searching, as Alfred has no wish to hurt her and Natalie is a fine-grained person who does not cotton to casual affairs. Alfred has become increasingly disenchanted with the success-and-status rat race, and his involvement with the sincere and self-immolating Natalie reinforces his conviction that his marriage and his career have proven cop-outs of

the first water. So when colleague Creighton Duffy (Howard Caine) attempts to blackmail Alfred into helping him promote a shabby investment scheme, by threatening to expose his affair with Natalie to the puritanical Mac Hardie, who is rigidly opposed to infidelity and divorce among his employees, Alfred decides once and for all that the moment of truth with himself and others has come. He tells his wife he is through, states his case openly before Mac Hardie and the outraged board of directors, and then goes off to what he feels will be a life of emotional integrity with Natalie.

REVIEWS

Holl. in *Variety*

The O'Hara name, the attention the novel received, although considered pedestrian O'Hara by the literary reviewers, the marquee value of Joanne Woodward, Paul Newman and Myrna Loy, and the promise of some hot sex scenes that goes with almost any O'Hara work may make the picture a popular success, but the more discriminating filmgoer will find *From the Terrace* seriously deficient... [it] builds up to one big cliché. ... Newman plays the success-seeker as if he were carrying the weight of the world's problems on his shoulders. Despite the slight insight into his background, it's difficult to comprehend the reasons for his actions . . . he seems more like a pawn being pushed than an individual who knows what he is doing.

In *Cue*
John O'Hara's turgid novel of contemporary (and commercial) love and marriage, "status"—and the chase for money that so often destroys all of these—has been given the lush treatment in this gilded colorfilm production . . . the scrubbed (although not quite purified) film reflects the wavering plot-and-character values that ran rampant through [the book]. . . . The story (discounting many flaws) is nevertheless interesting—slickly written even in its incredibilities. The actors suffer from script uncertainties—among them Paul Newman and Joanne Woodward as the couple who begin with love, and end in disaster.

In the *London Observer*
In the whole of this long film we encounter only one sympathetic character, and although she is poor and pure, she is practically a ninny. The other characters are rich, and either lustful or

With Felix Aylmer

With Myrna Loy

overbearing. *From the Terrace* is another treatise on Hollywood's favorite axiom, that wealth and power corrupt . . . at one point in the film some character observes to another character, "This won't last . . ." Unfortunately it lasts all too long.

John McCarten in *The New Yorker*

I was not amused . . . as played by Paul Newman, (the lead) is a dead ringer for Marlon Brando, complete with built-in pout. . . . Mr. New-

man is . . . encumbered with rhetoric, and in great, static closeups, he and Miss Balin schnooze so much that the spectator is inclined to wonder whether they are lovers or delegates to a political convention.

Howard Thompson in *The New York Times*

A handsome picture, well-performed and emotionally intriguing . . . however, it lacks real cumulative power. . . . Mr. Newman is fine throughout.

Exodus

1960   United Artists

CREDITS

An Otto Preminger Production released through United Artists. Produced and directed by Otto Preminger. Screenplay by Dalton Trumbo, based on the novel by Leon Uris. Photographed by Sam Leavitt. Music by Ernest Gold. Art Director, Richard Day. Set Decorations by Dario Simani. Film Editor, Louis R. Loeffler. Titles designed by Saul Bass. Sound by Paddy Cunningham, Red Law and John Cox. Sound effects by Win Ryder. Special effects by Cliff Richardson. Makeup by George Lane. Wardrobe by Joe King, Marge Slater and May Walding. Hairstyles by A. G. Scott. Miss Saint's clothes by Rudi Gernreich. Costume Coordinator, Hope Bryce. General Manager, Martin C. Schute. Production Manager, Eva Monley. Assistant to the Producer, Max

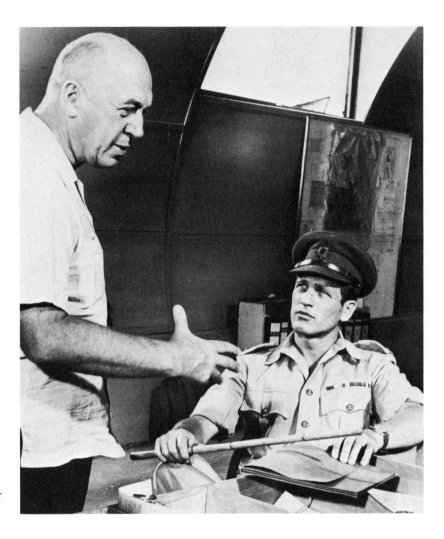

With director Otto Preminger

Slater. Assistant Director, Gerry O'Hara. Filmed in Israel. Technicolor and Super-Panavision 70. Running time, 212 minutes.

CAST
Paul Newman, Eva Marie Saint, Ralph Richardson, Peter Lawford, Lee J. Cobb, Sal Mineo, John Derek, Hugh Griffith, David Opotoshu, Jill Haworth, Gregory Ratoff, Felix Aylmer, Marius Goring, Alexandra Stewart, Michael Wager, Martin Benson, Paul Stevens, Betty Walker, Martin Miller, Victor Maddern, George Maharis, John Crawford, Samuel Segal, Dahn Ben Motz, Peter Madden, Ralph Truman, Joseph Furst, Paul Stassine, Marc Burns, Esther Reichstadt, Zeporrah Peled, Philo Hauser.

THE FILM
Otto Preminger's ambitious, 212-minute production of Leon Uris' best-selling novel *Exodus,* re-

plete with screenplay by Dalton Trumbo and assorted mountings by an army of technicians, seemed to have everything in it but the kitchen sink—and there were even a few of those! Preminger poured energy and organizational expertise into the film, marshalling stupendous crowd scenes, insisting on topnotch production values and transporting cast and crew to Israel itself for an all-out attempt at a huge and heroic Technicolor and Super-Panavision celebration of the Israeli courage and persistence which eventually led to independence and nationhood in 1947.

The subject was undeniably a stirring and glorious one, the aims not to be faulted, the intentions the best, and the picture boasted a number of stirring moments, but the critics for the most part opined that it was overlong, episodic, turgid, thematically inconclusive, and fell short of truly heroic proportions. Newman, as the young Hagannah leader Ari Ben Canaan, drew lukewarm reviews. His competence and his confidence in the role were credited but it was generally felt that he failed to inject sufficient humanity, stature and feeling into his role, of a kind that would have lifted his characterization to Oscar-calibre greatness.

Perfunctory, sound, competent, stout, capable—the critics damned Newman with faint praise. His failure to rise fully to the demands of the occasion in such a bravura and lengthy role is puzzling; ("Charlton Heston he ain't," the wags snickered). Some stories had it that he and Preminger were chemically and creatively antithetical; other reports had it that the lengthy and taxing role had depleted even Newman's prodigious energies, leaving him listless and perfunctory and devitalized to the point where he couldn't summon the extra effort required to redeem the total. It was also opined that Preminger's grandiose conceptions had drowned even the best characterizations in a sea of overproduced epic-style sound and fury. As it turned out, nobody won, with Newman and Preminger both meriting only B's for their respective contributions.

The well-known story of *Exodus* details the internment of some 30,000 Jews who have fled Europe to the island of Cyprus, their attempts to enter Palestine frustrated by the British. Ari Ben Canaan (Newman) an officer of the Jewish underground (the Palestine-based Hagannah) implements an heroic project designed to dramatize the Jews' plight and their determination to win through to dignity and freedom. Six hundred of them are engineered by Ari and his aides into an escape aboard the *Exodus,* a freighter ship. Then they engage in a lengthy hunger strike to protest the British destroyers who block the way. They then threaten to blow themselves up if the British come aboard. Also on the ship is Kitty Fremont (Eva Marie Saint) an American nurse whose newspaper-man husband has left her a widow. With Kitty is a refugee child, Karen (Jill Haworth) whom she has taken under her wing. General Sutherland (Ralph Richardson) commander at Cyprus, proves sympathetic to the Jews' plight and influences the British to permit the ship's journey to Haifa.

The refugees land and Ari and Kitty find that their relationship, shared amidst many tensions and hardships, is ripening into love. Kitty gets an

Paul Newman

The Journey

With Hugh Griffith

With Eva Marie Saint, Jill Haworth and Sal Mineo

intimate insight into the Jews' plight, bolstering Ari's morale as he comes into conflict, along with his father, Hagannah stalwart Barak Ben Canaan (Lee J. Cobb) with his uncle, Akiva (David Opotoshu) and Dov Landau (Sal Mineo) a young Auschwitz survivor who are members of the Irgun, a Jewish terrorist organization that disagrees with the Hagannah which tries to minimize violence. Ari, convinced that action at all costs is mandatory if Jewish aims are to be furthered, joins the Irgun despite his beliefs and helps it to plan and carry out a mass breakout of Jews from the prison at Acre. Though they succeed in the project, Akiva is killed. Israeli independence is achieved shortly thereafter.

REVIEWS

Hollis Alpert in *The Saturday Review*
We are witnessing . . . the birth pangs of a new nation. History may be skimped, the political complexities oversimplified, but the handling is intelligent and reasonably thoughtful. . . . If [the film] had been allowed to end forty to fifty minutes before its full running time, I suspect I would have left my seat with fewer mixed feelings . . . but Preminger relentlessly insists on going on, and the more he does, the more the lack of dimension of the characters becomes apparent. Figures who, up to then, had been heroic in size, become longwinded and lose our interest, even though they are played by such capable people as Paul Newman and Eva Marie Saint.

Bosley Crowther in *The New York Times*
. . . massive, overlong, episodic, involved and generally inconclusive "cinemarama" of historical and pictorial events . . . an ambiguous piece of work . . . so much churning around in it that no deep or solid stream of interest evolves. . . . Ari Ben Canaan, who is forcefully, albeit much too neatly, played by an always well-shaved Paul Newman, is a mighty stout fellow to have around, but it is

Independence is announced

hard to gather where he stands or what distinguishes him as an individual.

Paul V. Beckley in the *New York Herald Tribune*
Otto Preminger had a stirring subject in *Exodus* and in his movie version he has made his point eloquently in the first hour but let some clichés of romance and melodrama dim the vision in the later hours . . . Had the film continued in [the earlier] calmly definitive vein, one might well applaud a masterpiece. However, once in Israel, the characters of Newman and Miss Saint stiffen into the postures of stock film romance . . . [Preminger] is handling a good many points of view in this necessarily complicated subject, British, Hagannah, Irgun, Arab. For the most part he has tried to indicate the complexities. This air of intellectual honesty more than makes up for the lapses into romantic clichés.

Pyr. in *Variety*
Technically Paul Newman gives a sound performance, but he fails to give the role the warmth and deep humanity that would give the character distinguished stature.

With Piper Laurie

The Hustler

1961   20th Century-Fox

CREDITS

Produced and directed by Robert Rossen. Screenplay by Robert Rossen and Sidney Carroll. Based on the novel by Walter Tevis. Photography, Gene Shufton. Art Direction, Harry Horner and Albert Brenner. Set Decorations, Gene Callahan. Film Editor, Deedee Allan. Sound, James Shields. Technical Advisor, Willie Mosconi. Unit Manager, John Graham. Costumes, Ruth Morley. Makeup, Bob Jiras. Hairstyles, Deneene. Assistant Directors, Charles Maguire and Don Kranz. In CinemaScope. Filmed in New York City. Running time, 133 minutes.

CAST

Paul Newman, Jackie Gleason, Piper Laurie, George C. Scott, Myron McCormick, Murray Hamilton, Michael Constantine, Stefan Gierasch, Jake LaMotta, Gordon B. Clarke, Carl York, Alexander Rose, Carolyn Coates, Vincent Gardenia, Gloria Curtis, Charles Diercep, Donald Crabtree, Brendan Fay, Cliff Fellow.

THE FILM

If ever Paul Newman needed a first-rate picture—and a chance to deliver a first-rate performance—he needed it in 1961. In the three years since *Cat*

With Jackie Gleason

on a Hot Tin Roof he had known near-misses and false alarms, and even slickly commercial pictures like *The Young Philadelphians* were doing nothing to take him where he really wanted to go. What he needed at that juncture, Robert Rossen provided.

Rossen, the painstaking, toughly sensitive genius of *All the Kings Men* and other films that carried his unmistakable stamp, came up with a screenplay based on a novel by Walter Tevis, which he had co-written with Sidney Carroll. He got himself an able cameraman, Gene Shufton,

With Myron McCormick, left

With Piper Laurie

arranged to produce and direct the film for 20th Century-Fox—and persuaded a then somewhat worried and deflated Newman that *The Hustler* was the ticket. It proved to be a ticket to Newman's second Academy Award nomination.

The part of pool hustler Eddie Felson was perfectly tailored to his measure, and he had more-than-able support from Jackie Gleason and Piper Laurie. Eddie, jaded, disillusioned, filled with American-style *Weltschmerz,* a wanderer who is only a few cuts above a bum, is an adventurer who learns about love and its responsibilities too late. Eddie is a plum role for the actor whose chemistry and inner psychological processes mesh with its mechanics; Newman was right for it in every way. It had elements in it that Newman empathized with: the sense of a "buried life," the tired cynicism and grayish mental outlook, the flickering resiliencies of the guy who is down but not quite out.

For this performance, and justly, the critics accorded Newman some of the most glowing notices he had ever received, throwing out adjectives like "superlative," "excellent," "masterly," "dimensional," "depthful." Once again, Hollywood and the world of showbusiness were reminded that Newman, in the right role, was an actor to be reckoned with. Piper Laurie, George C. Scott and Jackie Gleason also scored heavily, and the film took Scott's career up several notches. Behind it all was the guiding intelligence of the resourceful Rossen, in one of his finest creative hours. The picture had the stuff of life in it; its psychology was true; its people real; it was free of mendacities or artificialities of any kind.

The story dealt with pool shark Eddie Felson (Newman) who hustles in billiard rooms cross-country, taking on suckers whom he allows to win until the stakes get high enough; then he clamps down with brilliant shots, makes a bundle, and

About to be roughed-up

disappears. With his manager-crony Charlie Binns (Myron McCormick) Eddie comes to New York to challenge the champion poolplayer of the fifty states, Minnesota Fats (Jackie Gleason). For many hours the two men battle it out on "the field of the cloth of green" and Eddie is the winner all the way—until overconfidence and too much drinking bring him low. He ends up beaten and financially drained. Later, at an all-night restaurant, he meets up with a crippled girl, Sarah Packard (Piper Laurie) who is a disillusioned, life-weary alcoholic. Eddie moves into Sarah's place and drifts around town hustling in third-rate pool places. One night he picks the wrong man and the loser's friends corner him and break his thumbs. He is comforted by Sarah and a mutual feeling dawns between them, though her feelings run deeper than his.

After he has recovered, Eddie gets involved with Bert Gordon (George C. Scott) a ruthless gambler who arranges topnotch matches for Eddie —for a 70 per cent cut. Eddie, Bert and Sarah go to Kentucky, where he challenges and defeats a millionaire billiard addict, Findlay (Murray Hamilton). Sarah has been deteriorating at a rapid rate, and Bert, who wishes to dominate Eddie com-

pletely, undermines her to the point where suicide seems the only way out for her. Her death sobers the glumly self-centered Eddie, who now realizes that his last chance for a meaningful relationship with another human being has gone. He returns to New York, soundly beats Minnesota Fats in a disciplined and brilliantly executed rematch, then refuses to cut Bert into the take, denounces his cupidity and gross inhumanity, and walks away. Life may not really improve for Eddie henceforth, but spiritually he has learned and grown.

REVIEWS

Frank Leyendecker in *Boxoffice*

Robert Rossen, who produced as well as directed, gets a superlative portrayal from Paul Newman.

In *Time*

Artistically speaking, it is an amusingly mangled myth, an epic in a pool hall, a ceremony of chivalric valor on the Field of the Cloth of Green ...the picture is much too long but it has strength as well as length. Cameraman Gene Shufton has artfully preserved what actor Gleason calls "the dirty, antiseptic look of poolrooms"—spots on the floor, toilets stuffed up, but the tables brushed immaculately, like green jewels lying in the mud. The pool shooting scenes are magnificently staged —the principals well coached by Willie Mosconi, top-ranking pool player in the U.S. . . . Newman is better than usual. . . . In the minds of many customers there may arise a certain doubt that playing pool is as lofty a theme as Director Rossen seems to think, but he doggedly insists on the point, and in the middle of the picture he carries it with a clutch of phrases ("I got oil on my arm") that breathe the smoky poetry of pool-rooms and ring true as a struck spittoon.

In *Variety*

Despite the excellence of Newman's portrayal of the boozing pool hustler, the sordid aspects of overall picture are strictly downbeat . . . Newman is entirely believable.

Alton Cook in the *New York World-Telegram & Sun*

Paul Newman is always a dominant figure in any scene, but there is something extra this time in his intense ardor as the man who treats a game with religious zeal that at times mounts to mania. His standard is high but he has surpassed it this time.

Bosley Crowther in *The New York Times*

It crackles with credible passions. It comes briskly and brusquely to sharp points. . . . Mr. Rossen and Sidney Carroll have provided their characters with dialogue that keeps them buoyant and alive . . . Paul Newman violently plays with a master's control of tart expressions and bitterly passionate attitudes.

Paul V. Beckley in the *New York Herald Tribune*

The writing, the directing and the acting all have that kind of intense unanimity that convinces you everyone involved understood and felt what they were concerned with. . . . I'm not sure Paul Newman has ever looked more firmly inside a role. . . . Rossen has been at pains to avoid that over-emphasis that is so often fatal to any emphasis at all. His movie is all of one piece. Its effect is built not alone out of the crises of the characters but of their quiet moments too [which] add much to the general impression of everything moving from first to last inevitably and rightly.

Playing pool

With Diahann Carroll and
Sidney Poitier

Paris Blues

1961   United Artists

CREDITS

A Pennebaker Production. Executive Producers,
George Glass and Walter Seltzer. Producer, Sam
Shaw. Directed by Martin Ritt. Screenplay by
Jack Sher, Irene Kamp and Walter Bernstein.
Adaptation by Lulla Adler. Based on a novel by
Harold Flender. Photographed by Christian Mat-
ros. Music by Duke Ellington. Second Unit di-
rected by Andre Smagghe. Art Direction, Alex-
ander Trauner. Film Editor, Roger Dwyre. Sound,
Jo De Bretagne. Production Manager, Michael
Rittener. Assistant Director, Bernard Farrel. Lo-
cation scenes filmed in Paris. Running time, 98
minutes.

CAST

Paul Newman, Joanne Woodward, Sidney Poitier,
Louis Armstrong, Diahann Carroll, Serge Reg-
giani, Barbara Laage, Andre Luguet, Marie Ver-
sini, Moustache, Aaron Bridgers, Guy Pederson,
Maria Velasco, Roger Blin, Helene Dieudonne,
Niko.

THE FILM

Paris Blues was Newman's second picture with
director Martin Ritt and his fourth with Miss
Woodward. A story about jazz musicians filmed
in Paris on location, and co-starring Sidney Poitier and Diahann Carroll, this picture's only assets
were the excellent musicianship of Louis Armstrong and Duke Ellington. Coming on the heels
of his signal triumph in *The Hustler,* this represented a disappointing setback for Newman, with
the critics complaining of the unreality of its
characters and the shallowness of its story line.
The drama seemed listless, pedestrian, one-dimensional, as were the characters, and both
played a distinct second fiddle to the music, nor
was the interracial casting particularly an asset,
though Newman, Woodward, Poitier and Carroll
played easily and well together.

Newman reportedly gambled on the picture
because he felt the attractive casting, the timeli-
ness of the racial angle, Ritt's sure directorial
touch and the fascinating background music

would bring home a crisply entertaining winner, but it didn't work out that way. A frothy and insubstantial concoction, *Paris Blues* was not the sort of thing Ritt did best, nor was Newman particularly suited to the role of the musician. One critic capsulized the film's failure when he noted that the audience couldn't be lured into caring about the characters, and that sums up its main deficiency.

The plot, such as it is, has to do with two expatriate American jazzmen, Ram Bowen (Newman) and Eddie Cook (Poitier) who live in Paris. Ram is after a serious musical career. Eddie enjoys the tolerant atmosphere and the freedom from U.S. racial tensions. They work at a Left Bank club owned by Marie Seoul (Barbara Laage) who is having a casual affair with Ram. Michel Duvigne (Serge Raggiani) a gypsy guitarist who is a narcotics addict, and Wild Man Moore (Louis Armstrong) a trumpeter, are among their friends. Ram and Eddie meet a couple of American tourists, Lillian Corning (Joanne Woodward) and Connie Lampson (Diahann Carroll) who are visiting Paris on a two-week vacation.

A romance develops between Eddie and Connie. Lillian and Ram also find that a feeling is growing between them. Ram, however, is determined to remain in Paris and pursue a classical career in music, and he is reluctant to give up his freedom and return to a second-rate career in the States. Eddie, on the other hand, lacks Ram's intense ambition and despite his aversion to racial discrimination back home, he determines to return and marry Connie. When an impresario tells Ram that his concerto leaves something to be desired, he is at first discouraged, and almost gives up and returns to America with Lillian. Eventually he decides that he must put his abilities to the ultimate test in Paris via persistent creative efforts in composing, no matter what the cost, and sadly he bids Lillian goodbye at the railroad station.

REVIEWS

Arthur Knight in *The Saturday Review*
The fundamental weakness [of the film] is that one couldn't care less what happens to its central characters. Superficially, they are unattractive people—and neither the script, the direction, nor the actors themselves ever carry them beyond that level.

Tube. in *Variety*
Crux of the picture's failure is the screenplay's failure to bring any true identity to any of these

With Joanne Woodward

With Sidney Poitier

With Joanne Woodward

With Barbara Laage

four characters. As a result, their relationships are vague and superficial. Furthermore, except for sporadic interludes, none of the four players can achieve clarity, arouse sympathy, or sustain concern. This is especially disappointing in view of the acknowledged calibre of performers such as Newman, Poitier and Miss Woodward . . . the film is notable for Duke Ellington's moody, stimulating jazz score. The music is likely to seem just too obtrusive and dissonant for more conservative taste, but there is no denying its importance as a driving factor in the sluggish dramatic proceedings and its intrinsic value as a jazz work. There are, however, scenes when the drama itself takes a back seat to the music, with unsatisfactory results insofar as dialogue is concerned. Along the way there are several full-fledged passages of superior Ellingtonia such as "Mood Indigo" and "Sophisticated Lady" and Louis Armstrong is on hand for one flamboyant interlude of hot jazz.

In *Cue*

The story is frothy and self-consciously "soci- ally significant": a loosely amoral, romantically dreamy-eyed, casually inter-racial, pseudo-realistic tale of music and music-makers, of love, conflict, boys-grab-at-girls, dope, tragedy, and raucously wild music. And all so slickly fricasseed and illogical as to add up to a Frenchified fairy tale that fobs off criticism. As such—and particularly in view of the extraordinarily beautiful outdoor photography all over Paris, it is an interesting even if incredible picture.

Paul V. Beckley in the *New York Herald Tribune*

The characters are no more than attitudes, so it is by no means the fault of Miss Woodward, Miss Carroll, Newman or Poitier that they come off so poorly.

Frank Leyendecker in *Boxoffice*

There is a marquee-mighty cast headed by Paul Newman, who gives an exceptionally fine performance.

Sweet Bird of Youth

1962   Metro-Goldwyn-Mayer

CREDITS

A Roxbury Production. Produced by Pandro S. Berman. Directed and written by Richard Brooks. Based on the play by Tennessee Williams. Photographed by Milton Krasner. Music Supervisor, Harold Gelman. Orchestra conducted by Robert Armbruster. Art Direction, George W. Davis and Urie McCleary. Set decorations, Henry Grace and Hugh Hunt. Special visual effects, Lee LeBlanc. Film Editor, Henry Berman. Recording Supervisor, Franklin Milton. Makeup, William Tuttle. Costumes, Orry-Kelly. Hairstyles, Sydney Guilaroff. Associate Producer, Kathryn Hereford. Assistant Director, Hank Moonjean. CinemaScope and MetroColor. Charles K. Hagedon, Color Consultant. Running time, 120 minutes.

CAST

Paul Newman, Geraldine Page, Shirley Knight, Ed Begley, Rip Torn, Mildred Dunnock, Madeleine Sherwood, Philip Abbott, Corey Allen, Barry Cahill, Dug Taylor, James Douglas, Barry Atwater, Charles Arnt, Dorothy Konrad, James Chandler, Mike Steen, Kelly Thordsen.

THE FILM

Some two years after appearing on the Broadway stage to rave notices in Tennessee Williams' *Sweet Bird of Youth,* Newman made the film version for Metro-Goldwyn-Mayer. Newman, Geraldine Page, Rip Torn and Madeleine Sherwood repeated their original roles. Replacing the stage's Sidney Blackmer, Diana Hyland and Martine Bartlett were Ed Begley, Shirley Knight and Mildred Dunnock.

The casting changes paled in comparison with the drastic emasculations inflicted on Williams' corrosive and piercing play in this Hollywood incarnation, and which blunted its points and compromised its integrity. Again Richard Brooks was called in to direct Newman in a Williams work. He also wrote the screenplay. Hobbled by the Production Code, whose inane restrictions in-

With Geraldine Page

sisted on dying a slow, piecemeal death, to say nothing of the Hollywood studios' continuing insistence on watering down and romanticizing Williams' conceptions, Brooks meddled and tampered as he had in *Cat on a Hot Tin Roof* and reinforced his burgeoning reputation as Chief Castrator of Honestly Cynical Stage Art by changing the ending around so that the hero, Chance Wayne, is merely beaten up, rather than castrated as he was in the play.

Brooks even allowed Chance to run away with his true love, Heavenly Finley, whereas in the play she was lost to him. In Williams' honest original, Heavenly had been infected by Chance with a venereal disease and had been hysterectomized. In the Brooks version she is let off with a pregnancy and abortion.

As is obvious from these sophomoric instances of Hollywood's craven panderings to what it regarded as 1962-style "great silent majority" conventions (and boxoffice power) it is apparent that, at the time, the West Coast film capital had a great deal of growing-up to do. Moreover, Brooks, though intelligent, industrious and well-meaning, was as a writer no match for Williams and as a director far below Elia Kazan—and the result was an uneasy blend of Hollywood frou-frou and Williams' tragic sense, which no amount of fustian

tampering could completely obscure. Since Brooks was no more than a craftsman at his best, and Williams was an artist, there was much criticism of this high-handed tampering with the perceptions and inner visions of America's most gifted playwright.

Despite all this, Newman managed to sneak through a robust, vigorous performance, though unlike Kazan, Brooks permitted him to lapse at times into the mannerisms that had in the past enhanced Newman's film-idol image at the cost of his integrity as an actor. Miss Page obviously had no intention of letting Brooks or anyone else dilute her strong stage performance as the fading movie star, and she was every bit as effective in the screen version. Miss Knight, Begley, Rip Torn, Miss Dunnock and Miss Sherwood all delivered in fine style. The reviews of the film were naturally equivocal, given all the circumstances, and words like "glossy," "slick," "toned-down," "altered," "weak" and "melodramatic" proliferated in their reviews. Miss Page drew adjectives like "superb," "mercurial," and "excellent" and Newman, despite some critics' references to his mannerisms, got off with "vital," "excellent," "assured," "very good," "fine" and even "memorable." But such kudoes, while sincere for Miss Page, seemed somehow to be addressed more to Newman's stage per-

With Shirley Knight

formance, or the memory of it. Brooks, to repeat, was no Kazan, and Newman had to contend with a watered-down characterization and situations. Significantly, he did not get a 1962 Academy nomination for this film; had Kazan been allowed to direct the film and had Williams written it in full-strength, Newman might well have won an Oscar. And certainly Miss Page deserved one.

The famous story deals with Chance Wayne (Newman) the beach boy and aspiring actor who has parlayed his good looks and sex appeal into a kept-boy spot with has-been screen star Alexandra Del Lago (Miss Page) whose influence, he hopes, will bring him a movie contract. Alexandra takes constant refuge in drink, hashish, oxygen masks—and compliant young male whores. She is convinced that her comeback picture is a failure, and she and Chance, after peregrinating restlessly

around the country, wind up in his Florida hometown, where Chance had left some dirty linen. It seems (according to Brooks' version) that he had impregnated Heavenly Finley (Shirley Knight), the daughter of corrupt and powerful politician Tom (Boss) Finley (Ed Begley). Chance plans a reunion with Heavenly but her father and brother, Tom Jr. (Rip Torn) conspire to keep them apart. Heavenly's Aunt Nonny (Mildred Dunnock) who is sympathetic to Chance, tries to help him but her efforts are frustrated by the Finleys. Heavenly fears for Chance's safety and Aunt Nonny warns him to leave town.

Meanwhile, Alexandra has learned from Walter Winchell that her comeback is a success and that she is again on the Hollywood rise. Once more arrogant and assured, she treats Chance with cynical disdain and prepares to leave. Outside her

With Geraldine Page

hotel a Finley political rally degenerates into a fiasco when Miss Lucy (Madeleine Sherwood), Finley's discarded mistress, arranges to have Finley's private life, including Heavenly's abortion, exposed publicly. Alexandra, sensing that Chance is in serious danger, offers to take him with her, but he declines, and goes to find Heavenly. Tom Jr. and his gang of toughs find Chance outside the Finley mansion and beat him and disfigure his face. But Heavenly defies her father and goes off with Chance, leaving an enraged Boss Finley and a triumphantly smiling Aunt Nonnie in front of the mansion. (For years the closing sequence of the film was referred to contemptuously in New York as "the cop-out ending to beat all cop-out endings," and that it certainly was).

REVIEWS

Tube. in *Variety*

One has to pry deep to find edification or human enlightenment in the raw melodramatic elements. But it's a glossy, engrossing hunk of motion picture entertainment, slickly produced. . . . In altering the playwright's Dixie climax (castration of the hero) Brooks has slightly weakened the story by damaging character consistency and emotional momentum. But he has accomplished this revision as if winking his creative eye at the "in" audience, saying, "Yes, we have compromised but you get the general idea." The "general idea" is that the menace, or grisly potential, can be equally as frightening as the act. . . . Newman brings thrust and vitality to the role but has some overly mannered moments that distract. Paradoxically these mannerisms, which tend to diminish his stature and versatility as an actor, serve to make him a star.

In the *London Sunday Times*

The Williams themes are here in strength: mob-savagery, sexual violence, the immolation of the pitifully, obstinately defenseless. Beginning handled excitingly, then a tailing off; Paul Newman [is] excellent, Geraldine Page superb as the ex star, insolent, hysterical, egomaniacal, a performance of magnitude.

Bosley Crowther in *The New York Times*

It is ironic that the work of Tennessee Williams, who is allowed to be the most powerful and prolific playwright (if not the most pleasant) writing for the American theatre today, has tended more and more to be unsuitable for translation to the screen—at least into the kinds of motion pictures that are conventional with Hollywood. We mean, of course, those pictures in which ugliness and violence are toned down and the logic of predestined frustration is hoisted into the illogic of some sort of halfway happy end...the total point of the play's conclusion in the emasculation and utter debasement of the principal character has been destroyed. Mr. Brooks has altered the ending so that the fellow is only beat up and kicked a bit by the brother of the young woman he has violated and then is oddly allowed to run off with her. In short, to satisfy the Hollywood hunger for gratification of the romantic ideal. Mr. Brooks simply has reversed the play's cold logic. He has turned defeat into victory. This tampering... knocks the final punch out of the picture and... reduces what might have been a really cruel spurt of honest cynicism to a weak splash of phony hope.

In *The New Yorker*

An actor can't do much more than feel ticklish under such circumstances, and I think I detected an occasional look of desperate longing on Mr. Newman's face, as if he were thinking how nice it would be to be ugly and fat and middle-aged and allowed simply to *act*.

Richard L. Coe in *The Washington Post*

Miss Page's nerve-wracked, mercurially-paced film queen is even more striking than on the stage. This is even more true of Newman, now wholly assured as Chance, despite the disappearance of his introspective lines to the audience.

Paul V. Beckley in the *New York Herald Tribune*

Newman...in these furious *tête-à-têtes* when Brooks' script lets him dive into his role's clammier depths, is very good indeed. Mildred Dunnock and Madeleine Sherwood likewise give performances with the sting of truth in them. It is too bad that such excitement is doused so often by the watery and melodramatic sequences that recur rhythmically as though devised to offset the corrosive effects of the film's high moments.

Frank Leyendecker in *Boxoffice*

The two original Broadway leads, Paul Newman and Geraldine Page, recreate their scintillating portrayals and both stand a good chance to be considered for the Oscar sweepstakes. Newman

With Geraldine Page

About to be beaten

is fine as the handsome hanger-on who has been defeated both in love and fame.

In *Time*
Newman as the young dog who is putting on the cat, creates a memorable portrait of a phony.

Stanley Kauffmann in *The New Republic*
Newman and Geraldine Page get excellent value out of the *humeur nôire* of the bedroom scenes.

Paul Newman

Hemingway's Adventures of a Young Man

1962   20th Century-Fox

CREDITS

A Company of Artists (Jerry Wald) Production for 20th Century-Fox. Produced by Jerry Wald. Directed by Martin Ritt. Screenplay by A. E. Hotchner, based on stories by Ernest Hemingway. Photographed by Lee Garmes. Music composed and conducted by Franz Waxman. Art Direction, John Martin Smith and Paul Groesse. Set decorations by Walter M. Scott and Robert Priestley.

Special Photographic Effects by L. B. Abbott and Emil Kosa Jr. Film Editor, Hugh S. Fowler. Sound: E. Clayton Ward and Warren B. Delaplain. Costumes, Don Feld. Hairstyles, Helen Turpin. Makeup, Ben Nye. Associate Producer, Peter Nelson. Assistant Director, Eli Dunn. Italian sequences filmed in Rome. CinemaScope. Color by DeLuxe. Running time, 145 minutes.

With Richard Beymer and
Juano Hernandez

CAST

Richard Beymer, Diane Baker, Corinne Calvet, Fred Clark, Dan Dailey, James Dunn, Juano Hernandez, Arthur Kennedy, Ricardo Montalban, Susan Strasberg, Jessica Tandy, Eli Wallach, Edward Binns, Whit Bissell, Philip Bourneuf, Tullio Carminati, Marc Cavell, Charles Fredericks, Simon Oakland, Michael Pollard, Pat Hogan and Paul Newman as The Battler.

THE FILM

This was one of the last films of the late producer Jerry Wald. It was based on ten of Ernest Hemingway's autobiographical "Nick Adams" stories and included an adaptation of Italian sequences from his novel, *A Farewell to Arms*. A. E. Hotchner, who wrote the screenplay, had been the official adapter of Hemingway's work prior to the novelist's death in 1961. Newman had the cameo role of The Battler, a punch-drunk fifty-five-year-old pug. This was a reprise of his 1955 television appearance in an adaptation of a Hemingway short story.

Starring throughout the film as young Nick Adams was Richard Beymer, who at the time was being boomed by 20th Century-Fox as a coming star. (Beymer appeared that year in another of Wald's final projects, *The Stripper*, with Joanne Woodward). A sensitive young performer, with real potential, Beymer weathered a series of adverse reviews that were, in retrospect, unduly harsh since his problem was not one of lack of ability, but of miscasting. In subtle, introspective roles (such as *Five Finger Exercise)* Beymer did much better, but Hemingway's busy extroversions, as projected in the Nick Adams part, proved outside his range, and in 1962 he was no one's idea of the life-hungry young Hemingway who in 1917 left his Wisconsin home to seek wider horizons, and got involved (as Nick Adams) in a succession of picaresque incidents.

Thrown off a train by a brakeman (Edward Binns) Beymer encounters the old prizefighter (Newman) and his kindly manager (Juano Hernandez). Heavily made up to resemble a battered pug of fifty-five, Newman turned in a solid characterization, and his sincere efforts to submerge the well-known Newman personality and mannerisms into a role in the best in-depth character-actor style, along with his ready and indeed enthusiastic aceptance of the short cameo, though he was by then a top star, were praised. The Battler, of course, is one of those pathetic has-beens of the ring, the pug who wasn't smart enough to quit when he was ahead. Now fifty-five, he has gone downhill step by step, from top stardom in the ring to second-rate bouts to prison to punchdrunk panhandling to the pathetic half-

113

brain, dependent on his only remaining pal, whom Nick Adams encounters in the forest by an open fire. The old pug and the boy sit and talk over food, and his stupefied brain wanders as he makes swinging gestures in the air and mumbles, at times incoherently.

Newman summed up thirty-five years of a man's life in this limited cameo, via shrewd touches of characterization and stance, gesture and vocal tone, and Juano Hernandez was likewise effective as the faithful sidekick. Significantly enough, young Beymer's scenes with Newman were better than his acting in the later sequences, and there is reason to believe that Newman gave him some extra help and that his professionalism enhanced Beymer's confidence.

This was Newman's third picture with director Martin Ritt. The rest of the film followed Nick Adams on his assorted encounters. He next meets a kindly telegraph operator (James Dunn) who subtly dissuades him from weakening and wiring his father for return-home money. He then becomes an aide to a drunken press agent (Dan Dailey) and replaces him on a journey to New York. In the big town he tries for a writing career, but is rebuffed in his efforts. He then goes to Europe, signing on with the Italian Army on the World War I Austrian front. As an ambulance driver he saves the life of his commanding officer (Ricardo Montalban) and later is wounded. While convalescing, he falls in love with his nurse (Susan Strasberg) but she is wounded and dies during a bedside wedding to Nick. Nick returns to America and is given a hero's welcome back in Wisconsin but his homecoming is marred by the news of the suicide of his father (Arthur Kennedy). Briefly, he remains at home, but the possessiveness of his strong-willed mother (Jessica Tandy) alienates him and he leaves home once more—this time to seek his manhood in ultimate terms.

REVIEWS

Stanley Kauffmann in *The New Republic*
The virtue of the film is that it has some of the quality of the title; there is considerable savor in it of the classic forms—a youth striking out from home to become a man by seeing the world: what can be called the downy-cheeked picaresque. The film's vulnerability in drama is that it is a succession of separate episodes . . . the scarred and

With Richard Beymer

With Richard Beymer

punchdrunk boxer that Paul Newman plays is, as any actor will see, a "show" part; grotesques are always easier than subtly distinguished characters. What actors will also see is that Newman does much more than merely have a holiday in it with gargoyle makeup and hoarse voice. He has begun at the roots and worked up, with artistic intelligence and responsive talent.

In *Time*

As the mentally woozy old "Battler," Paul Newman splats fist into palm in a ring-conditioned reflex, gropes spastically for the thoughts in his fogged-up brain and achieves a vividly unflawed integrity of characterization that rebukes every lazy actor who ever let his own personality rub off on a part.

Tube. in *Variety*

Newman's colorful and compassionate cameo merits credit not only for the performance but for the fact that, as a top star, he's not above the undertaking of a small character role when it represents an artistic challenge.

Paul V. Beckley in the *New York Herald Tribune*

A noticeable reverence for the author prevails throughout the film, but one can find little Hemingway influence on its characterizations or its style, which is rather slick. . . . Paul Newman is the fighter, but the makeup makes his face unrecognizable and diverts attention from his performance; this may be for the best, however, since it is essentially a caricature that fails to capture Hemingway's compassion for the indomitable in a man seemingly in the last ditch of defeat.

With Patricia Neal

Hud

1963   Paramount

CREDITS

A Salem-Dover Production. Produced by Martin Ritt and Irving Ravetch. Directed by Martin Ritt. Screenplay by Irving Ravetch and Harriet Frank, Jr. Based on the novel *Horseman, Pass By,* by Larry McMurtry. Photographed by James Wong Howe. Second Unit Photography by Rex Wimpy. Art Directors: Hal Pereira and Tambi Larsen. Music by Elmer Bernstein. Set decorations by Sam Comer and Robert Benton. Film Editor, Frank Bracht. Special Photographic Effects, Paul K. Lerpal. Process Photography: Farciot Edouart. Sound, John Carter and John Wilkinson. Costumes by Edith Head. Makeup by Wally Westmore. Hairstyles by Nellie Manley. Production Managers, Lloyd Anderson and Andrew J. Durkus. Assistant Director, C. C. Coleman Jr. Panavision. Filmed on location in Texas. Running time, 112 minutes.

CAST

Paul Newman, Melvyn Douglas, Patricia Neal, Brandon de Wilde, John Ashley, Whit Bissell,

With Patricia Neal

Crahan Denton, Val Avery, Sheldon Allman, Pitt Herbert, Peter Brooks, Curt Conway, Yvette Vickers, George Petrie, David Kent, Frank Killmond.

THE FILM

In 1963, Newman and director Martin Ritt, who found during three pictures together that they had conceived a mutual liking and an empathy with each other's creative aims, formed a partnership. Its intent: to work together independently within the framework of their own loose-structured company, joining forces when they felt strongly about a certain project and wanted to work on it together. Ritt was a sensitive and talented director who had worked with Miss Woodward in *No Down Payment,* with Newman and Woodward in *The Long Hot Summer* and *Paris Blues* and with Newman in the Hemingway film.

The two partners, along with screenwriters Irving Ravetch and Harriet Frank, Jr., conceived the character of Hud Bannon from a few lines in

With Patricia Neal

118

Larry McMurtry's novel, *Horseman Pass By.* Newman, along with his confreres, had chaffed under the compromises of the previous year's *Sweet Bird of Youth,* and he was determined that *Hud* and his characterization in it would be as honest and uncompromising as he could make them. Ritt and the writers fully agreed, and the result was a bitterly truthful portrait of a heel, limned by the actor and his director-writer combine with startling insight and raw veracity as the person Hud was—a guy "who didn't give a damn about anyone."

With both critics and public, this film proved to be Newman's high-water mark to date, and the adjectives this time around went along the lines of "memorable," "provocative," "tremendous," and "brilliant." Newman and Ritt also drove home another telling point: that a film could be dramatically and characterizationally uncompromising, yet still prove commercial. Little by little

the film medium was maturing, and Newman, Ritt and company contributed their fair share in helping the dynamic art, to which they had by now fully committed themselves, to gradually realize its potentialities as an adult dramatic form.

Newman received his third Academy Award nomination for this film, but ironically his co-stars Patricia Neal and Melvyn Douglas picked up Oscars for their portrayals, Miss Neal scoring for her wise and warm and deeply human portrayal of Alma the housekeeper and Douglas for his solid performance as the father. Newman's friend and *Paris Blues* co-star Sidney Poitier marched off with the Best Actor award that year for his excellent performance in *Lilies of the Field* and while his award was deserved, it became increasingly apparent, this third time around, that Newman was being unjustly slighted. However, he could take consolation in the fact that he was now Hollywood's top male star, as lionized by the critics and film intelligentsia as by the money-men and the public.

The story of *Hud* deals with a young rancher (Newman) whose father, (Douglas) a veteran Texas cattleman, disapproves of his inhuman approach to life and ever-ready opportunism and disregard for others' rights. Hud's sixteen-year-old nephew, Lon (winningly played by Brandon de Wilde) idolizes his uncle, whose good looks and jaunty charm conceal a total inability to feel for anyone else. The housekeeper Alma (Patricia Neal), a worldlywise cynic of decent instincts and warm heart, is physically attracted to Hud but recognizes his caddishness and rebuffs his crude advances. Hud's father, whose solid principles Hud affronts, fears the effects of his son's example on Lon. When one of Bannon's cows is discovered dead of foot-and-mouth disease, Hud as usual plumps for the easy way out, however unprincipled, and urges his father to sell the entire herd before the government inspectors can order a mass slaughter.

Bannon refuses, knowing as he does the catastrophic effects of disseminating diseased cattle. Hud contemptuously writes his father off as impractical and senile and attempts to have him declared mentally incompetent. Bannon, he claims, holds against him the death of Lon's father, Hud's

With Patricia Neal

119

brother, some years before in a car driven by Hud, and the hatred between father and son intensifies. Old Bannon attempts to give Lon insights into his uncle's essential negations-of-spirit.

After a drunken night on the town, Hud returns to the ranch and attempts to rape Alma, but is interrupted by Lon. Alma leaves in disgust the next day, to Lon's keen regret, and some time later old Bannon dies of heart failure. Lon through all this has gradually come to recognize his uncle's true character, and leaves the ranch to make his own way in life. Hud watches him leave, cynically shrugs his shoulders and opens a can of beer, his aloneness underlying the principle that "those who live for themselves are left to themselves."

REVIEWS

In *Time*

... a provocative picture with a shock for audiences who have been conditioned like laboratory mice to expect the customary bad-guy-is-really-good-guy reward in the last reel of a western. Paul Newman, the title-role bad guy, is a cad to the end.... Newman, Neal, Douglas and de Wilde are so good that they might well form the nucleus of a cinematic repertory company.

Arthur Knight in *The Saturday Review*

In this age of heel-heroes and beasts that walk like men, screen writers Irving Ravetch and Harriet Frank Jr. have pulled a switch that is both commercial and commendable. Working with a few lines from a novel by Larry McMurtry, they have created in Hud ... a charming monster who demonstrates by inversion that such old-fashioned virtues as honesty, loyalty and filial duty are still highly cherishable.... There can be no two thoughts about Hud: He is purely and simply a bastard. And by the end of the film, for all his charm, he has succeeded in alienating everyone, including the audience.... Always excellent with actors [Martin Ritt] has drawn memorable performances from his small, skilled cast. He uses Newman's considerable personal magnetism first to cover, then to reveal, the shallow, egocentric, callous nature of Hud. With his lean, muscular body and scornful smile, Newman's very essence is a threat poised over every scene.... Alma, played with warmth, dignity and astounding earthiness by Patricia Neal, is the film's counterfoil to Hud.

Judith Crist in the *New York Herald Tribune*

The distinction of *Hud* is that it presents an un-

With Brandon de Wilde

With Melvyn Douglas

pleasant truth about people without the pretty packaging, without the [sop] that easy answers and penny ante analysis provide, without the slightest sweetener to satisfy our sentimental yearnings. And perhaps the most encouraging aspect is that the making of such film and our appreciation of it indicates that we are getting out of the lollipop stage at last.

Bosley Crowther in *The New York Times*

While it looks like a modern western and is an outdoor drama indeed, *Hud* is as wide and profound a contemplation of the human condition as one of the New England plays of Eugene O'Neill. . . . The striking, important thing about it is the clarity with which it unreels. The sureness and integrity of it are as crystal clear as the plot is spare . . . with a fine cast of performers, he has people who behave and talk so truly that it is hard to shake them out of your mind. Paul New-

man is tremendous—a potent, voracious man, restless with all his crude ambitions, arrogant with his contempt and churned up inside with all the meanness and misgivings of himself. . . . Patricia Neal is brilliant as the lonely housekeeper.

Stanley Kauffmann in *The New Republic*

Paul Newman's new film *Hud* is the best American picture since Newman's *The Hustler*. Its distinctions are his and Patricia Neal's performances, Martin Ritt's direction, James Wong Howe's camera work, and the swift, sharp knifeplay in the dialogue. . . . Newman confirms his place in the front rank of American film actors.

Frank Leyendecker in *Boxoffice*

Brilliantly acted by Paul Newman in a completely unsympathetic role. He is to be commended for not attempting to soften his "ornery" hard-drinking, woman-chasing character.

A New Kind of Love

1963   Paramount

CREDITS

A Denroc Production. Produced, directed and written by Melville Shavelson. Photography by Daniel Fapp. Music by Leith Stevens. Additional Themes by Erroll Garner. Title Song sung by Frank Sinatra. Art Direction, Hal Pereira and Arthur Lonergan. Set Decorations by Sam Comer and James Payne. Editor, Frank Bracht. Costumes by Edith Head. Paris Originals by Christian Dior, Lanvin-Castille and Pierre Cardin. Sound by John Cartier. Makeup by Wally Westmore. Assistant to the Producer, Hal Kern. Production Manager, Andrew J. Durkus. Assistant Director, Arthur Jacobson. Technicolor. Color consultant, Hoyningen-Huene. Running time, 110 minutes.

CAST

Paul Newman, Joanne Woodward, Thelma Ritter, Eva Gabor, George Tobias, Marvin Kaplan, Robert Clary, Jon Moriarty, Valerie Varda, Robert Simon, Jean Staley and guest star Maurice Chevalier.

THE FILM

Perspicacious as he could be, Newman demonstrated in one area that he had distinctly not learned from experience. In 1963, he had fol-

With Robert Clary

lowed the superb *Hud* with the forgettable comedy *A New Kind of Love,* just as in 1961 he had followed the superior *The Hustler* with the lightweight *Paris Blues.* For some reason Newman could not face the evident fact that he was not at his best in lighter fare, especially farce comedy. Yet here he was again, teamed for the fourth time with Miss Woodward (who during this period always seemed to find herself teamed with her husband in his less creditable efforts) in a comedy that was soundly trounced by the critics as interminable and tasteless and unsubtle and obvious and thin.

Possibly Newman was still determined, come hell or high water, to prove that his range was greater than believed; or he may have felt that films like this gave him the needed comedy practice that might eventually metamorphose him into a tolerable farceur; if this were the case, it proved an expensive and highly attritional way to go about it. Co-workers have maintained that Newman expressed great faith in the comedy talents of Melville Shavelson, who had given excellent accounts of himself in prior films, and that New-

man felt that Shavelson might succeed in Svengaliing him into a Comic Wow as Ritt and McCarey had failed to do.

However, even Shavelson's resourceful pyrotechnics in his triple function of producer, director and writer couldn't turn Newman's glum silk purse into a gay-spirited sow's ear, and the reviews were distinctly bad. Shavelson threw in everything: Frank Sinatra, drafted to sing the title song; sight gags all over the place, endless camera tricks, gimmicky credits, snappy Shavelsonian quips, but this grab-bag of furbelows designed to work the miracle only seemed to bog the film down. Though imaginative enough with comedy, Shavelson's story sense left something to be desired, and the action (if it could be called that) gallumphed along fitfully for what seemed an endless 110 minutes, the weak, thin plot creaking ominously at strategic points.

What there was of it concerned a ladies' man newspaper columnist, Steve Sherman (Newman) who had been exiled to Paris for messing around with his publisher's wife. On the plane he meets Samantha Blake (Miss Woodward) a drab and

With Joanne Woodward

With Joanne Woodward

mannish career girl who is big in ladies' ready-to-wear. She is accompanied by her boss, Joseph Bergner (George Tobias) and store buyer Lena O'Connor (Thelma Ritter). Steve is repelled by Samantha's dowdy dullness and she thinks him an arrogant, alcoholic boor. Later, in Paris, the outwardly cool but inwardly love-starved Samantha finds herself at the St. Catherine's Day celebration, where young unmarried girls are expected to pray fervently for mates.

She gets drunk in the course of the evening, and imagines she has had a vision of St. Catherine, who gives her motherly advice on how to lure the male of the species. Spiritually reborn, Samantha rushes out to a beauty parlor the next day and does the ugly-duckling-to-swan bit. Replete with blonde wig, sharp clothes and a bewitchingly come-hither air, she then sets out to conquer fresh worlds.

Meanwhile, Lena, who is in love with Joseph, forlornly watches him romance Felicienne (Eva Gabor) their French agent. Steve encounters the new Samantha, fails to recognize her, and she impishly and ironically decides to help promote his impression that she is an expensive courtesan. Steve listens to her imaginative lies about her allegedly glamorous life as the Sultana of Sin, and uses them in his newspaper column, scoring a circulation hit. Gradually they fall sincerely in love. Eventually Steve learns she is really the drab Samantha of the plane journey, Lena gets a contrite Joe on the rebound when Felicienne gives him the air, and all ends happily for both pairs.

REVIEWS

Richard L. Coe in the *Washington Post*

This mess lumbers on interminably and tastelessly and not even a brief visit with Maurice Chevalier, several fashion shows or Thelma Ritter can get it out of its Miami Beach sands. Blame Melville Shavelson, who wrote, directed and produced it. Even were the material witty, I have the sad feeling the Newmans wouldn't be at home in it.

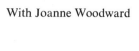

With Joanne Woodward

Judith Crist in the *New York Herald Tribune*

"It must be a new kind of love," says befuddled and hoaxed Paul Newman in this newest Melville Shavelson movie. "They ought to bottle it and label it 'instant stupid.'" Well, little does Mr. Newman know that Hollywood's been bottling instant stupid for years and labelling it things like *A New Kind of Love*. It's instant, all right. The pow-bam-sock-wow subtle sophistication of the jazzed-up now-it's-black-and-white-now-it's-Technicolor introduction, all to the tune of a Sinatra song, provides immediate stupefaction—and sets the tone for the ensuing banalities, commercial, juvenile sex play and sophomoric camera tricks that go on for nigh to two unsolid hours. . . . [Newman and Woodward], those two usually distinguished performers, are entitled to a fling—but Doris Day and Rock Hudson, they're not—and shouldn't aspire to be.

Tube. in *Variety*

A decided lack of comic restraint and subtlety and a tendency to be tricky for the sake of trickery mark the progress of what story there is. The situations are only fitfully funny, and the good conversational gags are widely scattered. . . . [The Newmans] are better at dramatic assignments than comedy.

A. H. Weiler in *The New York Times*

Mr. Shavelson's quips are fast, contemporary and polished to a bright slickness but his story is obvious and thin and his principals belabor the obvious to little avail. . . . But cute sight gags and bits do not make a satisfying or original examination of the grand passion. . . . As the unwitting object of [Miss Woodward's] affections, Mr. Newman is a decidedly unlikely, wooden citizen in decidedly transparent situations. . . . Mr. Shavelson and his hardworking troupe have strained mightily but their [film] is hardly new and only fitfully funny or farcical.

With Joanne Woodward

Paul Newman

The Prize

1963   Metro-Goldwyn-Mayer

CREDITS

Produced by Pandro S. Berman. Directed by Mark Robson. Screenplay by Ernest Lehman. Based on the novel by Irving Wallace. Music by Jerry Goldsmith. Photographed by William Daniels. Assistant Director, Hank Moonjean. Set Decoration, Henry Grace and Dick Pefferle. Film Editor, Adrienne Fazan. Special Visual Effects, J. McMillan Johnson, A. Arnold Gillespie, Robert R. Hoag. Hair Styles, Sydney Guilaroff. Makeup, William Tuttle. Associate Producer, Kathryn Hereford. Art Directors, George W. Davis and Urie McCleary. In Panavision and MetroColor. A Roxbury Production. Running time, 135 minutes.

CAST

Paul Newman, Edward G. Robinson, Elke Sommer, Diane Baker, Micheline Presle, Gerard Oury, Sergie Fantoni, Kevin McCarthy, Leo G. Carroll, Sacha Pitoeff, Jacqueline Beer, John Wengraf, Don Dubbins, Virginia Christine, Rudolph Anders, Martine Bartlett, Karl Swenson, John Qualen, Ned Wever.

THE FILM

Newman went back to Metro-Goldwyn-Mayer for this film. He was reunited with his *From the Terrace* director, Mark Robson, and so far as vehicle quality went, the two did not seem to be good luck for each other. The screenplay by Ernest Lehman from the rather fustian best-seller by Irving Wallace was a hodge-podge of comedy, melodrama, mistaken identity and chase intrigue, with enough messy subplots to succeed in dissipating the impact of occasionally-bright Lehman dialogue and fast-paced Robson direction. The net effect of this tale of Nobel Prize winners congregated in Stockholm who get involved in sexual escapades, international intrigue and clownish misunderstandings was less than felicitous, either esthetically or cinematically, and the Panavision and MetroColor served to vulgarize garishly rather than enhance attractively.

The Swedes protested the film because they felt it denigrated the dignity of the prizes; Newman was once again called upon to bumble through comedy sequences that he lacked the comic feel for, and the garbled, confused meanderings of the plot left viewers and critics alike with the feeling that here was a lot of ado about nothing served up with a lot of silly fuss-and-feathers. The critics threw around words like "claptrap," "purply passion," "vulgarity," "pretentious" and "silly," and though Mr. Newman was generally conceded to have the body for it, his flounderings and fumblings during his half-nude showings-off in a nudist colony sequence during his pursuit of the lighter muses, fell heavily flat. The "adventurous" sequences showcased Newman to only fair advantage, with the scurryings and chases keeping his character off-balance and poorly focussed. Mr. Newman's luck in the year 1963 was not holding up; *The Prize* was still another step down from *Hud* (even though Miss Woodward was not on

hand to share her husband's misfortune this time). Even blonde Elke Sommer's generous physical endowments in her role of the Swedish official assigned to Mr. Newman, somehow only served to vulgarize the scene rather than make it more palatable.

The story dealt with the group of Nobel winners clustered in a Stockholm hotel prior to the Award ceremonies. Andrew Craig (Newman) a hard-drinking lady-chaser, is on hand for the Literature prize. Dr. Max Stratman (Edward G. Robinson) is present for his Physics award. Doctors John Garrett and Carlo Farelli (Kevin McCarthy and Sergio Fantoni) are winners in the Medicine category and Dr. Denise Marceau (Micheline Presle) is being honored for her exploits in Chemistry. Dr. Stratman, whose companion is his niece Emily (Diane Baker), is kidnapped by the communists and spirited to a Russian ship in Stockholm's harbor. His twin brother is substituted. The communists plan to take the real Doctor Stratman back to Russia, leaving his communist-indoctrinated brother to make derogatory remarks about the United States when he makes his acceptance speech.

Craig, who has met the real Doctor Stratman,

With Elke Sommer, Edward G. Robinson and Diane Baker

With Micheline Presle

becomes suspicious of the imposter and begins investigating, his imaginative writer's mind working overtime in its search for clues. Soon communist countermeasures are endangering his life. The Swedish police and Lisa Andersen (Miss Sommer), who has been assigned to him by his hosts, discredit his insistence that "Stratman" is an imposter. Newman's search for Stratman takes him around Stockholm, in and around odd byways, including a nudist colony where he hides to avoid two communist agents intent on killing him. The men follow him in, so he is forced to mingle with the nudists. In order to escape he pretends to heckle the speaker at a nudist meeting and is rushed out.

Back on his travels again, he manages to find the ship where the real Stratman is being held prisoner. Almost singlehandedly, he smuggles him off and back to the hotel where, exhausted from his ordeal, Stratman suffers a heart seizure. Garrett and Farelli revive him. Later the real Stratman joins the other prizewinners at the ceremony, and at sight of him the imposter flees. He is later killed by a Russian agent to conceal the aborted plan. The denouement brings out the fact that the dead man was not Stratman's brother at all, but a professional actor. Stratman's brother had actually died years before in Russia. The award ceremonies are conducted with great dignity and pomp, and the winners, including Craig, go up to King Gustav to accept their awards. Craig, who during the course of the action had dallied with

Paul Newman, center

Denise and Emily, decides that Lise is his final romantic choice, and future happiness for them is indicated.

REVIEWS

Arthur Knight in *The Saturday Review*

Granting that it would be rather difficult to reproduce on the screen the greater part of Irving Wallace's sex-oriented study of a peculiarly libidinous group of Nobel winners, *The Prize,* still the scenario that Ernest Lehman has improvised on Wallace's theme is such a melange of claptrap melodrama and purply passion that the film could better be titled "Dr. No In Stockholm." . . . Substantial enough as a point of departure for a straight adventure yarn. it soon strains both patience and credulity. . . . Subplots abound, and all of them do more to hobble than help the central story [which] needs all the help it can get. The action is clouded from the very start. It breaks into the clear for some fairly exciting chase sequences. . . . But then come the explanations and reconciliations, complicated, confusing and un-

likely. . . . Neither the writer nor the director was quite certain whether he was serving his hokum straight or for laughs, or how strong was his commitment to Wallace's novel. Veering abruptly from place to place, they lost the novel, diluted the excitement and will probably be getting laughs where least expected.

Tube. in *Variety*

This is the story about the Nobel Prize, nude swimming and Nordic morals which upset the Kingdom of Sweden when first scheduled for filming. Swedes deplored what they foresaw as a vulgarization of the serious awards given annually under the will of the inventor of dynamite. So read on— Pandro S. Berman's screen version of the novel by Irving Wallace has the cast magnetism, glamorous production sheen and exploitable ingredients to lure the kind of audience that will respond to its cheerier aspects and dismiss its shortcomings. Such being the case, it should make its mark at the boxoffice. However, the film is marred by inconsistency of approach and, although it has a number of juicy moments and scenes, the whole is a rather uneasy, capricious concoction of such widely divergent elements as comedy, suspense, melodrama and political topicality. Reaction will be mixed. [The film] is a suspense melodrama played for laughs. Trouble is, the basic comedy approach clashes with the political-topical framework of the story, so that the audience continually has to make adjustments to the altitude. Although limited as a comic actor and confronted here with a rather difficult and unsubstantial character to portray, Newman tackles his task with sufficient vivacity to keep an audience concerned for his welfare and amused by his antics.

Louis Chapin in the *Christian Science Monitor*

It is easy to forget, until near the end of *The Prize,* that the Nobel award with which the film free-wheelingly concerns itself, is an award for service to peace. Most of the bickering people (in the screenplay) would be questionable candidates for a high school civics class essay contest. . . . Mr. Newman knows just when to smile wearily, when to knit his brows, and when to do both at once.

Judith Crist in the *New York Herald Tribune*

[The film] stands barefaced amid the pomp of Panavision, MetroColor and Elke Sommer's physique as a pretentious and silly spy story guaranteed to test—or rather try—Swedish-American relations, let alone the idiocy-threshhold of the moviegoer. Paul Newman seems intent on living down whatever artistic reputation he has earned. . . . He plunges into the detection game with all the efficacy of Charlie Chan's No. 2 Son although he never quite seems to achieve the dignity of that prat-falling young sleuth. Lest Miss Sommer fail to supply enough libidinous interest, Ernest Lehman's script also has Diane Baker and Micheline Presle horse around with Mr. Newman.

Bosley Crowther in *The New York Times*

This florid farrago of fiction plays fast and loose not only with the prestige of the Nobel affair but also with the simple conventions of melodrama and with the intelligence of the customers . . . at

Paul Newman, center

least it's a fast-moving picture. [Mark] Robson, who directed, hasn't looked at a lot of old Alfred Hitchcock pictures, including *The Lady Vanishes* for nought. And Ernest Lehman has provided some breezy, amusing dialogue, which Mr. Newman particularly delivers with infectious enjoyment. . . . But it's all just a bit too garbled, illogical and wild. This might happen at a bathing beauty contest—but please, not at the Nobel Prize affair!

With Elke Sommer

With Shirley MacLaine

What a Way to Go!

1964   20th Century-Fox

CREDITS

A J. Lee Thompson Production. Produced by Arthur P. Jacobs. Directed by J. Lee Thompson. Screenplay by Betty Comden and Adolph Green. Based on a story by Gwen Davis. The songs, "I Think That You And I Should Get Acquainted," and "Musical Extravaganza," Lyrics by Betty Comden and Adolph Green. Music by Jules Styne. Choreography by Gene Kelly. Music by Nelson Riddle. Photographed by Leon Shamroy. Art Direction by Jack Martin Smith and Ted Howarth. Set Decoration by Walter M. Scott and Stuart A. Reiss. Special Photographic Effects by L. B. Abbott and Emil Kosa, Jr. Unit Production Manager, William Eckhardt. Men's Wardrobe, Moss Mabry. Film Editor, Marjorie Fowler. Assistant to Mr. Kelly, Richard Humphrey. Dialogue Coach, Leon Charles. Sound, Bernard Freerich and Elmer Raguse. Assistant Director, Fred R. Simpson. Makeup, Ben Nye. Orchestration, Arthur Morton. Supervising Hair Stylist, Margaret Donovan. Miss MacLaine's Hair Styles, Sydney Guilaroff. Precious Stones, Harry Winston, Inc. Gloves, Kislav. Miss MacLaine's gowns, Edith Head. CinemaScope. DeLuxe Color. Running time, 111 minutes.

CAST

Shirley MacLaine, Paul Newman, Robert Mitchum, Dean Martin, Gene Kelly, Bob Cummings, Dick Van Dye, Reginald Gardiner, Margaret Dumont, Lou Nova, Fifi D'Orsay, Maurice Marsac, Wally Vernon, Jane Wald, Lenny Kent.

THE FILM

Oddly enough, it was director J. Lee Thompson who got a somewhat improved comedy performance out of Newman in the episodic money-and-marriage satire, *What a Way to Go,* which showcased him briefly as a Paris painter and the second of five husbands of an eccentric millionairess, played by Shirley MacLaine. This time the critics threw a few sops to Newman's comic venture, "acceptable" being the average adjective employed. They blistered the film itself as overblown and wrote that it lacked style, grace and wit.

The year 1964 seems to have been Newman's period for progress in the comic arts, in retrospect, as he garnered good personal reviews for his stage appearance under Frank Corsaro's direction in the satire, *Baby Want a Kiss.* Since Newman appeared in only about one-fifth the running time of *What a Way to Go!,* he did not suffer the usual critical attritions implicit in a full-length comedy performance. Because his stint here was more concentrated, it afforded him a chance to work more carefully to perfect his style in the comic genre he was anxious to master. The European setting of the sequence in which he appeared, and Thompson's shrewd suggestions, also helped him to carry it off with less trouble than

usual. The film was overproduced by Arthur Jacobs for 20th Century-Fox and the Betty Comden-Adolph Green screenplay offered an embarrassment (and that is the word) of riches. The film boasted lavish sets, overwhelming background music, Jules Styne songs, Comden-Green lyrics, Leon Shamroy photography, the garish wonders of 1964-style CinemaScope and DeLuxe Color—and the critics sat through it like sphinxes —and then went out and blasted it. Nor did Miss MacLaine fare well with the critics as a comedienne, though it might well have happened that the Brobdignagian buffooneries of the plot, laid on as they were with a heavy shovel where stiletto wit was called for, might have dampened her enthusiasm and exhausted her.

The story has MacLaine essaying the role of Louisa Benson, who at the start of the picture offers her entire 200-million-dollar wealth in a check to the U.S. Internal Revenue Service. Her offer is rejected, and she then visits psychiatrist Victor Stephanson (Robert Cummings) and tells him her life story via flashbacks.

She was, it seems, widowed shortly after each

With Shirley MacLaine

132

of her four marriages. After rejecting Leonard Crowley (Dean Martin), the richest boy in her home town, Louisa weds a happy-go-lucky clerk, Edgar Hopper (Dick Van Dyke) who becomes a fabulously successful merchant after Crowley goads him to success by ridiculing his poverty. But Edgar works himself to death, and Louisa is left a rich young widow. She then goes to Paris, where she meets taxi driver Larry Flint (Newman). Flint wants to be an artist but his modernist conceptions don't go over. He invents a machine that can convert sound into oil paintings. He and Louisa marry and all goes well until Louisa feeds classical selections into the machine. The result: a fabulously successful painting that turns Larry into the lion of Paris. Larry begins building more machines for conversion purposes, using shrewdly selected musical excerpts, and becomes an enormously rich artist.

One day he gets entangled in the mechanism of his invention and is killed. This leaves Louisa richer than ever, and as Husband Number Three she picks Rod Anderson (Robert Mitchum), a millionaire industrialist, feeling as she does that a man who is already rich has nowhere else to go.

Rod neglects his work for her, but this perversely serves to triple his estate. They retire to a farm but Rod is killed by a bull he has mistaken for a cow and is attempting to milk.

Husband Number Four is song-and-dance man Pinky Benson (Gene Kelly) whose showbusiness career has so far been a dismal failure. When he switches from an ill-advised clown act to straight comedy material he is a hit. Pinky rapidly becomes a bigtime film star, but is trampled to death at a premiere by over-enthusiastic fans. At this point in Louisa's narrative, Dr. Stephanson is told on the phone by the Internal Revenue Service that his patient really *is* worth 200 million (he had thought she was fantasizing) and he faints in surprise. While Louisa is reviving him, a janitor passes by. It is none other than her first beau, Leonard, now poor as a churchmouse. Louisa and Leonard resume their involvement and marry, living in contented poverty until oil is discovered on their property. Later, to Louisa's profound relief, they discover that the supposed bonanza was merely a break in an oil company's neighboring pipeline.

With Shirley MacLaine

With Shirley MacLaine

REVIEWS

In *The New Yorker*

Paul Newman . . . makes his obligatory appearance stripped to the waist—an odd trademark for a gifted man.

In the *London Sunday Times*

Paul Newman [is] Husband Number Two, a Paris actionpainter; Mr. Newman's comic gifts, and they are considerable, are for the fast throwaway, not the extravaganza, and anyway the joke about modern art is wearing a bit thick.

Richard Schickel in *Life*

A twice-told tale is bad enough, but to see a theme reworked five times in a single movie ex-

ceeds the dictates of common prudence . . . [the film] parodies its own overblown failures in devastating fashion as Miss MacLaine recalls Husbands One and Two in flashbacks that take the form of a) a black and white silent comedy, and b) a black and white, heavy-breathing sex drama. The narrow, colorless screen is a welcome relief from the insistent brightness of the rest of the picture, and the net effect is to call attention to the innocent pleasures movies can offer. . . . In the last analysis, the trouble with [the film] is that it's just not silly putty. It aspires to be, it tries hard, but it cannot escape its origins, which were a great big ball of wax. And wax, for all its splen-

With Shirley MacLaine and
Fifi D'Orsay

did qualities, simply can't be made to bounce, no matter how hard you throw it.

Bosley Crowther in *The New York Times*

It may be a funny idea, and some of the incidents by which it is revealed may have a certain sprightliness about them. But the whole thing, alas, lacks wit and grace. . . . J. Lee Thompson's direction has failed to coalesce a good film farce. It lets the whole thing flop wildly—and that's no way to make a film. Of course it is in dazzling color and is riotously overdressed.

Judith Crist in the *New York Herald Tribune*

. . . on and on and on Miss MacLaine mugs and traipses and cavorts in a fettle that becomes decreasingly fine and increasingly familiar. . . . Messrs. Newman and Mitchum are scarcely natural-born comedians . . . the movie satires are stale stuff, the pokes at avant-garde or pop art, big business and show biz even staler.

Stanley Kauffmann in *The New Republic*

The film's only interest is that Paul Newman, so admirable in serious roles, gives one of his rare acceptable comic performances as an American painter in Paris. And he manages this in a satire on modern art that, in this depressed field, is a new nadir.

In *Time*

[The film] is five or six big splashy movies rolled into none . . . [it] is so extravagantly overdrawn that the audience may well ponder where parody leaves off and plot begins. To furbish a frail spoof with all that Hollywood upholstery seems a bit like crossing a mountain stream aboard the *Queen Mary*—and why bother?

Paul Newman

With Claire Bloom

The Outrage

1964   Metro-Goldwyn-Mayer

CREDITS

A Martin Ritt Production. Produced by A. Ronald Lubin. Directed by Martin Ritt. Screenplay by Michael Kanin. Based on the Japanese Daiei film *Rashomon,* by Akira Kurosawa, from stories by Ryunosuke Akutagawa and the play *Rashomon* by Fay and Michael Kanin. Photographed by James Wong Howe. Music composed and conducted by Alex North. Associate Producer, Michael Kanin. Art Direction, George W. Davis and Tambi Larsen. Set Decorations, Henry Grace and Robert R. Benton. Special Visual Effects, J. McMillan Johnson and Robert R. Hoag. Film Editor, Frank Santillo. Assistant Director, Daniel J. McCauley. Costumes by Don Feld. Hairstyles by Sydney Guilaroff. Makeup by William Tuttle. Panavision. Running time, 97 minutes.

CAST

Paul Newman, Laurence Harvey, Claire Bloom, Edward G. Robinson, William Shatner, Howard Da Silva, Albert Salmi, Thomas Chalmers, Paul Fix.

THE FILM

Newman again teamed up with director Martin Ritt in a praiseworthy but somewhat abortive attempt to do a creditable screen version of the famed 1959 stage play, "Rashomon." They retitled it *The Outrage.* Rod Steiger had played the role of the bandit-rapist on Broadway, with Claire Bloom opposite him. Newman took over the Steiger part for the film, with Claire Bloom in her original role and Laurence Harvey as her husband. The play in turn had been derived from

With Claire Bloom

Akira Kurosawa's Japanese film, *Rashomon*.

The Newman-Ritt version, unlike either the original Japanese picture or the play, both of which had been set in ancient Japan, was played against a late nineteenth century Western background. *The Outrage* is one of Newman's favorite films. He went to Mexico to research it, studying the language and manners and customs of the inhabitants he felt most closely approximated the bandit characterization he was after.

Newman and Ritt worked carefully on the picture, and the Newman performance, flawed as it is, indicates that he was making a laudable attempt to expand his acting technique and effect a solid, in-depth characterization. The critics, unfortunately, did not for the most part agree with him, and while some of them praised his colorful dynamics and animal magnetism, it was felt that he overplayed, laying on the dialect and accent too thickly, and at times sounded like a parody of Mexican villains in old Western shoot-em-ups. One critic even compared him to the late Leo Carrillo!

It was apparent that in this instance Newman had overreached himself, however commendable his motivations. The picture also was castigated as not blending with, or being true to, its alleged Western milieu, and some critics declared flatly that it should never have been taken out of its eighth-century Japanese context. Nor was this sort of thing the All-American Martin Ritt's dish of tea (though he may have thought it was), the subtleties and motivations and complexities of the original being Oriental to the core—and medieval Oriental at that!

Though the film did not do well, Newman consistently defends it as containing in his view some of his best work. The bravura qualities of the part doubtless attracted him originally; it is possible that, being too close to it creatively, he subjectively has mistaken the intention for the accomplishment, and *The Outrage* was, regrettably enough, long on the first and short on the second.

A complicated exercise in the many aspects of reality, as exemplified in a murder and rape which a number of people have claimed to have witnessed, it opens with a clergyman (William Shatner), a prospector (Howard Da Silva) and a confidence man (Edward G. Robinson) talking at a Western railway depot. They discuss the trial of Juan Carrasco (Newman) a notorious outlaw. Carrasco has been sentenced to death for murdering a traveler (Laurence Harvey) and raping his wife (Claire Bloom). The trial had proven a strangely ambiguous affair because three of the witnesses to the crime had offered three different versions of what actually happened. Carrasco claimed that he had tied up the husband, raped the wife, then killed the husband in a duel. The wife maintained that Carrasco had raped her and fled; then, enraged, she had killed her husband when he had accused her of encouraging her assailant. An old Indian (Paul Fix) declares that he found the husband dying with a knife in his breast and the husband told him he had stabbed himself out of shame.

After further discussion of the crime, the three men at the depot discover an abandoned baby. The con man tries to steal the gold found on the child. The ensuing argument brings to light the suspect motives of the prospector who had witnessed the crime but didn't testify because he had purloined the jewel-encrusted dagger from the dying traveler's breast. According to the prospector, Carrasco was remorseful after the rape and begged the wife to leave with him. The wife, regarding herself as a prize to be attained, goaded her husband and Carrasco into a fight during which the husband had accidentally fallen on the dagger. The prospector offers to raise the abandoned child, though he has other children. The clergyman's faith in humanity, shaken by the trial, is reaffirmed in the face of this offer. A careful examination of truth's many colorations and ramifications, the story does not offer either a clear resolution or a cathartic focus.

REVIEWS

Whit. in *Variety*
Newman as the violent and passionate killer plays his colorful character with a flourish and heavy accent, reminiscent of the late Holbrook Blinn's portrayal in *The Bad Man*, which years ago set the model for demi-heroes (or badmen) of this type. He dominates the action, mainly told in flashback sequences, as the basic situation and consequent footage is recounted four times.

Louis Chapin in the *Christian Science Monitor*
The Outrage is an American film [deriving] from the Japanese cinematic masterpiece, *Rashomon*.

With Laurence Harvey and
Claire Bloom

Paul Newman

... It takes the original many-faceted study of 8th century motivation out to a post-Civil War West, and loses it ... (the) actors seem to be working out an improvisation assignment they don't quite understand. They start with a reasonable effort at melodrama which progressively, for kicks of some sort, deteriorates into half-hearted slapstick. The puzzle they finally hand us does not concern a murderer's motivation but a producer's. One of its clues reads: "Good Japanese may be no good in American." ... When this mixed-bag adaptation occasionally draws a laugh, it is more likely to be at than with the film.

In the *New York Morning Telegraph*

Mr. Newman, as a Mexican bandit, growls and snuffles and steams his way through the role of the supposed villain with notable effect, and Miss Bloom makes the figure of the ravished wife an oddly complex creation.

Judith Crist in the *New York Herald Tribune*

What should be a cogent, almost ritualistic exami-nation and re-examination of the many facets of truth emerges as little more than a story told and thrice re-told simply to provide three performers with exercises in acting. ... Paul Newman emerges as a sort of junior-grade Leo Carrillo, spitting and spewing and wallowing in dialect and playing the villain, the lecher, the social outcast, the lover and the coward to the hilt for his own very private edification. ... Perhaps *Rashomon* cannot stand the transition from East to West or to modern times. As it is, *The Outrage* emerges as a sen-tentious theme with dull variations.

A. H. Weiler in *The New York Times*

Mr. Newman's outlaw is perhaps played too broadly. From the top of his large sombrero to his matted hair, buckskin chaps and down to his large, jangling spurs, he is obviously a rough rene-gade seeking animal pleasures and self-preserva-tion. But he also, it is revealed, is not a gent who commits murder deviously. He sounds like a parody of the Mexican villains in old movies.

Paul Newman

Lady L

1965   Metro-Goldwyn-Mayer

CREDITS

A Carlo Ponti Production presented and released by Metro-Goldwyn-Mayer. Directed by Peter Ustinov. Screenplay by Mr. Ustinov from the novel by Romain Gary. Photographed by Henri Alekan. Music by Jean Francaix. Film Editor, Roger Dwyre. Running time, 124 minutes.

CAST

Sophia Loren, Paul Newman, David Niven, Claude Dauphin, Philippe Noiret, Michel Piccoli, Marcel Dalio, Cecil Parker, Jean Wiener. Daniel Emilfork, Eugene Deckers, Jacques Dufilho, Tanya Lopert, Catherine Allegret, Peter Ustinov.

THE FILM

Lady L, the film version of the Romain Gary novel, had originally been scheduled as a starring vehicle for Tony Curtis and Gina Lollobrigida by

With Sophia Loren

Metro-Goldwyn-Mayer but script and other problems intervened, and the project was shelved indefinitely. In late 1964, under a producing deal with Carlo Ponti, with MGM handling releasing arrangements, Sophia Loren and Newman undertook to do the film under Peter Ustinov's direction. Ustinov also wrote the screenplay. The picture was finished by April, 1965, but was not shown in Europe until late in the year, premiering in London in November, 1965. It was the only Paul Newman picture that underwent a lengthy release-delay and it was not seen in New York until May 1966, after the picture Newman made subsequently, *Harper,* had made its New York debut (March 1966).

There has been some speculation as to the reason for this one-year interval between *Lady L*'s completion and its U.S. debut. According to one theory, MGM powers-that-be, having gotten word that *Harper* would be a smash hit, delayed release until such time as *Harper* could carry the faltering *Lady L* along on its coattails, thanks to another fresh wave of audience interest in Newman. Whatever the reason, *Lady L* finally opened in

New York, two months after *Harper,* in the spring of 1966 to less than enthusiastic reviews.

Again the old charge of "miscast" was trotted out and leveled at Newman's performance. True, he played competently, but his personality seemed too American and modern and temperamentally wrong for the part of a bomb-toting 1905-style French anarchist. Nor did Miss Loren fare as well as usual, the role of the fey poseur *Lady L* being, by general agreement, not particularly suited to her earthy Italian temperament, always at its best when dealing with human basics, as against the coy subtleties of the Gary heroine's mystique. Ustinov came off best of all, and there was warm praise in some quarters for his writing and direction. Still, the picture seemed too tame, genteel and lightweight, and lacked the confident, epic sweep and fullsome, nostalgic glamor that its subject matter should have commanded. Though miscast, Miss Loren performed forcefully, her role overshadowing (indeed overwhelming) Newman's and even the scintillating David Niven's.

The story opens with an eighty-year-old Dowager Duchess telling the story of her life to Sir

With Michel Piccoli and Marcel Dalio

Percy (Cecil Parker) her poet laureate friend, in the summer house of her magnificent Blenheim-style English palace. The Duchess, it seems, has been playing a cosmic joke on British society for fifty years. She relates her humble beginnings as a Paris laundress who makes deliveries to a fashionable bordello, Le Moulin Bleu, presided over by LeCoeur (Michel Piccoli). Prominent officials, like French cabinet minister Philippe Noiret, frequent the house of pleasure. The future Lady L becomes the laundress for the house, and while she becomes friendly with the prostitutes and is admired by the male patrons, she remains technically chaste, being naturally a lady. At this point she meets Armand (Paul Newman), a roguish, Robin Hood-style thief and bank robber. Armand is sought by the police and seeks refuge in the bordello where Lady L, who has become his mistress, protects him.

Subsequently Armand joins up with an underground revolutionary movement led by Koenigstein (Eugene Deckers). This band of petty anarchists, sought by the frustrated Paris police head, Inspector Mercier (Claude Dauphin), is planning the assassination of the visting Prince

Otto (Peter Ustinov). Lady L foils the assassination attempt. She meets Dicky, Lord Lendale (David Niven), a British aristocrat looking for a wife. He offers her a bargain: if she'll marry him, he will save her lover from the police. Lord Lendale closes his eyes during the following years to his lady's continuing affair with Armand.

Fifty years later she is a widowed Dowager Duchess and her son, the Duke, and her other ostensibly noble children are actually the offspring of Armand, who though now an old man, works as the Duchess' chauffeur. It then develops that the ex-laundress who had climbed to high estate isn't even a legitimate duchess; she had never actually married Lord Lendale, but they had set up housekeeping anyway!

REVIEWS

Frank Leyendecker in *Boxoffice*
Paul Newman's portrayal of an urban Robin Hood, obsessed with his mission of stealing from the rich with perilous audacity to give to the poor, is delightfully entertaining.

Harold Rogers in the *Christian Science Monitor*
Lady L doesn't give (Sophia Loren) the scope
she requires for her best work. An actress who
has depths within depths, she is limited when
dealing with superficial and sometimes tasteless
pleasantries. . . . Paul Newman as Armand . . .
gives us only a pale reflection of what he can do
in a film like *Harper*.

In *The New Yorker*

Mr. Newman has not troubled to think himself
very deeply into his silly role, and seems about as
far from Paris and anarchism as, say, Akron and
the Young Republicans are.

In *Time*

Paul Newman performs behind a large moustache,
possibly to conceal the fact that he is hopelessly
miscast as a bomb-toting French anarchist.

Rich. in *Variety*

Paul Newman, though turning in a thoroughly
competent performance, is not happily cast [as]
his role [calls out for] the dependable mixture of
solidity and lightness . . . there's been much attention to set and costume detail which will please
the attentive. But, over-all, the film jerks genteelly
rather than sweeps through what could have been
a still witty, but more boisterous and extravagant
joke.

Eliot Fremont-Smith in *The New York Times*

[Paul Newman] plays the Corsican anarchist as a
matter-of-fact, very contemporary American. His
devotion to the anarchist cause is on the same
level as some modern's devotion to, say, a career
of auto racing—that is, strictly surface. But with
the same plot results: difficulties with the girl. It
is not Mr. Newman's fault; he . . . is more than

With Paris policemen of 1905

competent at playing himself, which remark is not intended to be snide—and he has, in this sense, been miscast. . . . Whatever the causes of the minor dissatisfactions inherent in this film, its major rewards are due to Peter Ustinov's sensitive conception and superb direction. The pacing is fast, the wit is sure, the scenes are gorgeous . . . pictorially, a sumptuous treat from beginning to end . . . imperfect (but) droll, rewarding and technically very interesting entertainment.

Kate Cameron in the *New York Daily News*

The characters of Gary's novel have come to life on the screen in a brilliant fashion. The picture has been elegantly produced. . . . There are a number of surface twists and turns to the story and the ending, although it departs somewhat from the novel, gives an extra fillip to the delightful tale, as the film retains most of the book's spicy flavor.

Archer Winsten in the *New York Post*

The picture takes full advantage of the colorful times to extend itself in Panavision and color, suiting extravagant action to the scene, and vice versa. It runs down a bit at the end, being unable to top its brave beginnings in word, deed or spectacle, but this is inevitable when the single biographical jest runs out of invention. The lady, it seems, was never really what she seemed, and since she did seem a bit shocking, you can gather that the final unshocking revelation is sentimental rather than merry.

Leo Mishkin in the *New York Morning Telegraph*

Through it all, Miss Loren glows with her customary beauty and splendid presence. As her two lovers, Paul Newman and David Niven both seem to be somewhat overshadowed and lost in the background.

Harper

1966   Warner Bros.

CREDITS

Warner Bros. release of a Jerry Gershwin-Elliott Kastner Production. Directed by Jack Smight. Screenplay by William Goldman based on the novel *The Moving Target,* by Ross MacDonald. Music by Johnny Mandel. Song "Livin' Alone" by Dory and Andre Previn. Photographed by Conrad Hall. Film Editor, Stefan Arnsten. Assistant Director, James H. Brown. Technicolor. Running time, 121 minutes.

CAST

Paul Newman, Lauren Bacall, Julie Harris, Arthur Hill, Janet Leigh, Pamela Tiffin, Robert Wagner, Robert Webber, Shelley Winters, Harold Gould, Strother Martin, Roy Jensen, Martin West, Jacqueline de Wit, Eugene Iglesias, Richard Carlyle.

THE FILM

Harper, made after *Lady L* and released in the United States two months before it, proved to be an ironically timely event in the Newman career. For at this point (1966) a succession of also-ran pictures had begun to make inroads on his cinematic image and his boxoffice pull. *Harper* recovered all the lost ground and more; it made Newman a blockbusting super-star. Another surprising element about the film was its theme; no one had connected Newman with hard-eyed private-detective roles of the Bogart stripe, and in fact he had never played such a role in any of his previous twenty-two films. And oddly enough, despite *Harper*'s enormous success and the recurring talk of a *Harper*-type sequel or follow-up film for him, Newman to date has not again essayed on the screen a private-eye of this sort. Why not is one of those casting mysteries buried in darkest Hollywood. Possibly there had been one instance too many of sequels or follow-ups to proven hits that had boomeranged, or perhaps it was that Newman simply wanted to continue varying his roles.

This was Newman's first picture with director Jack Smight, and they proved to be happy discoveries for each other. Working with economy and precision, exact about what he wanted, Smight guided Newman through a lithe, cat-like, enormously self-assured and resourceful performance that had no apologies to make to the memory of Bogart or any other famed movie-sleuth shade. William Goldman prepared a well-paced, well-written screenplay based on famed detective storyteller Ross MacDonald's novel, *The Moving Target*. An interesting touch was the inclusion of the former Mrs. Bogart, Lauren Bacall in the cast, which was packed with such solid name players as Robert Wagner, Julie Harris, Janet Leigh and Shelley Winters. This film, incidentally, was Newman's first Warner release since winning his freedom (for $500,000) from his Warner contract seven years before.

Throughout the film Newman's character is the coolest of the cool, hip, cynical, wisecracking, resourceful and at times quite human, an antihero detective without illusions but plenty of drily aware insight into the human condition. He needs every quality he can summon to survive as he combs the dregs of Los Angeles searching for a millionaire kidnap victim. This time around, the critics trotted out their choicest adjectives for Newman's performance: "authoritative," "droll," "versatile," "admirable," "splendid," "perfectly cast," "ideal," etc.

The plot, as in the usual detective dramas of this type, has Newman up against a variety of "struggle and flight" situations replete with assorted maneuverings and plots and counterplots on the part of those he runs afoul of. He is estranged from his wife Susan (Janet Leigh) and would like to renew his marriage, but she feels that his work has destroyed their happiness, and asks for a divorce. Elaine Sampson (Miss Bacall)

With Shelley Winters

commissions Harper, through their mutual friend, lawyer Albert Graves (Arthur Hill) to trace her wealthy husband who has been kidnapped. A $500,000 ransom demand has been received. There is no love lost between Miss Bacall and her missing husband and she frankly hopes that Harper will find him dead—which eventually he does.

Mrs. Sampson's spoiled daughter Miranda (Pamela Tiffin) is having a casual thing with Alan Traggert (Robert Wagner) the family pilot, who in turn is involved with junkie nightclub singer Betty Fraley (Julie Harris). Harper gets to meet one and all during his peregrinations, including aging actress Fay Estabrook (Shelley Winters) who had known the missing Sampson and her husband Dwight Troy (Robert Webber) who is the brains behind a wetback smuggling ring operated by a religious maniac named Claude (Strother Martin). Harper, upon instructions, delivers the ransom money, chases the car that picks it up and gets involved with more wetbacks, who put him temporarily out of commission. At Betty Fraley's home, Harper finds her being tortured by Troy, Fay and Claude, who are after the missing

ransom money. Harper shoots Troy and Betty flees later in her car. Harper's persistent and continuing investigations eventually untangle the complex skein.

REVIEWS

Rose Pelswick in the *New York Journal-American*
Paul Newman checks in just about the best performance of his career . . . developed in a mood that's remindful of the early Raymond Chandlers, this is a hugely entertaining thriller that manages to come up with suspense and excitement and comedy and yet never gets out of hand. . . . Newman as the cynical and oh-so-hip Harper, is perfectly cast in the role, playing it cool no matter what comes up, tossing off flip lines and slugging it out with the best of 'em.

Richard Schickel in *Life*
Screenwriter William Goldman, director Jack Smight and star Paul Newman all play their film as straight as the novelist (Ross MacDonald) habitually does his books. Goldman's script is full

With Janet Leigh

With Julie Harris

of snap-crackle-pop dialogue and he adorns the essentially simple plot (Harper is trying to find a kidnapped millionaire) with Byzantine twists and turns, around which nearly always lurks a grotesque and curious minor character. Smight has a good feel for the tawdry, *nouveau gauche* Southern California atmosphere. More important, he has directed with nary a shock cut nor an over-fancy angle, giving us a good approximation of the pell-mell pace and bluntness of exposition one used to be able to count on in American films and which nowadays (1966) one receives mainly from the French imitation of the old school. As for Newman, this is the kind of superficial role— plenty of action, wisecracks and manly sentiment—for which his superficial talent is ideally suited. . . . *Harper* delivers us an unemotional memo on the way things too often are in our society, then shrugs and cracks wise. But in the prevailing conscienceless climate of American moviemaking, it is good to see a film with at least that much awareness of its social context, that much critical objectivity.

Alan N. Bunce in the *Christian Science Monitor*
In an effort to give it color and impact, the makers of *Harper* have so laden their film with bizarre episodes and artificial characters that it barely gains the momentum a private-eye mystery requires. In the title role, Paul Newman plays a tough, offhand, antiheroic detective trying to track down a missing wealthy husband. Mr. Newman

With Strother Martin, Julie Harris, Shelley Winters and Robert Webber

is authoritative, versatile, and frequently droll in the part, but *Harper* is a self-consciously hard-boiled sleuth who speaks in a stilted pattern of caustic punchlines and coarse cracks.

In *The Saturday Review*

One of the best things about [the film] is that its detective hero, Paul Newman, goes about his business with the same undeflectable, no-nonsense attitude that once endeared Humphrey Bogart to a whole generation of moviegoers. His path is not strewn with luscious dropouts from the James Bond series, nor is he aided in his grubby labors by any assortment of fantastic gadgetry. Like Bogart, Harper is a loner, with nothing beyond his own brains and muscle to help him untangle the web. . . . Newman as the hard, sardonic shamus, works with the same skill and consistency that marked his performances in *Hud* and *The Hustler*.

Murf. in *Variety*

Director Jack Smight has inserted countless touches which illuminate each character to the highest degree. In this he complements Goldman's sharp and often salty lingo. All principals acquit themselves admirably, including Newman, Miss Bacall, Webber, and particularly Miss Winters, who makes every second count as the once-aspiring film star now on the high calorie sauce.

Frank Leyendecker in *Boxoffice*

Male and female fans alike will hail Paul Newman for his splendid performance as the engaging Harper.

With Julie Andrews

Torn Curtain

1966   Universal

CREDITS

Produced and directed by Alfred Hitchcock. Screenplay by Brian Moore, based on his story. Art Director, Frank Arrige. Photographed by John F. Warren. Unit Production Manager, Jack Carrick. Pictorial Designs, Albert Whitlock. Sound, Waldon O. Watson and William Russell. Miss Andrews' costumes by Edith Head. Production designer, Hein Heckroth. Music by John Addison. Set Decorations, George Milo. Film Editor, Bud Hoffman. Makeup Supervision, Jack Barron. Costume Supervisor, Grady Hunt. Assistant to Mr. Hitchcock, Peggy Robertson. Hair styles for Miss Andrews, Hal Saunders. Hair Stylist, Lorraine Roberson. Assistant Director, Donald Baer. Technicolor. Running time, 126 minutes.

CAST

Paul Newman, Julie Andrews, Lila Kedrova, Hansjoerg Felmy, Tamara Toumanova, Wolfgang Kieling, Gunter Strack, Ludwig Donath, David Opatoshu, Gisela Fischer, Mort Mills, Carolyn Conwell, Arthur Gould-Porter, Gloria Garvin.

THE FILM

If *Harper* took Newman ten giant steps forward careerwise, his next, *Torn Curtain* yanked him at least two steps back. He himself has expressed his dislike of the picture, and well he should, for his reviews in this, his first encounter with director Alfred Hitchcock, were not flattering. Newman and Hitchcock were simply not made for each other, nor were either in prime form in this picture, which at the time was widely heralded by Universal as Hitchcock's Fiftieth.

A dull, plodding hodge-podge of cold war spy clichés, the film drew such notices as "pathetically

With Julie Andrews and Lyle Sudrow

undistinguished," "blah script," and "unbelievable." There are stories that Newman and Hitchcock did not get along too well during the shooting. Hitchcock reportedly expected Newman to perform less literally and adopt a tongue-in-cheek approach to his characterization, à la Cary Grant of sacred memory, and Newman it is said, felt that The Master should accept him on his own terms and guide him accordingly. Whatever the facts of the matter (and there is no denying that Hitchcock himself was not in top form this time around), Newman and Julie Andrews, despite the appropriate enthusiasm they put into the vulgarly overpublicized bundling scene at the picture's start, did not seem to comprehend their roles or how they should be played, and the usually sharp and knowing Hitchcock touches were considerably muted, often to the vanishing point.

The picture had, moreover, a tired *déjà vu* look. Everyone concerned had been this way before; Hitchcock certainly had, and Newman, after scurrying around with Red agents in *The Prize* addressed himself to *Torn Curtain* in a style natural to him—a style that had worked well in other films for other directors of a newer stylistic persuasion but—as the final result starkly demonstrated—went over like a lead balloon in a Hitchcock opus.

The story is still another of those excessively convoluted affairs that by 1966 were beginning to grow tiresome and in fact would have proven so even had Brian Moore's script been less perfunctory, mechanical and predictable. Newman is Professor Michael Armstrong, a brilliant U.S. atomic scientist who passes himself off as a defector to East Germany in order to learn the secret antimissile formula he is after. The formula is in the possession of a Leipzig scientist to whom Newman intends to make a bee-line despite all the Red agents in East Germany.

The picture opens on a cruise ship in a Norwegian fjord where Armstrong is bundled in bed under many covers with his fiancée Sarah Sherman (Julie Andrews). The ship's heating system is being repaired, so Harper and Mary Poppins have no recourse but to bundle intimately, or so Moore's script insists. Michael is not at liberty to tell Sarah of his iron curtain-penetrating intentions. Cut to the East German border, after a few cloak-and-dagger forays in intervening cities, with Sarah tagging along after Michael and determined to believe in his patriotism and integrity despite the sinister evidence to the contrary piling up.

Once in East Germany Michael and Sarah run a complicated gauntlet of Red agents, including one that they messily murder in a farmer's house. At Leipzig, Michael tricks the professor he seeks (Ludwig Donath) into revealing the antimissile formula by luring him into an contest-of-intellects debate which elicits in time (via blackboard diagrams chalked up by the professor and which Michael memorizes) the information he has come to East Germany to obtain. One Countess Kuchinska (Lila Kedrova) offers to help Michael and Sarah to get out of the country if they will in turn aid her in obtaining a U.S. visa.

In a race for the border, the pair are detoured to a ballet performance crawling with Red agents. Panic breaks out in the hall and the always-on-the-job CIA sneak Michael and Sarah to a dress-

With Julie Andrews

ing room where they are hidden in large costume-baskets. The baskets are loaded on a ship and with freedom within reach, the Red operative on board demands that the baskets being debarked be opened. When CIA agents fail to comply, the baskets, hanging on cranes in mid-air, are riddled with bullets, but they are, of course, the wrong ones. Michael and Sarah escape from the ship by swimming to land, where they find themselves once more on the right side of the iron curtain. Bundled shivering in a blanket in a waiting room, they refuse to be photographed and pull the blanket up over their heads. Wearily but contentedly, they bundle together, their troubles conclusively over.

REVIEWS

Richard Schickel in *Life*
Brian Moore's script lacks that constant crackle of smart dialogue that one usually associates with a Hitchcock enterprise. . . . Newman and Miss An-drews have small ability to play with the high style of such previous Hitchcock leads as Cary Grant and Ingrid Bergman, and . . . there is a distracted air about much of the film—as if the master were not really paying attention to what he was doing. Therefore our emotional involvement never grows to the point where it overrules rational disbelief or blocks out those flaws of logic which should not be noticed until we emerge into daylight.

Bosley Crowther in *The New York Times*
A pathetically undistinguished spy picture . . . a collection of clichés . . . the idea is not insufficient for a fictitious spy film of the sort that Mr. Hitchcock has many times managed to make scamper and skip across the screen. The locale and circumstances should do for a characteristic lark. But here he is so badly burdened with a blah script by Brian Moore, and a hero and heroine, Paul Newman and Julie Andrews, who seem to miss the point, that he has come up with a film

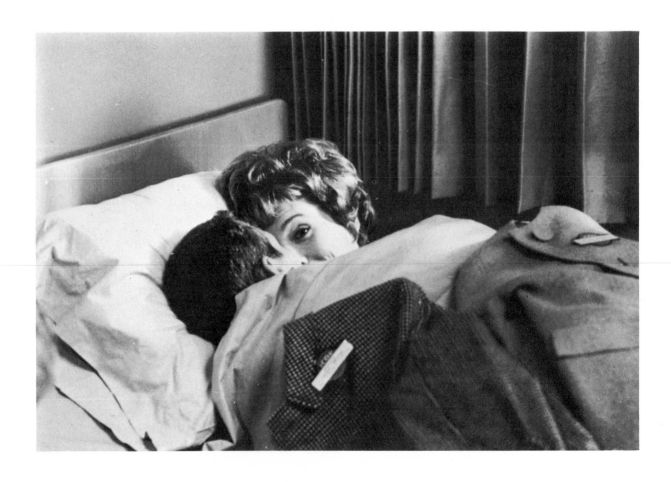

that plows through grimly, without any real surprises, suspense or fun. . . . [Newman and Andrews] seem to have no sense whatsoever of the fancifulness of the piece, no ability or willingness to play it strictly with tongue in cheek. Mr. Newman goes at it really as though he meant to pick a German scientist's brain and Miss Andrews is like an English nanny who means to see that no harm will come to him. The scene of the two under covers at the beginning of the film—a scene as harmless as it is notorious—is a fraud. They never get that close again. . . . In these times, with James Bond cutting capers and pallid spies coming in out of the cold, Mr. Hitchcock will have to give us something a good bit brighter to keep us amused.

Archer Winsten in the *New York Post*

Newman simply doesn't add up as a nuclear physicist. Maybe he was Harper too recently and was too good in it. And Julie Andrews doesn't resemble in any way the assistant to a nuclear physicist.

She has been too much the Baroness and Mary Poppins or even Americanized Emily, to fit this chore.

Murf. in *Variety*

An okay cold war suspenser. . . . Alfred Hitchcock's direction emphasizes his earlier suspense and ironic comedy flair in a series of often intriguing scenes, but some good plot ideas are marred by routine dialogue and a too relaxed pace contributes to a dull overlength . . . Hitchcock fishes up his bag of tricks—a mysterious book, a mathematical symbol, his own silent bit in a hotel lobby with a baby on his lap, imminent violence and actual crowd panic in a cultural setting—in a good pot pourri which becomes a bit stale through a noticeable lack of zip and pacing. . . . Newman gives a good underplaying to his role, while Miss Andrews' charming voice and appearance lend grace to a limited but billed-over-title role. Pair's necking sequence at the start is tastefully sexy, reminiscent of "Rear Window."

With Julie Andrews (left)

155

Paul Newman

With Martin Balsam

Hombre

1967   20th Century-Fox

CREDITS

Produced by Martin Ritt and Irving Ravetch. Directed by Martin Ritt. Screenplay by Irving Ravetch and Harriet Frank, Jr. Based on the novel by Elmore Leonard. Second Unit Director, Ray Kellogg. Photographed by James Wong Howe. Music composed and conducted by David Rose. Film Editor, Frank Bracht. Art Direction, Jack Martin Smith and Robert E. Smith. Set Decorations: Walter M. Scott and Raphael Bretton. Sound: John R. Carter and David Deckendorf. Orchestration: Leo Shuken and Jack Hayes. Costumes: Don Feld. Hairstyles: Margaret Donovan. Makeup, Ben Nye. Production Manager, Harry A. Caplan. Assistant Director, William McGarry. Filmed on location in Arizona. Panavision. De-Luxe Color. Running time, 111 minutes.

CAST

Paul Newman, Fredric March, Richard Boone, Diane Cilento, Cameron Mitchell, Barbara Rush,

With Diane Cilento and Margaret Blye

Peter Lazer, Margaret Blye, Martin Balsam, Skip Ward, Frank Silvera, David Canary, Val Avery, Larry Ward, Linda Cordova, Pete Hernandez, Merrill C. Isbell.

THE FILM

Fresh from the Hitchcock wars, Newman teamed again with Martin Ritt to make *Hombre.* Irving Ravetch and Harriet Frank, Jr., who by now had become part of the Newman-Ritt creative ensemble with frequent contributions, wrote a taut, tight screenplay from the Elmore Leonard novel, and Ravetch co-produced with Ritt, who gave the film careful direction. A strong cast was recruited, including Fredric March, Richard Boone, Cameron Mitchell, Barbara Rush and Diane Cilento. Newman's dialogue was at a minimum in his stoical, strong-fibered characterization of John Russell, a Caucasian separated from his parents in childhood and raised as an Indian.

He finds himself on a stagecoach with other passengers of varying backgrounds and beliefs, and serves as the catalyst which brings out their true selves. Newman believed in the screenplay and went into the project with enthusiasm because he felt it had something to say about tolerance and cooperation and the common human ties that bind us all. Nor did he and Ritt stint with the action that is a customary Western staple.

It was about this time, with *Hombre,* that the jokes grew more frequent concerning Newman's penchant for films whose titles began with the letter H. Cited were *The Hustler, Hud* and *Harper,* but people tended to forget that there had been two others along the way, *Hemingway's Adventures of a Young Man* and *The Helen Morgan Story.* And instead of remarking, "That Newman film has everything but the kitchen sink in it," Holywood wags began cracking, "It had everything but Joanne Woodward."

Newman received a mixed set of reviews for his performance in this film, some critics hailing his conscientious attempts to achieve a detailed, in-depth characterization, and others calling his portrayal implausible. But it was typical of Newman that he should undertake still another experimental-type role in an effort to find the outer limits of his range. Russell (Newman), a white man raised by Apache Indians, finds himself on a stagecoach in the Arizona of the 1880's. He has

158

With Cameron Mitchell

inherited a boarding house which he has traded for a herd of horses, and is now on the way back to his home. Russell has been advised by his only white friend Henry Mendez (Martin Balsam) to shed his Indian clothing and get a haircut, so as to make himself acceptable to the whites on the stagecoach. Among the other passengers (with Mendez, the driver) are Alexander Favor (Fredric March) an Indian agent who has been mulcting the Indians out of their money by selling dogmeat passed off as beef; his wife Audra (Barbara Rush); a young married couple (Peter Lazer and Margaret Blye); Jessie Brown (Diane Cilento), an earthy type who had once managed the boarding house; and a brusque stranger, Cicero Grimes (Richard Boone).

Favor's mean prejudices compel Russell, known as The Hombre, to sit outside. Four gunmen, secretly in Grimes' employ, hold up the stagecoach and rob Favor of some $12,000 he has embezzled from the government for Indian beef contracts. The gunmen flee, taking Andra as a hostage, but before they get too far away the Hombre shoots and kills two of them. The money is recovered, but the Hombre warns the others that the outlaws will return and he leads them to an abandoned mine to undergo the inevitable siege. The outlaws come back the next day and offer to trade Andra for the $12,000. The Hombre tells the others that the offer should be refused, on the grounds that Andra made no protest during all the time her husband, with her full knowledge, was grossly cheating the Indians. Jessie attempts to take the money to Grimes, but the Hombre sends her back and goes in her place. A pitched battle breaks out between the gunmen and the besieged group, but though all the bandits die, Hombre also is killed saving his companions' lives.

REVIEWS

Joseph Gelmis in *Newsday*

In *Hombre* the H is silent, and so is Paul Newman. He's strong and silent and mean. If he has more than a page of dialogue in the film, it would be a surprise. Hombre has less impact than his previous gallery of H films—*Hud, Harper, The Hustler*. I liked *Hombre*. It is rough, funny, exciting. But I couldn't take it very seriously. Newman's blue-eyed Indian, a Caucasian raised by the Apaches, is somehow implausible, even when he is being his most nasty, inscrutable or violent. The heroic gesture at the end of the film is unbelievable, or, at least, out of character.

Robert Robinson in the *London Sunday Telegraph*
Newman might have been made for the asperities

With Martin Balsam, Margaret Blye, Peter Lazer, Barbara Rush, Fredric March, and Diane Cilento

of this kind of role. His face assumes extra edges, his cowboy hat sits on his Indian head, refusing to look easy there. His movements grow out of a stillness that seems to have been with him a long time; his preambles to action are impassive, remote. All this happens under faded blue skies and dusty trails, picked up by the camera like places instead of scenery.

Murf. in *Variety*

A well-executed film which develops the theme that socially and morally disparate types of people are often thrown into uneasy, explosive alliance due to emergencies. Paul Newman heads a uniformly competent cast . . . a conscious social commentary on greed, nobility, prejudice and resignation. Newman is excellent . . . Fredric March scores in a strong, unsympathetic—but eventually pathetic—role.

Leo Mishkin in the *New York Morning Telegraph*

Another stark, hard-bitten western in which some deep significance might be found if you have the time and patience to look for it, but which is so laden with old clichés and worn-out confrontations as to have you come away with the impression that there's very little new in it that you haven't seen before. . . . Mr. Newman plays his *Hombre* with dour one-note grimness, hardly changing any expression on his face.

Lawrence J. Quirk in *Screen Slants*

Hombre is a well-intentioned "western-with-built-in-think" (to coin a phrase, but it cannot escape an aura of *déjà vu*). Yes, it's all been done before, this business of a group of people of varying ethical and moral persuasions coming together via fortuitous circumstance. Such strong assets as Fredric March and Richard Boone try to lend conviction to the proceedings, some of which tax even their considerable talents, but the casting of Paul Newman as an Indian who *isn't* an Indian (he's a Caucasian adopted by Indians in early life) lends a strong impression that in attempting to reach out once more for a "versatile" image, he is again essaying a role that is ill-suited to his admittedly narrow but nonetheless depthful talents. Give Newman a part suited to his chemistry and personality and he delivers, *in depth* (as in, say, *The Rack, Cat on a Hot Tin Roof* or *Hud*), but take him out of his proper milieu and Newman is invariably and automatically forced to resort to a variety of surface postures and gimmicks which only serve to highlight the fact that he is not a character, first; individual-personality, second; thespic type but rather an actor of more confined range who delivers with solid intensity when allowed to tap his own unique inner resources. This he does not—and cannot—do with a gimmicky part like *Hombre*.

160

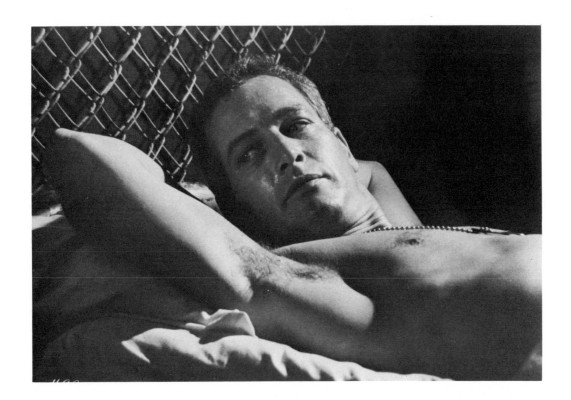

Cool Hand Luke

1967   Warner Bros.

CREDITS

A Jalem Production. Produced by Gordon Carroll. Directed by Stuart Rosenberg. Screenplay by Donn Pearce and Frank R. Pierson. Based on the novel by Donn Pearce. Photographed by Conrad Hall. Music by Lalo Shiffrin. Film Editor, Sam O'Steen. Art Director, Cary O'Dell. Set Decorations, Fred Price. Sound, Larry Jost. Costumes, Howard Shoup. Makeup, Gordon Bau. Hairstyles, Jean Burt Reilly. Associate Producer, Carter De-Haven, Jr. Production Manager, Arthur Newman. Assistant Director, Hank Moonjean. Filmed on location in the San Joaquin area near Stockton, California. Technicolor. Panavision. Running time, 129 minutes.

CAST

Paul Newman, George Kennedy, J. D. Cannon, Lou Antonio, Robert Drivas, Strother Martin, Jo Van Fleet, Clifton James, Morgan Woodward, Luke Askew, Marc Cavell, Richard Davalos, Robert Donner, Warren Finnerty, Dennis Hopper, John McLiam, Wayne Rogers, Dean Stanton, Charles Tyner, Ralph Waite, Anthony Zerbe, Buck Kartalian, Joy Harmon, Jim Gammon, Joe Don Baker, Donn Pearce, Norman Goodwins, Charles Hicks, John Pearce, Eddie Rossen, Rush Williams, James Jeter, Robert Luster, Rance Howard, James Bradley, Jr., Cyril "Chips" Robinson.

THE FILM

At last came a picture that showcased Newman's distinctive gifts so forcefully and vividly that to many it stands as his top acting achievement. *Cool Hand Luke* won Newman his fourth Academy Award nomination, and his admirers loudly protested when he failed to win for this. He was perfectly cast, projecting the somehow valiant rebelliousness of a chain-gang loner in a Southern prison camp.

Guided this time by Stuart Rosenberg, one of the creative young directors who were constantly shifting from the television to the film mediums, Newman exhibited a freshness of approach, a raw vitality, a complete spectrum of emotions, all of them right and true, and a sure command of his technical acting-resources that were breathtaking in their impact. Location scenes at the San Joaquin River Delta highlighted with their grim, authentic-looking ambience, the strong sequences in the script by Dean Pearce and Frank R. Pierson from Pearce's novel, and George Kennedy and a fine supporting cast backed up the star all the way.

Here then was Paul Newman at forty-two, within his range one of the finest screen actors of his or any era, at the peak of his powers, in perfect rapport with his role, perceptively invading its every nuance and implication, and this time around he brought the critics to their feet shouting superlatives in their honest admiration for a sterling talent well projected in a movie perfectly tailored to his measure. It was a long overdue recognition of the fullest kind, and that missing Oscar was the only cloudy speck on Newman's clear-blue career horizons.

The plot deals with Luke Jackson, who has been sentenced to two years with a chain gang in a Southern state for unscrewing the tops from parking meters while on a drunken spree. Luke is a loner of the first water. Even when consigned to the toughest physical details, he maintains his cool, though the sun blazes down and the environment is hostile. Dragline, the chain-gang leader (George Kennedy), takes a dislike to the independent Luke and their mutual hostility results in a fierce fist fight before the other prisoners in which Dragline beats Luke brutally but is unable to make him quit. From this point on, Dragline and the other men develop a new respect for Luke, especially when he refuses to take mistreatment from the camp's brutal guards.

Luke takes on a bet—that he will eat fifty eggs one after the other—and this adds to his growing popularity among the men, who see him increasingly as a tough symbol of the defiance they themselves do not dare to let out beyond a point. Luke's dying mother, Arietta (Jo Van Fleet) comes to the camp to visit him. She is too frail to leave her bed in the back of a truck. When, a short time later, he is informed that she has died, he goes berserk and is disciplined.

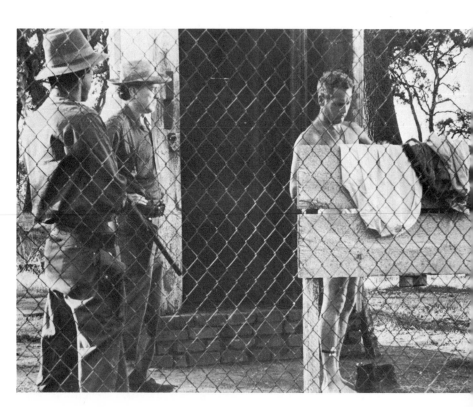

With prison guards

162

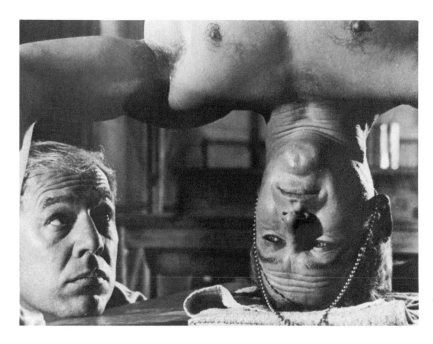

With George Kennedy

Confinement grates on him to the point that he actively plots escape. He saws a hole in the floor under his bunk and gets away but is captured, beaten and put in ankle chains. Later he breaks out again—and again is captured. The camp authorities begin an active campaign to break Luke's spirit, for they sense that he is a troublemaker who may influence the other prisoners to more aggressive actions. Mistreatment follows on mistreatment until he begs the guards for mercy in an abject manner in front of the other prisoners. In doing this he shatters the image he has built up of himself, and the inmates turn from him with contempt.

Again he escapes, this time in a dump truck. Dragline follows. Luke takes refuge in a church in a nearby town and after sending Dragline away, tries to achieve his own brand of eternal peace and reconciliation. Dragline returns, however, to the church with the prison guards, partly to save Luke and partly to win clemency. Luke, however, has had enough of living like an animal, and is shot to death. Donn Pearce, who collaborated on the screenplay based on his novel, was also the technical adviser for the movie. Pearce, a onetime safecracker, knew his subject, having served time in a prison camp. He also played a bit part as a prisoner.

REVIEWS

Bosley Crowther in *The New York Times*
Paul Newman is superb in this forceful portrait of a man born to lose . . . that traditional object of sorrow and compassion in American folk song and lore, the chain gang prisoner, is given as strong a presentation as ever he has had on the screen.

Hollis Alpert in *The Saturday Review*
Paul Newman's case is that of a very good, if somewhat limited, actor who took to leaning more on his popular personality than on his abilities. He also took on a few roles not particularly well suited to him (the unfortunate *Lady L* and *Torn Curtain* among them). But in *Cool Hand Luke* he is not only back on the beam—he has raised himself quite a notch above his previous best. Of course he is exactly right for the role of a rebellious prisoner in a concentration-camp-like Southern jail system (it would have been almost impossible to find anyone *more* right); yet this wouldn't have automatically guaranteed the emotional charge he generates. Newman manages a considerable gamut: he is funny at times, stalwart, submissive, defiant, pathetic, and eventually tragic. Obviously he and Stuart Rosenberg (an-

other of the crop of youngish directors who have emerged from television prep school) worked in a harmonious relationship, notably aided by a good script. . . . If there is such a thing as tasteful violence, this film has it. We are made to understand what is going on, why it is going on, and what is right or wrong about it. *Cool Hand Luke* may not be humane but it is certainly human.

Murf. in *Variety*

Downbeat but well-made. . . . Newman gives an excellent performance . . . directed and edited in superior fashion, it practically leaps off the screen.

Lawrence J. Quirk in *Screen Slants*

When Paul Newman is good he is very very good, and when he is bad he is—miscast. He is certainly *not* miscast in this strong prison drama; in fact he is superbly in his acting element, and very very good he is, indeed; in fact Mr. Newman is simply wonderful here, and that Oscar he has long been outrageously denied for a slew of distinguished performances should certainly come his way for 1967 if there is any justice in the world. If Mr. Newman would stick to the roles he does well,

and if he would avoid trying to Cary Grant-it with Hitchcock and Eli Wallach-it in films like *The Outrage* or *Hombre*—if he would just realize that he can't be all things to all audiences—he might wind up imagewise, with the critics and with cinematic posterity, as an actor of admittedly narrow range but within that narrow range superbly gifted. Comedian he is not; farceur, hardly; fey anarchist, no. He should let Gig Young handle farce and David Niven manipulate comic nuances, and even the likes of young Terence Stamp could beat him out at the anarchist bit. Let Mr. Newman, then, stick to the guns that are fashioned to his unique individuality, and he can make them boom like cannon. The cannons boom proudly in *Cool Hand Luke,* a gutsy and powerful and well-made drama in its own right. But with Paul Newman heading its cast it approaches grade-A artistry. He is given able support by always-dependable George Kennedy and a group of "cons" who look and act like they're really seething and rotting in their Southern hellhole. A great acting ensemble they make, with Mr. Newman their grimly shining centerpiece.

Paul Newman, center

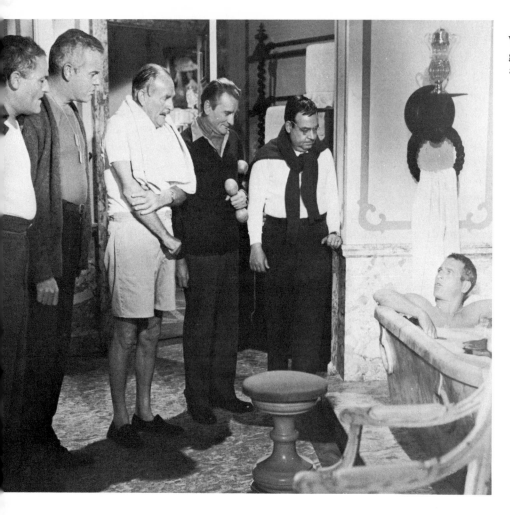

With Charles Gray, Andrew Duggan, John Williams, Jacques Roux and Tom Bosley

The Secret War of Harry Frigg

1968   Universal

CREDITS

An Albion Production for Universal. Produced by Hal E. Chester. Directed by Jack Smight. Screenplay by Peter Stone and Frank Tarloff. Based on a story by Frank Tarloff. Photographed by Russell Metty. Music by Carlo Rustichelli. Musical Supervision, Joseph Gershenson. Art Direction, Alexander Golitzen and Henry Bumstead. Set decorations, John McCarthy and John Austin.

Sound: Walden O. Watson, William Russell and Ronald Pierce. Costumes by Edith Head. Makeup by Bud Westmore. Hairstyles by Larry Germain. Associate Producer, Peter Stone. Production Manager, Arthur S. Newman, Jr. Assistant Director, Terence Nelson. Location scenes filmed in Sierra Madre area of Southern California. Technicolor. Techniscope. Running time, 110 minutes.

With Andrew Duggan

CAST

Paul Newman, Sylva Koscina, Andrew Duggan, Tom Bosley, John Williams, Charles D. Gray, Vito Scotti, Jacques Roux, Werner Peters, James Gregory, Fabrizio Mioni, Johnny Haymer, Norman Fell, Buck Henry, Horst Ebersberg, Richard X. Slattery, George Ives.

THE FILM

The critics solidly roasted this picture as well as Newman's performance in it. The old charges were trotted out again: that excellent as he could be when working with dramatic material suited to him, Newman came across as forced and gauche when essaying comedy. True, director Frank Corsaro had gotten some good comic effects out of Newman in the stage play, *Baby Want a Kiss,* in 1964, and for this the New York theatre critics had accorded Newman his just due (though how much of his improved comic sense in that play had been due to Corsaro's directorial insights and how much to Newman's natural bent remains moot).

The Secret War of Harry Frigg, however, got a negative reaction, and more than one critic im-plied that the film's producers were trying to carry the war for honesty in films too far in using such a surname (even with an extra 'g') in the title and that such specious gimmickry smacked of pre-release boxoffice anxiety. However that may be, Newman came across as dismally heavy-handed in scenes that a Cary Grant would have invested with a gossamer touch, and the story was generally far-fetched, unbelievable and an embar-rassment in its constant straining for non-existent comic effects.

The plot concerned five World War II Allied generals (Andrew Duggan, Tom Bosley, John Williams, Charles D. Gray and Jacques Roux) who were captured in a Tunisian turkish bath by the Italians and forthwith transported to deten-tion in a luxurious Italian villa. The villa is under the command of Lieutenant Colonel Ferrucci (Vito Scotti). The five generals are not the bright-est lot as generals go, and they cannot agree on an escape plan. General Homer Prentiss (James Gregory) of Army Public Relations decides to enlist the services of Private Harry Frigg (Paul Newman) in arranging the generals' escape. Frigg, it seems, is famous for his cleverly-expedited escapes from stockades, and it is reasoned that he might well apply his unique skills to spring the generals. Immediately Frigg is promoted to Major General, so as to enable him to order the one-star generals in the villa about without back-talk. He is then smuggled into Italy. He reaches the villa, and begins engineering the generals' escape, but when he meets the owner, Contessa Francesca de Montefiore (Sylva Koscina), who resides for the duration in the gatehouse, Frigg slows down his escape plans. Via a secret passageway he visits the Countess nightly and meanwhile he delays the generals via a series of diversionary escape maneuvers.

When the escape night finally arrives, another postponement becomes necessary, for it seems that the Italian commandant is to be made a general at midnight and the conspirators do not wish to cramp his style at such a time. During the midnight celebration, Nazi officers come to the villa and announce the surrender of Italy and the imminent transportation of all prisoners to a German stalag. Once deprived of the Countess' company and the luxurious villa existence, Frigg snaps back to his old self and shrewdly engineers the generals' escape. For this he is cited for a commission. He winds up, of course, stationed at an Army radio station in the Countess' villa.

The picture purports to show the maturing of the Frigg character under the stress of responsibility, but he seems as frivolous at the end of the picture as at the beginning. It was one of Newman's critical lowpoints during recent years, but his other 1968 picture (this time as a director) more than recovered the lost ground.

With Sylva Koscina

REVIEWS

Elaine Rothschild in *Films in Review*
The double "g" in the surname of the title character of *The Secret War of Harry Frigg* does not rescue it from being offensive, nor the film from the fate of farce that doesn't come off. . . . NYC's Radio City Music Hall played this picture because, it would seem, it could get nothing else when its preceding movie faded sooner than was expected. Whatever the reason, the MH ill-served its patrons. An uninteresting, as well as unbelievable, story-line is *not* helped by tired jokes, poor performances (especially Paul Newman's incapacity for comedy) and couldn't-care-less direction by Jack Smight. The only woman in this pastiche about a U.S. private being made a general during World War II so he can lead the escape of five allied generals whom the Italians have captured, is Sylva Koscina. She is also the only thing in *The Secret War of Harry Frigg* worth looking at.

Lawrence J. Quirk in *Screen Slants*
Oh, Mr. Paul Newman, why, oh why, do you insist on essaying these comic spoofs? This latest ill-advised venture into a métier in which you are not at your best goes over like a lead balloon. Back to the chain gang with you, Mr. Newman. Back to the wide-open-spaces villainies of *Hud* and the sure control of *Harper*. Turn backward oh backward, Mr. Newman, to the roles that have won you your enormous prestige and follow-

With Sylva Koscina

ing, but if you insist on moving forward with a series of roles like this, then do not seek to know for whom the bell tolls, it will toll even for a glistening star like thee. Mr. Newman is one of the few authentic stars of the 1960's. He has won that stardom with hard work and worry and thorough professionalism in the roles for which he is best suited—and he should not jeopardize it with any more of these gross miscastings.

Renata Adler in *The New York Times*

As Private Harry, Newman is supposed to be slope-shouldered, floppy and comic—and it is clear from his first appearance during the credits that he has no talents in this direction at all. He sits, in a rag doll way, on a prison truck and fakes a yawn, and the part won't bend. The scene becomes a charade in which Paul Newman is trying to communicate that he is not playing *Hud* this time and what we have here, as *Cool Hand Luke* would say, is a failure to communicate. The

screenplay is uneven and boring. It gets a lot of unearned mileage out of the hero's name. (Hollywood's secret war for frank speech in movies ought to be waged more nobly than in surnames).

Murf. in *Variety*

Despite some latter-day casting as a flip, hip character, Newman herein is essaying a different kind of comedy role—that of a perennial goof-off, who achieves a measure of self-confidence and maturity under pressure. Sympathy is with him all the way, for he remains a likeable actor. Fortunately for the pic, Newman's weakest and least believable scenes occur at the very start, when in establishment of the character, he's allowed to overdo in mugging and grunting, coming across as a poor caricature of the hoods once played in pix by Sheldon Leonard. At best, Newman does not appear to be a particularly strong comedy actor, but with such a competent surrounding cast, he is most acceptable.

Directing his wife

Rachel, Rachel

1968   Warner Bros.

CREDITS

A Paul Newman Production for Warner Bros. Produced and directed by Paul Newman. Screenplay by Stewart Stern. Based on the novel *A Jest of God,* by Margaret Laurence. Photographed by Gayne Rescher. Music composed and conducted by Jerome Moross. Song lyrics by Stewart Stern. Performed by The Phaetons. Film Editor, Dede Allen. Art Direction, Robert Gundlach. Set Decorations, Richard Merrell. Sound, Jack Jacobsen and Dick Vorisek. Costumes by Domingo Rodriguez. Associate Producers, Arthur Newman and Harrison Starr. Production Consultant, Larry Sturhahn. Production Manager, Flo Nerlinger. Assistant Director, Alan Hopkins. Filmed entirely in Connecticut, at Bethel, Georgetown and Danbury. Technicolor. Running time, 101 minutes.

CAST

Joanne Woodward, James Olson, Kate Harrington, Estelle Parsons, Geraldine Fitzgerald, Donald Moffatt, Terry Kiser, Frank Corsaro, Bernard Barrow, Nell Potts, Shawn Campbell, Violet

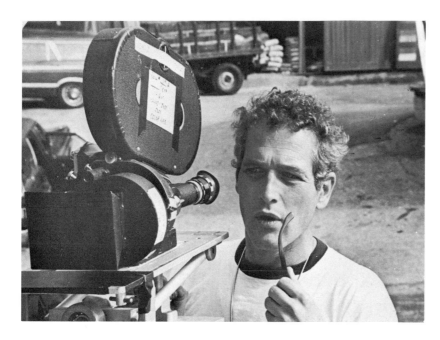

Directing the film

Dunn, Izzy Singer, Tod Engle, Bruno Engl, Beatrice Pons, Dorothea Duckworth, Connie Robinson, Sylvia Shipman, Larry Fredericks, Wendell MacNeal.

NOTE

Newman won the New York Film Critics Award for 1968 as Best Director for *Rachel, Rachel*. Miss Woodward won as Best Actress, also for *Rachel, Rachel*.

THE FILM

Rachel, Rachel was truly a labor of love for Newman and Miss Woodward. It was significant that as his first directorial stint he should choose this deeply human and profoundly heartbreaking tale of a repressed schoolteaching spinster in a small New England town who is bedevilled by a selfish mother and has become spiritually ill from the denial of love.

Rachel Cameron at thirty-five feels that life has

Joanne Woodward with
Kate Harrington

Estelle Parsons and
Joanne Woodward

passed her by, and this time movie conventions are flouted in the suggestion implicit in the closing sequence that she might well be right, though she is making attempts to get a fresh lease on life by moving away. Newman the director revealed another side to his personality—the melancholy, compassionate brooder over human loneliness, lovelessness and waste. He also proved with this film that he could hold his own with any pro director you would want to name, and the lean economy of his technique combined with his sure feel for the poignant and true, stamped him as a director of unlimited promise.

He had had directing in the back of his mind for some years, but it took his wife's enthusiasm for the Margaret Laurence novel, *A Jest of God,* and the Stewart Stern screenplay to convince him that this was right for him as a maiden effort. Miss Woodward and Stern had encountered much difficulty in getting financial backing for the film, as it was regarded as too introverted and drab, hence uncommercial. After Newman got into the act, the project got off the ground, and it revealed itself, upon completion, to be a film of which the Newmans could well be proud.

Earnest, sincere, subtly tragic, a perfect delineation of one "life of quiet desperation," *Rachel, Rachel,* dealing as it did with the drab ambience of an ordinary young woman's inner torments,

concentrated on depths rather than surfaces. The film won Joanne Woodward her first Academy Award nomination since her winning year of 1957, and her husband, who understood every facet of her nature and creative resources, after ten years of marriage and five co-starring movies, as no one else in the world did, got from Miss Woodward what would probably go on the record as her finest, most mature and feelingful performance.

Rachel and her mother (Kate Harrington) live in an apartment over the funeral parlor where her now-dead undertaker father had once presided. Her closest friend is another spinster teacher, Calla Mackie (Estelle Parsons). Rachel at thirty-five is love-hungry, life-battered, frustrated in the extreme. Calla persuades her to attend a revival meeting conducted by Reverend Wood (Geraldine Fitzgerald).

Rachel, to her shocked horror, finds herself caught up in the emotionalism unleashed by a visiting young preacher (Terry Kiser) who urges full expression of needs, and when she finds herself fleeing the Lesbian implications of the protective love Calla offers, she realizes that it is imperative that she expose herself to life before it is too late. A former high school friend, Nick Kazlik (James Olsen), back for a visit with his parents, seduces a willing Rachel and she falls into the

172

trap of mistaking sexual fulfillment for love and becomes emotionally involved with him. But Nick is turned off by her serious approach and lets her believe that he is married. He then breaks off with her completely.

Later Rachel imagines herself pregnant, and plans to have the child, but after Calla has aided her in finding a teaching spot in far-off Oregon, Rachel learns that her supposed pregnancy is merely a cyst. Nonetheless she determines to widen her horizons and move to Oregon anyway. She leaves town with her mother, hopeful of the future and determined to remain open to experience henceforth. Whatever her fate may be, she will no longer back away from it.

REVIEWS

Marya Mannes in *McCall's*

. . . an extremely auspicious debut in production and direction for actor Paul Newman and a triumph for Joanne Woodward in the title role . . . [here is a] revelation of love long denied and desperately sought. Like the rest of the film, from cast to photography, the conclusion is neither contrived nor expected. It is restrained, sensitive, engrossing—and right.

Arthur Knight in *The Saturday Review*

Newman, who has long wanted to direct, had the good sense as producer to surround himself with first-rate talent: New York editor Dede Allen, who cut last year's *Bonnie and Clyde,* cameraman Gayne Rescher, a resourceful recruit from the TV commercials with a knack for making New England's red barns and brick schoolhouses look like Charles Sheeler's clean, needle-sharp version of Americana; and composer Jerome Moross, who probably remembered from his ballet days that a simple phrase on a piano can often convey more than an entire symphony orchestra in full cry. . . . The cast, also largely New York based, he apparently chose less for name value than for character verisimilitude, and their ability to act. . . . But, quite properly, it is Miss Woodward who carries the picture, and makes it the affecting thing it is—and reminds us, incidentally, how long it has been since she had a picture worthy of her talents. No ravishing beauty, she projects instead an inner radiance, a winning wholesomeness and integrity that is the essence of Rachel Cameron. . . . Docile or desperate, hysterical with fear or with laughter, whether loving or brooding over the rejection of her love, she brings to the mobile surface of her face, without self-consciousness or any sense of "acting," the full force of what is felt inside. One recalls Helen Hayes and Barbara Stanwyck in films of the Thirties—actresses with a similar intensity and range—and suddenly we realize how much has been lost in the name of underplaying or "cool."

William Wolf in *Cue*

Directing his first movie, Paul Newman is off to

James Olsen and Joanne Woodward

an auspicious start in a new career. If he hasn't set the industry afire, he shows a truth-seeking directness that stamps his film with conviction and honesty. He also possesses a key quality; he knows how to be lean and judicious instead of cinematically verbose. . . . Joanne Woodward . . . is a marvelous actress, and her husband obviously knows what she can do in a part and helps her to make the most of this one . . . [The film] contains enough truth about people and loneliness to earn interest and admiration. There are many eloquent touches—flights of fancy into what Rachel would like to see happen and sequences capturing small-town Americana. Admirers of Paul Newman will now have an additional reason for their esteem.

Richard Schickel in *Life*

The film was clearly undertaken in a spirit entirely too rare in American life. That is to say, a star, Joanne Woodward, and a screenwriter, Stewart Stern, discovered a novel, Margaret Laurence's *A Jest of God,* that was, to them, something more than a mere property. Instead, it was a difficult and delicate thing that challenged them as artists, something they felt they simply had to make. They apparently encountered enormous difficulties in obtaining the relatively modest backing they required, and it was not until Miss Woodward's husband, Paul Newman, put his plentiful clout behind the project by agreeing to direct it that they could go ahead. Everyone involved thereupon did his work with taste, conviction, and solid, sometimes brilliant, craftsmanship. Stern's script, despite a tendency to tell rather than show, rings with gentle irony and rueful truth. Miss Woodward demonstrates again that she is perhaps the only major female star of our day capable of genuine naturalism, submerging self and image in a subtle, disciplined performance that avoids showiness, excessive sentiment, self-consciousness. As a director Newman is anything but the bouncing boy-o we are accustomed to seeing on our screens. He has a sensitive, slightly melancholic eye for something most American movies miss— the texture of ordinary life. He displays, moreover, a feel for emotional nuances and a technical sureness; he is neither too radical nor too conservative. That is remarkable in a first film.

Joanne Woodward and James Olsen

Joanne Woodward

174

With Joanne Woodward

Winning

1969   Universal

CREDITS

A Universal-Newman-Foreman Production. A Jennings Lang Production. Produced by John Foreman. Directed by James Goldstone. Screenplay by Howard Rodman. Photographed by Richard Moore. Music by Dave Grusin. Art Director, Alexander Golitzen, John J. Lloyd and Joe Alves. Set Decorations, John McCarthy and George Milo. Film Editors, Edward A. Biery and Richard C. Meyer. Sound, Weldon O. Watson and James T. Porter. Makeup, Bud Westmore. Hairstyles, Larry Germain. Associate Producer, George Santore. Production Manager, Wally Worsley. Assistant Director, Earl Bellamy, Jr. Location scenes filmed at the Indianapolis Speedway and at Elkhart Lake, Wisconsin. Technicolor. Panavision. Running time, 123 minutes.

CAST

Paul Newman, Joanne Woodward, Richard Thomas, Robert Wagner, David Sheiner, Clu Gulager, Barry Ford, Bob Quarry, Eileen Wesson, Toni Clayton, Maxine Stuart, Karen Arthur, Paulene Myers, Ray Ballard, Charles Steel, Alma Platt, Harry Basch, Allen Emerson, Marianna Coe, Carolyn McNichol, Bobby Unser, Tony Hulman, George Mason, Mimi Littlejohn, Pat Vidan, Bruce Walkup, Timothy Galbraith, Lon Palmer, Joy Teynolds.

THE FILM

Winning first saw the light of day in 1967 when it was projected as one of MCA's "World Premiere" items for NBC-TV presentation. Plans changed along the way, and it wound up eventually in 1969 as a $7,000,000 movie designed for theatrical release, and starring the Newmans. Some spectacular footage was caught in 1968 at the seventeen-car crash during the Memorial Day

Indianapolis 500, and it was incorporated into the picture.

An exciting and fast-paced racing drama in its own right, *Winning* profited enormously from the Newmans' presence, as they contributed a pair of performances that were quietly underplayed and expertly forceful. Newman's underplaying, especially, attracted attention, and the mannerisms that in so many films had been part of his stock-in-trade seemed to have been subtly planed away. The critics, who had developed an increasing respect for the Newmans as a team since *Rachel, Rachel,* lavishly praised both performances. One viewer got the distinct impression that his successful debut as a director had given Newman a fresh concept of his esthetic potential, that he was at last fully conscious of his powers, and rested confidently in them, and that past desires to pour extra adrenalin into proving what didn't *need* proving, had to a degree subsided, leaving him mellow.

The story dealt with Frank Capua (Newman) a top auto racing driver who meets a divorcee (Joanne Woodward) with a teenage son (Richard Thomas). An attachment grows between them, and eventually they marry. He also offers to adopt Charley, her son. But marital felicity is jeopardized by Frank's absorption in his racing

career and when he runs into bad luck and loses a number of races to his chief rival Luther Erding (Robert Wagner) he becomes increasingly self-absorbed and neglectful of his duties as husband and father. Lonely and neglected, Elora has a strictly physical affair with Erding, but this ends abruptly when Frank finds the two in bed together. Frank moves out of the motel and when he and Erding cross swords in the competitive driving life in which they are both involved, Frank grows even more bitter, especially when Leo Crawford (David Sheiner) a car owner, notes Frank's declining morale and allows Erding to race a car Frank has coveted. Charley sympathizes with his stepfather and tends to blame his mother for the break-up and hitchhikes to the track to watch Frank race Erding at Indianapolis.

His morale bolstered by the boy's affection and admiration, Frank decides to rebuild the car that Erding had burned out in a qualification run. He gets it in shape and qualifies it in time for the 500. A mammoth seventeen-car pile-up takes place during the race and Erding is knocked out when his engine fails. Frank wins the race. The next day, when Erding attempts to apologize for sleeping with his wife, Frank slugs him. He then learns that Elora and Charley have returned to their home town. Realizing that his neglect of her had

With Joanne Woodward and
Richard Thomas

176

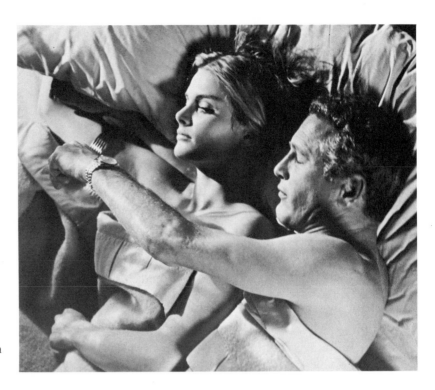

With Toni Clayton

played a large part in her infidelity with Erding, Newman goes after Elora and suggests a reconciliation.

Newman refused to use a double for some of the race sequences, and the studio had him insured for three million dollars.

REVIEWS

Whit. in *Variety*

A love story set against an auto racing background . . . Newman underplays his part throughout, resulting in one of his better performances. He is ideally cast as the racer, and those sequences in which he is racing are convincingly portrayed. . . . Miss Woodward, who makes no attempt at glamor or any other goal except as Newman's earthy wife, turns in a ringingly effective characterization. As the young son, Richard Thomas delivers a winning delineation which should get him future roles. Some of the slickest racing sequences in memory add top interest, one sequence in particular, causing a brief audience gasp as seventeen cars pile up at the beginning of the Indianapolis race.

Arthur Knight in *The Saturday Review*

The script has posed a recognizable, and thoroughly human, dilemma—and posed it in terms of thoroughly recognizable, and human, people. There is a sense of growth in Newman's character and a sense of depth in Miss Woodward's that carry the film far beyond the surface excitement of auto racing.

William Wolf in *Cue*

Paul Newman and Joanne Woodward are zooming in stature as a film world couple. They are doing it without leading private lives that catapult them into headlines. Their own special ingredient is *talent* . . . the driver and his woman come vividly alive, thanks to the Newmans' ability to create flesh and blood people. . . . In addition to having a keen eye for mood and detail [director James Goldstone] maintains a pace that supplies tension to the relationships. He makes us care. While racing itself may have a measure of excitement, the real nervousness concerns the outcome of life for the protagonists. In other hands they might well be cardboard figures. But the Newmans—well, they are just a special combination.

Leo Mishkin in the *New York Morning Telegraph*

Newman and Miss Woodward both invest this formula with the sensitivity and compassion of exquisitely fine performances, as honest, as real and as true as anything either, or both, have ever done. One scene alone, with the two of them sitting in a garden rocker, drinking beer out of cans, comes as close to their own marriage, I suspect, as could be depicted in a fictional motion picture.

Howard Thompson in *The New York Times*
Probably the best-rounded and most appealing personalized film of this kind ever made. . . . The Newmans are both splendid, he as the brooding, fiercely delineated "winner" and she in a complex characterization that Miss Woodward shades with wise reserve . . . even with motors roaring full-blast, in *Winning* it's the people that matter.

Susan Lardner in *The New Yorker*
Mr. Newman, who is not susceptible to unflattering angles, has less opportunity to develop a character [here] but he is very good within the limits imposed by the part of an impassive sports hero, which is to say that he successfully conveys the discomfort of being strong and silent.

Stanley Kauffmann in *The New Republic*
What keeps the picture from tedium, besides its hard action, is Paul Newman's performance. . . . Newman simply seems incapable of making a false move or sound.

Judith Crist in *New York*
Howard Rodman's screenplay and dialogue has

With Toni Clayton

more clichés and cornball phrasing than the telephone book has Smiths and Joneses [but] since Paul Newman and Joanne Woodward could, for my money, just stand there and read the telephone book—who's to quarrel?

With Joanne Woodward

178

With Katharine Ross and
Robert Redford

Butch Cassidy and the Sundance Kid

1969   20th Century-Fox

CREDITS

A 20th Century-Fox release of a George Roy Hill-Paul Monash (Campanile) Production. Directed by George Roy Hill. Produced by John Foreman. A Newman-Foreman Presentation. Camera (De-Luxe Color) Conrad Hill. Screenplay by William Goldman. Music by Burt Bacharach. Song "Raindrops Keep Falling on My Head" by Burt Bacharach and Hal David, sung by B. J. Thomas. Editors, John C. Howard and Richard C. Meyer. Art direction, Jack Martin Smith, Philip Jeffries.

Second Unit Director, Michael Moore. Assistant Director, Steven Bernhardt. Sound, William E. Edmondson, David E. Dockendorf. Running time, 112 minutes.

CAST

Paul Newman, Robert Redford, Katharine Ross, Strother Martin, Henry Jones, Jeff Corey, George Furth, Cloris Leachman, Ted Cassidy, Kenneth Mars, Donnelly Rhodes, Jody Gilbert, Timothy Scott, Don Keefer, Charles Dierkop, Francisco Cordova, Nelson Olmstead, Paul Bryar, Sam Elliott, Charles Akins, Eric Sinclair.

THE FILM

The quietly assured underplaying and the mellow affirmation that Newman first displayed full-force in *Winning* is in ample evidence in this actionful, gently humorous and feyly imaginative picture, and in fact so great is Newman's unassertive confidence in himself that he even lets Robert Redford outplay him in spots. But note: Redford outplays but does *not* outshine his co-star, who was never in better form. A spoof of every bad-man Western ever made, it is improvisationally brilliant. When Newman does a trick bicycle ride to the tune of Burt Bacharach's "Raindrops Keep

Falling on My Head," it is a show-stopper.

Butch Cassidy and the Sundance Kid are, let's face it, not very bright outlaws, but they are human and delightful, and the role of Butch provided Newman with a complete change of pace and gave him, moreover, a chance to demonstrate that, in the proper context and under the proper conditions, he *could* deliver the comedy after all.

Of course, this is a unique picture in every way. William Goldman's screenplay is full of iconoclastic touches, and most if not all of the western clichés (or is conventions a gentler word?) are swept away. John Foreman, with whom Newman had formed a rewarding production partner-ship, sees to it that the mounting is impeccable, and Katharine Ross, Strother Martin, Henry Jones and others give able support.

The plot, such as it is (for this is a comic spoof replete with moods and fey surprises) deals with Butch Cassidy (Newman) who runs a Wyoming gang known variously as the Wild Bunch and the Hole in the Wall Gang. Along with the Sundance Kid (Robert Redford) one of the West's deadliest young guns, Butch gets involved in one train hold-up after another. Along the way they get into a series of scrapes that are as comic as they are actionful.

A young Denver schoolteacher, Etta Place

With Robert Redford and
Katharine Ross

(Katharine Ross), is romantically involved with the Kid, and when Union Pacific President Harriman sends out agents hell-bent on stopping the train robberies for all time by eliminating Butch and the Kid from the scene, the trio decide to light out for greener pastures.

They stop first in New York, en route to Bolivia, where they have heard there are good pickings, and there they enjoy themselves like three kids. In Bolivia, they are disillusioned by the terrain and the people and the slim returns on outlawry, and when Etta realizes that they will keep pushing their luck until they are killed, she sadly bids them goodbye and returns home rather than see them killed before her eyes. Soon Butch and the Kid, with characteristic recklessness, have maneuvered themselves into a cul-de-sac in a Bolivian town, and come out of their hiding places with guns blazing at hundreds of Bolivian soldiers. The last shot of them, aggressively advancing, though hopelessly outnumbered, is frozen—we know they are about to die, but we (as the screenwriter and director knew so well) want to remember them in action.

Though Goldman's screenplay was in part based upon authentic files of the Pinkerton Agency, he did soften the characters of his legendary heroes. Butch in real life was a deadly outlaw and the Kid was likewise deadly with a gun and a vicious killer to boot. The film incarnation of Butch is friendly as a puppy, cheerful, playful and though he can get tough with the best of them when he has to, he prefers a life of cheerful relaxation. The evil in the true Sundance Kid is glossed over in the Redford portrayal as limned by Goldman's dialogue and action, and he emerges as gun-happy but human and replete with honest sentiment under a stoical exterior.

The picture's story does not convey its essence; it is a sort of mood piece, a complex fugue of

With Robert Redford

interlacing buffooneries and bitter-sweet commentary on the passing of an individualistic way of life. Butch and the Kid were truly the last of the Great Outlaws of legend. And this is a beautifully serio-comic tribute to them.

REVIEWS

Lawrence J. Quirk in *Screen Slants*

Paul Newman at 44 is mellowing and maturing as an actor, and with a quiet magnificence. Cast here in the role of flamboyant outlaw Butch Cassidy (and granting that the picture is a clever spoof of the last days of the Great Western Badmen) Newman performs in a delightfully light and at times even fey style, underplaying shrewdly, essaying comedy scenes (like a trick bicycle-riding sequence) with an ease and an insouciance I have never seen him display in such measure before, and graciously (and even magnanimously) blending into an ensemble playing-style with the other actors. And because Newman's style here is (I suspect deliberately) more subtly muted and nimbly self-effacing, he all but hands the picture to Robert Redford, who as the Sundance Kid is given a chance to display his arresting and distinctive talents as never before on the screen.

Redford infuses his characterization with a compelling synthesis of lethal malevolence and human sentiment. Here, however, is the Newman who has given promise of emerging on the screen for some time now—the stock mannerisms of the old days are radically diminished in this film; the slick, cocky, at-times-overblown aplomb is gradually being refined into a lithe performing style that bespeaks an ultimate confidence in his talent that I have in the past suspected Newman of not possessing one hundred percent. Newman's screen portrayals henceforth, in what promises to be his Golden Era, may some day be seen to date from this picture, in which artistic humility and professional sureness produce a Newman on-screen essence that exemplifies a great talent at last commencing to strike exactly the right balance. We can only hope that now that his acting style appears to be keeping pace with the sensitivity, compassion and wise balance that his superb direction last year of his wife Joanne Woodward's film, *Rachel, Rachel* displayed, he will not altogether abandon acting for directing. He has waited some fifteen years now for the Academy Award that Hollywood has perversely and unfairly denied him for picture after picture—while lesser talents with a greater bent for politics-playing and pub-

With Robert Redford

licity-saturation have sneaked away with the prize. We need both director Newman and actor Newman—and we hope he will not sacrifice one for the other. A one-time intense-but-narrow-ranged talent seems unmistakably to be broadening, and the Paul Newman of the 'seventies should have rich characterizations to offer his admirers.

Judith Crist in *New York*

It could, with its original screenplay by William Goldman, be termed a turn-of-the-century all-male version of *Bonnie and Clyde,* a Western badman spoof that's a blood relative of *Cat Ballou,* a deromanticization of a phase of Western mythology much in the manner of *The Rounders.* But with all these elements, Mr. Goldman has given a special dimension to his story of a couple of not-very-bright badmen on the run much as he gave a special depth to *Harper*—and the presence of Paul Newman in both is scarcely coincidental. For beneath the literacy and the wit that make the script sparkle, Mr. Goldman makes the stuff

of legendry human, telling the tale of two men who run their crooked route with gusto and guts and wouldn't take the straight road if they could . . . it is essentially a game—as the perfectly capped teeth of the leading players testify and as Katharine Ross's pure Hollywood portrait of a schoolmarm proves . . . but in the hands of Newman and Redford . . . and Goldman and Hill . . . it's a glorious game, an affectionate one—and one made meaningful. . . . And not the least of the pleasures is the emergence of Redford as the fine actor he is in a role worthy of his talents, which include keeping Newman from making the movie entirely his own. And that, as we Newman addicts know, is some talent!

Whit. in *Variety*

The John Foreman production is episodic, but George Roy Hill's direction is so satisfying in catching the full value of the Goldman screenplay that a high degree of interest is sustained. Film opens engagingly with flash-on of the titles, as a small portion of the screen is devoted to the unreeling of what appears to be an old silent flicker of the earliest days of motion pictures, showing Butch and his gang staging a train hold-up. The click of the old-fashioned projector is heard to further set the mood for what is to come. . . . Newman and Redford both sock over their respective roles with a humanness seldom attached to outlaw characters, and Miss Ross . . . is excellent.

Director George Roy Hill in a *Newark Evening News* interview:

"The Western became an American morality play and, practically up to today, good guys wore white hats. They were clean-living men who could out-ride, out-shoot and out-fight any villain because their hearts were pure. And bad guys were real varmints—black-hearted, one-dimensional villains. . . . Ours is more than even an adult Western—it's not a Western at all. It's a character study, and a retelling on the screen of the specific adventures of a specific gang and their leader. And as a character study, Butch Cassidy's story couldn't have been put on the screen before. He was an affable man who chose to be an outlaw as others decided to be lawyers and dentists. He never killed anybody until he and the Sundance Kid were in South America, and, in fact, he rode away from a train robbery when it became apparent that bloodshed would be unavoidable. Unlike the stories of the Jones, Younger and [other] gangs, there are official records of Butch and his "Hole-in-the-Wall" gang, and screenwriter William Goldman's screenplay is based on the files of the Pinkerton National Detective Agency.

Holding Up The Train

With Joanne Woodward

WUSA

1970   Paramount

CREDITS

A Rosenberg-Newman-Foreman Production for Paramount Pictures. Produced by John Foreman. Directed by Stuart Rosenberg. Associate Producer, Hank Moonjean. Screenplay by Robert Stone from his novel, *A Hall of Mirrors*. Photographed by Richard Moore. Art Director, Philip Jefferies. Set Decorator, William Kiernan. Unit Production Manager, Arthur Newman. Assistant Directors, Hank Moonjean, Howard Koch, Jr., Les Gorall. Film Editor, Bob Wyman. Sound Recording, Jerry Jost. Costumes by Travilla. Music composed and conducted by Lalo Shiffrin. Men's Wardrobe, Nat Tolmach. Women's Wardrobe, Norma Brown. Script Supervisor, Betty Crosby. Hair Styles by Sydney Guilaroff. Makeup artists, Lynn Reynolds and Jack Wilson. Technicolor. Panavision. Running time, 115 minutes.

CAST

Paul Newman, Joanne Woodward, Anthony Perkins, Laurence Harvey, Pat Hingle, Cloris Leachman, Don Gordon, Michael Anderson, Jr., Leigh French, Moses Gunn, Bruce Cabot, Lou Gosset, Robert Quarry.

THE FILM

While *WUSA* will certainly not go down in cinematic lore as anybody's favorite Paul Newman film (certainly it wouldn't make the top three-quarters of my own list) it does seem to this writer that it has been dealt with rather harshly by the critics. I tend to agree with Vincent Canby, who in a retrospective discussion of the film in *The New York Times* remarked, "[It] is not a good movie but it does, at least, prompt one to want to talk back to it—and recently, there haven't been too many movies to do even that."

Paul Newman holds this film in high regard, and has called it one of his most significant works. In an October 1970 TV interview with David Frost, Newman insisted that this exposé of neo-Fascist conspiracy in the United States was "tough-minded" and "should be in a time capsule to be seen 100 years from now" and that it was designed "to get people to ask themselves a lot of questions," adding, "if it does that, it has served its purpose." Newman on the same program also referred to WUSA as "an emotional exercise—a humanity exercise" and said it was not a well-made play type of thing so much as an emotional experience that "paints a picture of our times."

He went on to express his "paternal interest" in the picture. Contrary to his usual withdrawn and reclusive approach to the film promotion scene (he simply doesn't help promote at all), Newman *did* stump for *WUSA,* going beyond the call of duty in his efforts to put it over with critics and public. He told Frost that he had co-produced and acted in the film because he wanted to see a reversal in this country of "corporate greed" and "gimme gimme philosophy" and "apathetic indifference to our national future."

My own impression of the film is as follows: Its sincerity is apparent and its passionate quality unmistakable but its techniques and general approach went awry somewhere along the line with the result that its philosophic and ethical points are blunted, indeed obscured. While not quite so good as in *Butch Cassidy and the Sundance Kid,* Newman continues to demonstrate a refreshing tendency to underplay and restrain those "star" mannerisms that were so much a part of his cinematic past, and Miss Woodward gives one of her most touching and true performances as a prostitute with a set of convictions uniquely her own. Anthony Perkins as the addled idealist who is exploited by deep-dyed opportunists continues to demonstrate growth in his characterizational insights and acting expertise in general, and Pat Hingle is excellent as the neo-Fascist millionaire radio station operator who uses the cynical Newman as his cat's paw, as is Laurence Harvey in a somewhat skimpy part of a con-man turned preacher.

There is perhaps too much talk and too much

With Anthony Perkins

"think-think" and these liabilities militate against pace, coherence and audience interest. There is also a tendency to explain rather than show, and to preach rather than entertain, but there *are* a number of right-lively scenes and the acting in most instances is top-notch. I do not think it fair that the Newmans be so severely faulted for trying to make what, in their judgment, and doubtless director Stuart Rosenberg's, was a sincere and honest contribution to current thought.

But they had the wrong soapbox, obviously, and the wrong approach. Some insights into *WUSA* and the reasons, conscious and subconscious, why Newman threw himself so enthusiastically into the film and plugged it so avidly can be deduced from other remarks he made that night on the Frost show. Asked what element in his nature kept him ambitious, he replied "terror." He described himself as "a very private person, not good in front of people," adding that if supported by, say, Tennessee Williams dialogue, he got by, but on his own found it tough to say what he wanted to say. Asked what sex appeal was, he replied that he had no idea and was bored by the thought, and he insisted that his celluloid life had nothing to do with his real life and was only play-acting. Asked what picture roles corresponded most closely to the realities of his true nature, he said none of them did but such pictures as *The Young Philadelphians* and *From the Terrace* were "closest to the roots of the way I was raised." He said the reason his thirteen-year marriage has lasted is that "Joanne and I have no common interests at all," describing his wife as a lover of theatre and ballet and himself as more "primitive," with an interest in fishing, politics and "current events." He added that there is too much emphasis on youth today, that one doesn't need youth to be sensual, and added, "I carry my forty-six years with pride." Professionally, he added, there is great mutual respect between himself and his wife and a deep cooperative empathy. Asked by David Frost his future plans for his life, Newman said, "I just want to get through it with some kind of grace and style, both as an actor and a human being."

WUSA, in the face of all this, doubtless does exemplify Newman's sincere desire to make a

With Laurence Harvey

With Bruce Cabot

contribution to his fellows and to the current quality of American life. Unfortunately, most of the critics felt he had stumbled on a turgid detour on his route toward social-consciousness-style helpfulness, but any fair observer must concede that he and Miss Woodward merit creditable grades for good intentions, especially when their profession is so chockful of indifferentists and nihilists of all descriptions.

The plot of *WUSA,* for those who still care, deals with one Rheinhardt (Newman), a rolling-stone disk jockey and radio newscaster who hits New Orleans, meets up with Geraldine (Miss Woodward) a tart with a scarred face and a noble soul who becomes his mistress; and Morgan Rainey (Anthony Perkins) a social worker who finds himself duped by a corrupt neo-Fascist radio station operator, Bingamon (Pat Hingle), into investigating alleged welfare chiseling via fixed set-ups designed by Bingamon to discredit the entire welfare system and cheat honest, needy people of aid. Newman latches on as the station's star, furthering Bingamon's purposes (a sort of right-wing takeover of the United States) with existentialist cynicism fortified by frequent bouts with the bottle.

At a grotesque rally staged by Bingamon to sponsor and promote his phony brand of "big, clean, sound" Americanism, an enraged Rainey, now aware he has been rooked, attempts to assassinate Bingamon, but kills his assistant instead, and is then brutally trampled to death by the crowd. Rheinhardt goes to the microphone and cynically pokes fun at the befuddled crowd. Geraldine has drugs planted on her and lands in jail, where she decides she is fed up with everything and kills herself. At the fadeout, a shocked and mildly-chastened but still negative-minded

189

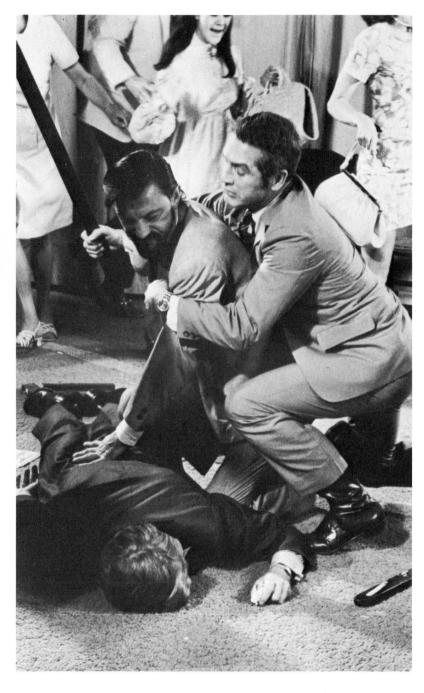

With Laurence Harvey

and existentialist Rheinhardt leaves Geraldine's potters-field grave to cut out for other regions. And that, as they say, is that.

REVIEWS

Roger Greenspun in *The New York Times*
If it were an ordinary bad movie (and it is a very bad movie), *WUSA* might, in spite of the distinguished names, and less distinguished pres-ence, of its leading actors, be dismissed with no more than a nod to the tension between Rosen-berg's ponderously emphatic direction and Rob-ert Stone's ponderously allusive screenplay. I suspect Stone wins out, for *WUSA* feels more like poor theatre than poor movie-making—so that it continually suggests a failed version of *The Balcony* even though it strives to fall short of *The Manchurian Candidate*.

But at least in its ambitions, *WUSA* is not an

ordinary bad movie. For in its climax, a huge white-power rally sponsored by WUSA (the patriotic hate station based in a Southern state), it means to hold a mirror up to middle America, to show the hate behind the innocence, the chaos implicit in the call to law and order. . . . Newman prepares to purge himself, to tell the country what it is, like it is. . . . In this sequence, during which Newman explains Vietnam to a panic-ridden, rioting mass of the thin-lipped, pinch-faced silent majority, *WUSA* has its crucial image, and, presumably, its rational. But in this sequence it displays most brazenly the utter gratuitousness of all its images, the bad faith that informs its self-righteous view of Southern demagoguery, the poverty not of mainstream America but of its own ideas about mainstream America. . . . Lacking either the grace of art or the vitality of guerrilla theatre, it can offer only the coarsest nourishment—and only to the elaborately self-deceived.

Judith Crist in *New York*

This is the kind of mess that results when moviemakers haven't got the courage of their intentions, let alone their convictions, and lack the guts to tackle a subject head-on or the faith in their public's intelligence. We need think back only to such films as *Black Legion* or *All The Kings Men* or *A Face in the Crowd,* to see that the coming or reviving American fascism can be dealt with openly. Fiddling around with lame-brained cynicisms and stereotyped philosophising, deluding oneself and beclouding the screen with pseudo-sophistications and pretended subtleties will not even convert the converted; it serves only to placate the know-nothings and convince them that they're far from alone. Of course Newman can be a charming alcoholic, cynical as all get-out; Miss Woodward an appealing lost lady . . . and Perkins is still the sweet psycho. But what they're all about in the frenetic context of N'Awlins and White Power in our time is beyond the ken of the unblown mind.

Kathleen Carroll in the *New York Daily News*

WUSA . . . was a complete turnoff for this reviewer. They, I suppose Newman and his co-producers, are trying to bury us with the message

With Cloris Leachman

that this country's current trend toward neo-fascism is a dangerous thing. Their message is only loud, not clear; and the movie itself amounts to nothing more than a lot of sounding off.

Frances Herridge in the *New York Post*

In spite of its flaws, *WUSA* is one of the most provocative and relevant films this year. . . . It is another joint effort of Paul Newman and his wife Joanne Woodward, and they are both superb. So is the direction by Stuart Rosenberg. . . . Pat Hingle creates an impressive atmosphere of evil power as the superpatriot, but his corrupt activities are too vaguely defined. The machinery of dictatorship is there, but its uses are minor. . . . Moses Gunn adds menace. . . . Laurence Harvey is amusing. . . . But it is the Newmans who carry the picture and keep it absorbing throughout. Never for a moment do they drop out of character. Their gestures, their expressions, their mannerisms—particularly Miss Woodward's—are original and honest. Their dialogue—intelligently written—is always fresh. A fascinating pair, and well worth a visit.

With Lee Remick and
Michael Sarrazin

Sometimes a Great Notion

1971   Universal

CREDITS

A Newman-Foreman Production in association with Universal Pictures. A Jennings Lang Presentation. Produced by John Foreman. Directed by Paul Newman. Associate Producer, Frank Caffey. Screenplay by John Gay from the novel by Ken Kesey. Technicolor and Panavision. Photographed on location in Oregon.

CAST

Paul Newman, Henry Fonda, Lee Remick, Michael Sarrazin, Joe Maross, Richard Jaeckel, Sam Gilman, Cliff Potts, Jim Burr, Linda Lawson, Roy Poole.

THE FILM

Sometimes a Great Notion represented the fourth collaboration of the Newman-Foreman Company with Universal and Jennings Lang. The film was plagued with troubles from the start of its production, which began on location in Newport, Oregon, on June 22, 1970. On July 29, while rehearsing for a racing sequence, Newman hit a dirt slick on his motorcycle, was thrown to the ground, and broke his ankle. After the ankle was set and placed in a cast, it was announced that production would be closed down for at least a month. Five weeks of additional filming were required to complete the film, with Newman in most of the remaining scenes.

Newman fretted restlessly over the costly delay. Then director Richard Colla, who had done only one previous film, *Zig-Zag,* left *Sometimes a Great Notion* and Newman himself, foot cast and all, took over the direction. By September things

were getting back to normal again, and Newman rushed the film to completion within a few weeks, this being his second directorial stint on a film. (The first was *Rachel, Rachel.*) For Newman as director, if not as actor, this was a change of pace, as the new film was chockful of extroverted action and physical brawling and assorted logging exploits, in contrast to the introspective, internalized mood-piece that *Rachel, Rachel* represented. John Gay's fast-paced screenplay, from the vigorous outdoor novel by Ken Kesey, offered Newman a role that was a sort of cross between *Hud, Cool Hand Luke,* and *The Long Hot Summer,* and though his new character, Hank Stamper, was not occupationally or environmentally similar to the other three, he was emphatically their brother under the skin.

As the scion of a rough-and-ready logging

With Richard Jaeckel

With Henry Fonda

family, always ready for whatever variety of excitement presented itself, Newman was exactly in his element. The always reliable veteran Henry Fonda was on hand as Henry Stamper, Newman's father and indomitable patriarch of the logging clan. After ten years, Hank's half-brother Lee (Michael Sarrazin) returns to the Oregon timberlands, full of bitter, vengeful feelings because of the memory of Hank's love-making with Lee's mother, Hank's stepmother, who has since committed suicide. Lee has difficulty adjusting to the Stampers, a close-knit, tough-sinewed clan with a logging history that goes back for generations. Henry is openly scornful of Lee's hippie-style locks and college airs, and Hank is gloweringly puzzled at his sudden advent.

Lee and Viv (Lee Remick) Hank's pretty wife, take an instant liking to each other, which later blossoms into something more intimate. Meanwhile, the Stampers have gotten into a labor dispute and find themselves, as independent, non-union operators, at odds with the striking townsfolk of the logging community. Henry is determined to fulfill his contract to deliver logs to the mill, and disregards union warnings that violent reprisals may result.

A series of incidents confirm these warnings.

Cables snap, logs crash unexpectedly, and Lee, who has decided to pitch in with the family during the crisis, narrowly escapes injury. At the annual Lumberman's Field Day, the Stampers get into a fight after a football game on the beach degenerates into fisticuffs when one of the townsmen casts slurs on Lee's mother's onetime intimacy with Hank. Later, the strikers attempt to dynamite a Stamper log boom and then tamper with the log truck, which plunges over a cliff and is demolished.

Henry decides to float the logs down to the mill on the river. The river is rising and the difficulties are many. Henry loses an arm when a log falls on him, and Joe Ben Stamper (Richard Jaeckel) is knocked into the river by a log and drowns despite Hank's efforts to save him. Henry dies in a hospital later. Then Hank finds out about Lee's involvement with Viv, who leaves home after telling Lee that there is no future for them. Hank beats up Lee, who does not resist. Later Hank rents a tugboat to tow the logs downstream. The river is high and rolling and the danger is great. Lee shows up to help Hank, who now realizes that his half-brother is a true Stamper. Despite the dangers, Hank's and Lee's operation is a success.

195

REVIEWS

Paul D. Zimmerman in *Newsweek*

Too many actors find a fantasy figure that connects with their own psychic needs and play him over and over again at the expense of their artistic growth. Sidney Poitier has Detective Virgil Tibbs. And Paul Newman is risking the same kind of dead end. As director and star of [this film] Newman plays the familiar, tough, lone-wolf hero of *Hud, The Hustler* and *Cool Hand Luke*. [Here] Newman does virtually nothing that we haven't seen before. He is still beautiful to look at and he still projects that sense of integrity that Bogart had. But there is no fresh information, as if Newman had nothing left to tell us.

Vincent Canby in *The New York Times*

Mr. Newman's handling of the logging and action sequences, some of which are as melodramatic as anything I've seen since Edward G. Robinson lost his hand in Hawks's *Tiger Shark,* is also surprisingly effective, not because of our contemporary fanciness, but because of what looks like a straightforward confidence in the subject. My only real objection to the film, I think, is a certain impatience with the screenplay, which lumberingly sets up almost every physical and emotional crisis that can (and, indeed, must) erupt before this kind of movie can be said to have decently met its obligations. Mr. Newman knows how to direct actors, and he has obtained lovely performances from [the cast].

Judith Crist in *New York*

[The cast] manages, under Newman's directorial hand, to surmount some incredible plotting and a lot of overripe dialogue and even a country-music ballad by Henry Mancini for openers. And in the surmounting, they succeed in hooking those among us who have a nostalgic feel for the old Hollywood mechanicals. In this second demonstration of his [directorial] skill [Newman] shows that he can go beyond the introspection and sensitivities of *Rachel, Rachel* and deal with the harsh primitivism of man and of nature. And oh, that Oregon scenery!

With Lee Marvin

Pocket Money

1972   National General Pictures

CREDITS
A First Artists/Coleytown Production for National General Pictures. Produced by John Foreman. Directed by Stuart Rosenberg. Screenplay by Terry Malick based on the novel *Jim Kane* by J. P. S. Brown. Adaptation by John Gay. Photographed by Laszlo Kovacs. Art Director, Tambi Larsen. Music by Alex North. Editor, Robert Wyman. Title Song by Carole King. Running time, 100 minutes. Technicolor.

CAST
Paul Newman, Lee Marvin, Strother Martin, Wayne Rogers, Christine Belford, Kelly Jean Peters, Fred Graham, Hector Elizondo, R. Camargo, Gregg Sierra, Wynn Pearce, G. Escandon, D. Herrera, E. Baca, John Verros, N. Roman, R. Manning, Terry Malick.

THE FILM
The critics and the public found the initial presentation of the much-ballyhooed First Artists Production Company a major disappointment. Shot in the spring and summer of 1971 and released in 1972, it was originally called *Jim Kane,* and Martin Ritt was to direct. Soon the film had a title change and a new director, Stuart Rosenberg. Neither helped the result.

Newman and company obviously were trying for new territory and wanted to show the cowboy as a not-too-bright loner, subject to the attri-

With Lee Marvin

tions of time and custom and circumstance. They later claimed, in the face of adverse reaction to the film, that they were aiming at a comic spoof of the western genre and that the aimless directorial style and scenes held too long for sustained audience interest had been deliberately employed to make certain points and to avoid the usual clichés to which westerns were given. ˈ

The trouble with this story of a naïve, not-too-bright cowboy jack of all trades (Newman) and his con-man pal, Lee Marvin, who turns out to be a bigger goof-off than he is, was that the "new and fresh" ideas ostensibly injected into the story lacked the power and force and attention-holding propensities of the time-proven "clichés" they were trying to get away from. The

Newman-Rosenberg-Marvin-Foreman combine had forgotten that old truism that to *become* a cliché, an idea has to have a lot of proven force and magnetism behind it and hence should be revised and expanded rather than tossed out the window. Another truism the ambitious "trail-breaking" foursome had disregarded was that if you get rid of one approach, you have to substitute something equally effective.

The dreary plot details the travails of the not-so-bright and the would-be-crafty pair of loons as they try to maneuver a herd of Appaloosa horses from Mexico back into Texas. They make every mistake in the book, shortchanging themselves with the horse dealer, getting their herd quarantined, and so on, and they wind up a study

198

in futility on a drab railroad-station platform. Newman, in trying for a fresh characterization, falls flat; he is coy and self-effacing, going against his screen persona and erasing his usual authoritative charm. Marvin has absolutely no gift for comedy, his appearance, mannerisms and chemistry invariably suggesting menace and cold masculine authority.

The story drags terribly, and Rosenberg seems to have directed in absentia, so badly are scenes set up and performed. The critical reaction for the most part was: a hopeless dud. That it was.

REVIEWS

Stanley Kauffman in *The New Republic*

It ambles and rambles, there are sections in it that almost audibly ask to be overlooked, it doesn't arrive anywhere much or deliver any great thump while getting there, but I certainly was pleased to be sitting in front of it. [The film] has two principal aims: the first is to parody the conventional Western by blatantly sidestepping all its conventions—the shoot-out, the chase, and

With Lee Marvin

With Lee Marvin

PM-17

so on . . . the second aim is the characterization of the two principals. These are good, largely successful attempts at American rural comedy. Newman is determined and not very bright, good-hearted and knowingly gullible, hot-tempered and quickly repentant. . . . Newman found himself a model or models, fashioned this man in his mind, and is that man, from his first onscreen breath. People sometimes say that they are hungry for valid Americana in American films. Here is an American folk comedy today. Expect little, get lots.

Paine Knickerbocker in *The San Francisco Chronicle*

The entire adventure is a waste of [Newman's and Marvin's] time and that of the audience. Everything meanders. It is as if certain footage was shot, and then someone decided to piece it together, hoping a story might develop. It does not. Included are aimless bargainings, fights, troubles, an attractive girl, a cattle drive, and then more trouble. Nothing seems to disturb the lackadaisical air of Newman and Marvin for very long, not even the conclusion of the film, which doesn't end—it merely stops. The film was toyed with, rather than directed, by Stuart Rosenberg.

Joseph Gelmis in *Newsday*

When you start nodding off into the z-z-z-s during a flick co-starring Newman and Lee Marvin, somebody has goofed. . . . Stuart Rosenberg, who stylishly guided Newman through *Cool Hand Luke,* gets lost in this one. It bogs down in flabby, uninspired performances. Nothing works. It's supposed to be a funny contemporary western about a naïve cowboy and his inept con-man pal. There's not a laugh in the film. [The adventures] consist of throwaway lines, non-sequiturs and anticlimaxes. I respect Newman. He tries. He cares. But someone counseled him badly on [this film]. Newman's Mr. Innocent isn't a Cool Hand Newman but a boob.

With Lee Marvin

The Effect of Gamma Rays on Man-in-the-Moon Marigolds

1972   20th Century-Fox

CREDITS

Produced and directed by Paul Newman, Assistant Director, John Nicolella. Executive Producer, John Foreman. Screenplay by Alvin Sargent from the play by Paul Zindel. Photographed by Adam Holender. Editor, Evan Lottman. Music by Maurice Jarre. Production design by Gene Callahan. Set decoration by Richard Merrell. Sound, Dennis Maitland, Robert Fine. Color by DeLuxe. Running time, 101 minutes.

CAST

Joanne Woodward, Nell Potts, Roberta Wallach, Judith Lowry, Richard Venture, Estelle Omens, Carolyn Coates, Will Hare, Jess Osuna, David Spielberg, Lynn Rogers, Ellen Dano, Roger Serbagi, John Lehne, Michael Kearney, Dee Victor.

THE FILM

Marigolds demonstrates an odd and arresting fact about Paul Newman. When he chooses a film to *act* in, he seems to seek out pretentious directors like Robert Altman and George Roy

Roberta Wallach, Nell Potts and Joanne Woodward

Hill, with whom he generates macho-style, insensitive spoofs like *Buffalo Bill and the Indians* or foul-mouthed, actionful studies in chaos like *Slap Shot.* The surface, negatively experimental, unsure Newman comes across in those films. But for the most part, when he picks a subject to *direct,* like *Rachel, Rachel* or *Marigolds,* he gets off his beer-swilling, existential, macho donkey and reveals himself for the intelligent, sensitive artist he in actuality is.

Newman therefore presented a strange duality that the 1970s public was forced to contemplate: Newman the somewhat false and forced extrovert of trivial pretension and badly cast macho projections as an actor; Newman the inspired and creatively illuminative introvert of the films he directed that starred his wife, Joanne Wood-

ward. In the latter he revealed, through subtle, compassionate directorial insights, his inner schematics far more affirmatively (and far more clearly) than in the acting stints he chose.

This was an odd shift: in his thirties, Newman seemed much less scared (as an actor) of honest emotion, as in *The Rack* and *Cat on a Hot Tin Roof;* in his fifties he seemed to be on a macho kick (in private life with his racing cars and on-screen as a performer) and seemed to be telegraphing that something in his unconscious seeks to hide his sensitivity; but behind the camera, it came out true and clear and unashamed.

Marigolds is a Newman-Woodward work of art. From the fine play by Paul Zindel, it tells of a frustrated, disappointed widow, Woodward, whose two daughters suffer from the infection of her negative, defeated attitudes. "Betty the Loon," as her elder daughter derisively calls her, is a failure as mother and as woman; she lives in pretentious dreams of fancy tea rooms she will own and manage. Her younger daughter (her actual daughter Nell) wins a science prize at school for deciphering the secret of the effects of gamma rays on marigolds (hence the plot symbolism), and at the end it is implied that she will rise above her environment and find beauty and fulfillment.

Woodward is masterful in her depictions of the many moods of the floundering Betty the Loon. "My heart is full," she repeats drunkenly, at the high school observance honoring her daughter's award; she is too far gone to rescue her own life, too sullenly self-involved to be aware either of the catastrophic effect of her defeatism on her daughters or of her youngest's eventual release. A masterpiece.

REVIEWS

Joseph Gelmis in *Newsday*

I can't remember when I've been more depressed and more moved on a nearly documentary level than I was with [this film]. There's a subtle change of mood at the end, an abruptly hopeful note that may allow you to leave the theatre feeling fairly exhilarated. I'm afraid that it didn't quite lift my spirits. . . . Though it's so grim a film that I wouldn't want to see it a second time, I am glad to have been exposed to it once—like an unpleasant inoculation against mean-spiritedness. And because I know what a work of love the film was for [Newman and Woodward], I feel sympathetic with their aims and hope they reach the wide audience they are aiming at. . . . What makes the film depressing is the frustration and the sense of helplessness you endure while watching someone pick psychic scabs and inflict pain on herself and the young in her charge. . . . But it's superior drama, because it's about basic human needs and thwarted desires and stunted emotional growth. . . . It is a socially significant drama presented in neo-realistic human terms. The performances . . . are exquisite. Newman's direction is unobtrusive, subordinated to the material.

Nell Potts (top), Joanne Woodward and Roberta Wallach

Nell Potts and Joanne Woodward

Kevin Thomas in *The Los Angeles Times*

The problem isn't that Zindel (the original playwright) hasn't created real people but that he and his screen adaptor Alvin Sargent don't know what to do with them. Zindel is at his best in conveying the potentially destructive impact of the embittered, negative parent upon children. However it's terribly hard to work up sympathy for [the Woodward character] mainly because she is so relentlessly, determinedly ignorant. Everyone seems to be acting, reciting dialog, rather than living his part under Newman's stagy direction. . . . [The film is] one of those high-minded, well-meaning undertakings—but hasn't been undertaken well.

Kathleen Carroll in *The New York Daily News*

Newman proves he is a remarkably sensitive filmmaker with a deep understanding of human nature. [Woodward's performance] is a triumph. . . . Her natural warmth takes some of the curse off Beatrice. She makes her capable of arousing our compassion. And in the end we bleed for not only what she has inflicted on her children but for what life has inflicted on her.

The Life and Times of Judge Roy Bean

1972   National General Pictures
Cinerama Releasing (UK) Ltd.

CREDITS
A First Artists Production. A John Huston Film. Produced by John Foreman. Directed by John Huston. Frank Caffey, Associate Producer. Screenplay by John Milius. Edited by Hugh S. Fowler, A.C.E. Music composed and conducted by Maurice Jarre. Song: "Marmalade, Molasses and Honey." Lyrics by Marilyn and Alan Bergman. Sung by Andy Williams. Director of Photography, Richard Moore. Art Director, Tambi Larsen. Costumes designed by Edith Head. Unit Production Manager, Arthur S. Newman, Jr. Sound, Larry Jost. Panavision. Technicolor. Running time, 124 minutes.

CAST
Paul Newman, Victoria Principal, Anthony Perkins, Frank Soto, Tab Hunter, John Huston, Neil Rivers, Howard Morton, Stacy Keach, Billy Pearson, Roddy McDowall, Stan Barrett, Don Starr, Alfred G. Bosonos, Anthony Zerbe, John Hudkins, David Sharpe, Jacqueline Bisset. Ava Gardner as Lily Langtry and Bruno as Watchbear.

With Anthony Perkins

THE FILM

Many Newman admirers felt he might have come up with something more dignified, controlled and artistically disciplined than *Judge Roy Bean* in the 196th year of America's Independence. Instead, in the peculiarly negative on-screen tradition he seemed to have set himself for the 1970s, Newman elected to be represented in 1972 in John Huston's badly directed and John Milius' badly executed screenplay, which set out to debunk the Roy Bean legend.

Huston insisted that the film "was a romp not intended to portray actual events," and Newman said that the film was "a fairy tale as far as being factual about Bean." In a decade in which the sober, serious, tasteful and yet highly entertaining *Adams Papers* were translated onto TV screens, educating and enlightening as well as enthralling the public, this misguided filmic tomfoolery perpetrated by Milius, then a callow twenty-six, and Huston, then what appeared to be a rapidly gone-over-the-hill sixty-six, aroused the consternation of everyone except possibly the undiscriminating young audience that the bankers keep telling the moviemakers they must film down to because "all they understand is noise, chaos and destructiveness."

By thus maligning the millions of America's youth that are serious, scholarly and questioning, moviemakers such as those who bankrolled *Roy Bean* show a contempt for the very audience from which they are trying to tease five bucks a ticket. The result in this case was a critical and popular flop of major proportions.

Milius, who in the fifties might have written passable Beach Blanket Bingo films (which were, incidentally, far more disciplined and far better paced than his mishmash here), imagines Bean as a capricious fellow who hangs people on impulse without proper trial, has a silly devotion to Lily Langtry, for whom he names the town he dominates, becomes a terror in the town and returns twenty years later as an old man, like a ghost of Halloween past, to wreak some more havoc among the oil derricks and auto-congested streets before dying courtesy of a blazing derrick.

Ava Gardner is handsome and dignified in the last scenes when she comes to the town to see memorabilia of herself and to read a letter Bean had written her—she is one of the few rational elements in the movie, playing Lily like a recognizable human being and not an overwrought caricature as is true of Newman, Jacqueline Bisset, Tab Hunter, Anthony Perkins and the rest. Maurice Jarre tries to make like Steiner or Korngold in his "poignant" theme music, but the goings-on are so sterile and pointless and foolish that his melodic inspirations seem highly misplaced.

REVIEWS

Goff in *Variety*

Newman is good as Bean. [The film] is a strange melange of fact, fantasy and violent melodrama. . . . The two-hour running time is not fleshed out with anything more than scenic vignettes—sometimes attempting to recreate the success of *Butch Cassidy and the Sundance Kid,* sometimes at-

With Victoria Principal

tempting honest spoofing of Westerns, and sometimes trying to play the story straight. . . . The overkill and the underdone do it in.

Roger Ebert in *The Chicago Sun-Times*

It's an incredible lapse in a movie of this size and ambition—but they've failed to make Judge Roy Bean interesting. He's one-dimensional, predictable, propped up by Paul Newman's acting style, with no personality of his own. There are a lot of characters in the background, however—too many. They walk onscreen, do their bits, and either get hanged or ride off into the sunset. Milius' script turns them into caricatures. [The film] doesn't have much flow and keeps stopping and starting.

Joseph Gelmis in *Newsday*

The film is not only anti-heroic, it's anti-dramatic. . . . Its self-mockery finally reduces it to a superficial joke.

Gary Arnold in *The Washington Post*

Milius modulates from the facetious to the vicious to the sentimental and back again . . . an episodic structure relying on crude jokes, dumb wheezes and gratuitous killings.

Kevin Thomas in *The Los Angeles Times*

As Bean, Newman may not seem quite dumb enough but he is genuinely moving and has great authority. Surely his performance here is a high point in a notable career. [The film] may not succeed in all that it so boldly attempts, but it is as big in spirit as it is in scope. Above all, it abounds with a rare and zesty sense of life.

Kathleen Carroll in *The New York Daily News*

[Newman's] tart, truly topnotch comic performance is the real gut pleasure of this movie.

With grizzly bear

The Mackintosh Man

1973   Warner Bros.

CREDITS

A Newman/Foreman/John Huston Production. Produced by John Foreman. Directed by John Huston. Associate Producer, William Hill. Second Unit Director, James Arnett. Assistant Director, Colin Brewer. Screenplay by Walter Hill, based on the novel *The Freedom Trap* by Desmond Bagley. Photographed by Oswald Morris. Editor, Russell Lloyd. Special Effects by Cliff Richardson and Ron Ballinger. Musical Director, Maurice Jarre. Running time, 99 minutes.

CAST

Paul Newman, Dominique Sanda, James Mason, Harry Andrews, Ian Bannen, Michael Hordern, Nigel Patrick, Peter Vaughan, Roland Culver, Percy Herbert, Robert Lang, Jenny Runacre, John Bindon, Hugh Manning, Leo Genn, Wolfe Morris, Noel Purcell, Donald Webster, Keith Webster, Niall MacGuinnis, Eddie Byrne, Shane Briant, Michael Poole, Eric Mason, Ronald Clarke, Anthony Viccars, Dinny Powell, Douglas Robinson, Jack Cooper, Marc Boyle, Marcelle Castillo, Nosher Powell, Terry Plummer, Joe Cahill, Gerry Alexander, John McDarby, Donal

McCann, Joe Lynch, Seamus Healy, Tom Irwin, Pascal Perry, Steve Brennan, Vernon Hayden, Brendan O'Duill.

THE FILM

"*Mackintosh Man* Strictly Applesauce," one reviewer proclaimed in a headline over her copy for this film. And applesauce it was. Having learned nothing from his previous negative experience with director John Huston, Newman joined with him again for a pointless Walter Hill screenplay (from a somewhat more professionally written novel by Desmond Bagley) about a British intelligence officer who is masquerading as an Australian in league with Iron Curtain types—Russians, of course. To worm himself into the good graces of those whom he seeks to expose, he gets himself jailed alongside a Russian spy, with whom he makes an escape. Then for illogical reasons he lands in Ireland, then on Malta, where he is soon confabbing with James Mason, a dissident member of Parliament who wants the spy who escaped from jail with Newman to escape to Russia, for reasons that are as obscure as all the other goings-on in this murkily constructed and mistily motivated spy drama.

Halfway through the film, one has lost interest in the proceedings and concentrates instead on watching Newman essay various accents in his assorted "disguises," some of them deft, more of them ridiculous.

Dominique Sanda won some critic or other's award for Worst Actress of 1973, with an accent so thick it would take a buzz saw to cut it, and Newman grimaces, struts, vaults assorted obstacles (to imply he is twenty-eight, not forty-eight, we suppose) and makes third-rate Actors Studio attempts to imitate Lord Olivier's knack of losing himself in the character. He gets kicked in the groin by a nurse in a hospital where he finds himself (maybe it's Germany, because she sports a German accent; maybe it's Timbuktu, so senseless and so rapid are the shifts of scene in this film). Of course, Newman being Newman, he kicks *her* in the face before exiting from the hospital, in the best nihilistic antihero tradition.

There is a lot more frenetic backing and filling and coming and going and skulking and hurrying—all of which makes for the dullest "action" stuff perpetrated on the screen in many a moon. Newman acts as if he were in a hurry to get through the film to meet an auto-racing engagement, and the talents of James Mason, Ian Bannen, Michael Hordern, and Nigel Patrick are all woefully misapplied.

Director Huston, who after the iniquities of *Roy Bean* should have seen the writing on the wall and retired permanently to his Irish castle, gums up this film with awkwardly choreographed scurryings and group ensembles that wax and wane like sluggish sewer water. Once more Newman displayed the bad judgment that had characterized his choice of acting assignments in the 1970s. But his next picture was to recover some lost ground.

REVIEWS

William Wolf in *Cue*

It's hard to believe John Huston made this drab film about secret agents trying to crack a gang that facilitates the escape of prisoners from

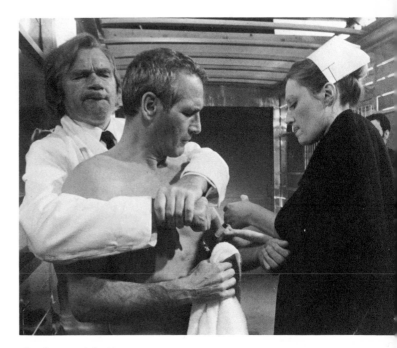
Getting an injection

Taking a beating

England, including a spy. Even watching charismatic performers isn't enough to compensate. The effort to find a way to escalate violence sums up the problem of this action film. Secret-agent plots are about as common as movie kicks in the groin. Nothing either new enough or exciting enough is found here to compel our interest.

Kathleen Carroll in *The New York Daily News*

The point is, none of this action means anything. By the time it is at last made a little clearer, one is long past caring what happens to any of these people. They are all so impossibly dreary. What is most appalling is the total waste of such fine talents as Mason, Harry Andrews, Michael Hordern and Nigel Patrick. Newman gives a flat, colorless performance in keeping with the flat, colorless look of the movie. John Huston seems to have directed the picture by remote control. It has no feeling, no tension, no nothing.

Rex Reed in *The New York Sunday News*

To tell you the truth, I had a decidedly unpleas-

ant sensation that I was never going to figure any of this movie out, and I was right. It is cold, unthinking and totally lacking in cohesion, and when it does threaten to shed some light on who all the spies are, it is almost drowned in obnoxious music by Maurice Jarre that seems like a direct steal from the *Third Man* theme. This is John Huston on a sick leave.

Penelope Gillatt in *The New Yorker*

Paul Newman [is] handsomely like Richard Burton when Burton first dazzlingly played Prince Hal on the English stage, but speaking in a slippery complex of excellent Australian, natural American and a trace of high-nosed Englishness. The script takes involved care to explain the Newman accent edifice; the baroque speech ornamentation could otherwise easily seem the work of a very wild mind. [The film] has very little humor, no drive of intellect, some dazed factual mistakes about England, and a lot of holes in the plot.

With Dominique Sanda

The Sting

1973   Universal

CREDITS

A Bill/Phillips production of a George Roy Hill film. A Zanuck/Brown presentation. Produced by Tony Bill and Michael and Julia Phillips. Directed by George Roy Hill. Robert L. Crawford, Associate Producer. Screenplay by David S. Ward. Photographed by Robert Surtees. Henry Bumstead, Art Director. James Payne, Set Decorations. William Reynolds, Editor. Edith Head, Costumes. Marvin Hamlisch, Music Adaptor. Piano Rags by Scott Joplin. Running time, 129 minutes.

CAST

Paul Newman, Robert Redford, Robert Shaw, Charles Durning, Ray Walston, Eileen Brennan, Harold Gould, John Heffernan, Dana Elcar, Jack Kehoe, Dimitra Arliss, Robert Earl Jones, James

With Robert Redford

J. Sloyan, Charles Dierkop, Lee Paul, Sally Kirk-
land, Avon Long, Arch Johnson, Ed Bakey, Brad
Sullivan, John Quade, Larry D. Mann, Leonard
Barr, Pauline Myers, Joe Tornatore, Jack Col-
lins, Tom Spratley, Ken O'Brien, Ken Sancom,
Ta-Tanisha, William Benedict.

THE FILM

Anxious for a hit after a run of flops, Newman
reteamed with Robert Redford, his co-star in the
highly successful *Butch Cassidy and the Sundance Kid* of four years before, and, under
George Roy Hill's direction, made *The Sting* as
a Richard Zanuck–David Brown presentation
for Universal release.

Once again Newman had involved himself
with a plot and characterization of stunning su-
perficiality (as noted, he seemed to save all the
more thoughtful, subtle characterizations for his
wife, Joanne Woodward, to project), but the
brew served up this time, despite its 127-minute
running time, was fast paced, well written and
highly entertaining, not to add extremely well
acted by Newman, Redford (their co-starring
chemistry was working away full time here) and
the fine British actor Robert Shaw, whose authoritative, indeed menacing presence added
immeasurably to the film.

Again this was a case where style and treatment were all, with the plot merely a convenient
(albeit highly convoluted) peg on which to hang
performances, directorial techniques and clever
photography (cinematographer Robert Surtees
went in for subtle brownish tones, lending a roto-

gravure look that suited the period, the 1930s, very well). Marvin Hamlisch, otherwise a good musician, came in later for some criticism by using Scott Joplin ragtime music at a time anachronistic for it, but it did add (for the nonpurists) some flavor.

In Ward's original screenplay, Redford is a novice con artist whose mentor is murdered by a mark who turns out to be part of Shaw's regional syndicate. The tangled trail lends Redford to Newman, a top con artist, who is planning a fake bookie joint setup, with accomplices Eileen Brennan, Ray Walston and John Heffernan, to trap Shaw in a major betting loss. Among the outstanding scenes, deftly acted and consummately directed and photographed, are Newman's sly feinting with Shaw during a poker game on a train, Redford's interlude with a compliant waitress (Dimitra Arliss) and the denouement, in which the protagonists square off to determine who is top man in all the games played throughout the film.

As before noted, style, pacing, and period atmosphere, combined with vital, ingenious performances from Newman, Redford and Shaw, inventive photography and deft direction from Hill—all these elements coalesced to make a hit picture. It was a film very much of the 70s, to be sure, with its style-over-content, action-over-analysis approach, but it was a hit combination of ingredients that Newman badly needed in 1973.

REVIEWS

Murf. in *Variety*

[The film] has all the signs of a blockbuster. Paul Newman and Robert Redford are superbly re-

With Eileen Brennan

Concentrating on the game

teamed. George Roy Hill's outstanding direction of David S. Ward's finely-crafted story of multiple deception and surprise ending will delight both mass and class audiences. . . . Although nearly every element in the film lends credibility to the story, the three stars make all the difference between simply a good story and a superior one. Newman, in a somewhat older role than normally, opens the door wide to another facet of his career: he rounds out his characterization of an old pro making his last big score.

Dilys Powell in *The London Sunday Times*

The few moments when the film falters in entertaining come when you are distracted from pleasure by the desperate ingenuity of the con men's plot. There is a puzzling twist towards the end; but that, too, I think, works. Anyway, [the film]

is directed and played with great verve; the 1936 underworld is re-created with delight; and the victims deserve what they get. You can sit back and enjoy their discomfiture.

Stanley Kauffman in *The New Republic*

It's more than two hours long, but if you can edit out about 20 minutes in your mind as you watch, it's passably entertaining. Three fine actors are wasted. Newman and Redford have, as actors, virtually nothing to do, although they are on screen a lot. Robert Shaw, [as] the racketeer, hulks well, but tries too hard to find the center of a role that has none. Hill, the director, is mildly competent but has no style or flavor. Robert Surtees, the vastly experienced cinematographer, gets more out of the picture than the director knows how to use.

The Towering Inferno

1974   20th Century-Fox/Warner Bros.

CREDITS

An Irwin Allen Production. Directed by John Guillermin. Action sequences directed by Irwin Allen. Wes McAfee, Newton Arnold, Malcolm Harding, Assistant Directors. Screenplay by Stirling Silliphant, based on the novels *The Tower* by Richard Martin Stern and *The Glass Inferno* by Thomas N. Scortia and Frank M. Robinson. Photographed by Fred Koenekamp. Director of Action Photography, Joseph Biroc. Edited by Harold F. Kress and Carl Kress. Sidney Marshall, Associate Producer. Music by John Williams. Costumes by Paul Zastupnevich. Art Direction by Ward Preston. Set Decorations by Raphael Bretton. Sound by John Bonner. Pana-

vision. Color by DeLuxe. Running time, 165 minutes.

CAST

Paul Newman, Steve McQueen, William Holden, Faye Dunaway, Fred Astaire, Susan Blakely, Richard Chamberlain, Jennifer Jones, O. J. Simpson, Robert Vaughn, Robert Wagner, Susan Flannery, Sheila Mathews, Norman Burton, Jack Collins, Don Gordon, Felton Perry, Gregory Sierra, Ernie Orsatti.

THE FILM

Having tasted Box-office Bonanza Blood with *The Sting,* Newman was in no frame of mind to let his guard down, and in 1974 he got into the "disaster film" act with *The Towering Inferno,* which had to do with a 135-story San Francisco

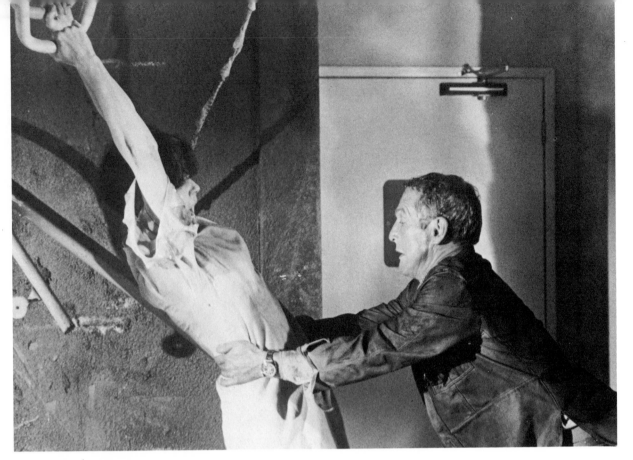

Newman to the rescue

structure, billed as the world's tallest building, and the night that faulty electric wiring and inadequate fireproofing led to a conflagration. Geared, as one critic declared unabashedly, to Neanderthal sensibilities, it is very 1970ish in that it evokes a great deal of terror but not one ounce of pity. But sex is not stinted—one stellar couple makes love until one of them notices that suspicious smoke beneath the door.

Two studios, Warners and Fox, and two directors, Irwin Allen (for the horrifics) and John Guillermin (for the relatively placid goings-on), got together for this film, to the tune of many millions of dollars, and the special-effects department had a field day, as it always does in films like this.

The plot? At the gala opening of the building, guests are trapped a number of floors above the origin of the blaze. Enter Paul Newman, the architect, William Holden, the builder, Richard Chamberlain, the cad responsible for cut-rate wiring and fireproofing. And then there's intrepid

With Steve McQueen

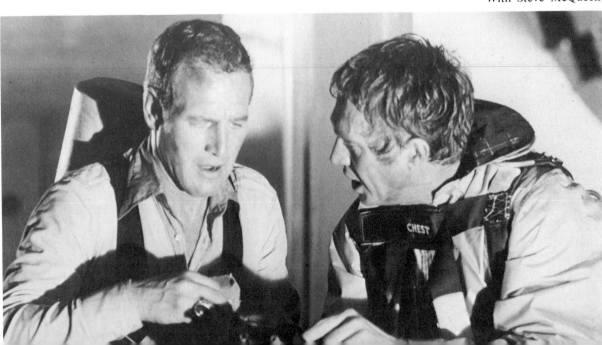

fire chief Steve McQueen, who holds lengthy, tension-filled colloquies with Newman while bodies fall, assorted extras scream, and all tarnation breaks loose.

Jennifer Jones comes out of retirement to fall many feet to her death (she'd have been better left on Wimpole Street in 1845 with the Barretts or in the convent with Gladys Cooper in *Bernadette*), and Fred Astaire just looks embarrassed as an old con man metamorphosed into a hero of sorts. Robert Vaughn and Faye Dunaway have little to do but look scared-concerned-fascinated, and the fires rage and the special effects bewilder and awe the Great Unwashed who paid enough into the till to make *The Towering Inferno* one of the box-office hits of 1974.

The perpetrators of this arrant piece of commercialism, having secured big names Newman and McQueen to make the box office absolutely cinchy, have used every trick in the book to entertain the audience. Newman is given scant chance to emote, being too busy figuring out what to do about it all, and the same goes for McQueen. Elevators fail, lifelines snap, tanks on an upper floor unleash a Noah's flood, as per engineers' attempt to extinguish the hellish flames. Result: Newman found himself in his second commercial success in one year.

REVIEWS

Vincent Canby in *The New York Times*

A nearly three-hour suspense film for arsonists, firemen, movie-technology buffs, building inspectors, worry warts—a gigantic cautionary tale for people who want the worst to happen . . . an almost interminable succession of rescue episodes involve lovers, frauds, villains, a little girl, a small cat, a mayor and his wife and other assorted characters whose life spans conform roughly to their billing. Actors at the head of the cast live longest. The special effects are smashing; the technological work is old-fashioned Hollywood make-believe at its painstaking best. . . . It has an advantage over most movies of this sort in that it has a really classy cast. Though the actors are not required to do much except behave well according to type, their presence upgrades a secondary form of movie melodrama.

Judith Crist in *New York*

The unique achievement is that all involved have managed to produce an asbestos film about a fire, one that even two—count 'em—stars like Paul Newman and Steve McQueen cannot ignite. Four babyblues prove no more efficacious than two. McQueen and Newman [carry on] a sort of Quirt and Flagg dialogue between suicide missions and such. . . . A film designed for the intelligence of cave-dwelling neanderthals.

Pauline Kael in *The New Yorker*

Despite the gruesome goings-on inside the world's tallest funeral pyre, a few performers manage to be minimally attractive. Paul Newman has the sense to look embarrassed, which, in addition to his looking remarkably pretty and fit, helps things along.

Rex Reed in *The New York Daily News*

Newman and McQueen could make me believe anything. The sheer force of their opposing presence ignites and gives the film an aura of excitement it might otherwise not have without them.

Dilys Powell in *The London Times*

I am left reflecting that addiction to Great Disaster cinema is lowering to the sensibilities. To save animal-lovers from fretting, I should add that despite the paucity of human survivors, somebody saves the cat.

In the drowning pool

The Drowning Pool

1975   Warner Bros.

CREDITS

A Coleytown Inc./Turman-Foster Production. Produced by A. Lawrence Turman and David Foster. Directed by Stuart Rosenberg. Assistant Director and Producer, Howard W. Koch, Jr. Screenplay by Tracy Keenan Wynn, Lorenzo Semple, Jr., and Walter Hill. Based on a novel by Ross MacDonald. Photographed by Gordon Willis. Edited by John Howard. Music by Michael Small. Art Director, Ed O'Donovan. Set Decorations by Phil Abramson. Sound by Larry Jost. Production Manager, Arthur Newman. Filmed on location in Louisiana and California. Panavision. Technicolor. Running time, 108 minutes.

CAST

Paul Newman, Joanne Woodward, Tony Franciosa, Linda Haynes, Murray Hamilton, Gail

With Joanne Woodward

Strickland, Melanie Griffith, Richard Jaeckel, Paul Koslo, Andy Robinson, Coral Browne, Richard Derr, Helena Kallianiotes, Leigh French, Cecil Elliott.

THE FILM

Newman in 1975 tried for the proverbial Three—meaning three hits in a row—but didn't make it with *The Drowning Pool,* in which he reprised his Harper character of 1966, who had been created by that prime crime novelist Ross MacDonald as Lew Archer for spectacular book-sales results.

This time around Newman based his Harper maneuverings on a 1950 novel by MacDonald, set in New Orleans. Newman answers the urgent call of a former romantic involvement (Joanne Woodward), who claims she is being black-mailed. Soon Newman-Harper is up against a

bevy of unsavory characters, ranging from mean cop Tony Franciosa to Woodward's man-crazy daughter (Melanie Griffith), someone's wealthy mother-in-law Coral Browne, a chauffeur up to blackmail (Andy Robinson), and an oil baron who is surrounded by beefy, sadistic henchmen and snarling attack dogs. Murray Hamilton plays this last character with unctuous deadliness.

It seems there's scrambling for an estate, and oil is mixed up in it. All winds up in the pool the film is named for—a drowning pool indeed, a hydrotherapy room that floods. Newman finds himself breathing hard as the water reaches the ceiling, but he manages to get out of it, you can bet, as all good detective-heroes do (or there would be no sequels). Newman tries hard to in-ject life into all this, but it has an aura of *déja-vu,* and though the cast tries right along with him, matters are too pat, the goings-on too predictable, and some of the performances too arch when they're not being heavy-handed. Stuart Rosenberg's direction is strong on hefty handling but short on precision and subtlety; he lets some promising situations depart before they have been properly exploited, and the screenplay emphasizes crude action at the cost of characterizational interest and plot-teasing. The result is that many situations are blunted where they should be rapier-sharp.

Woodward is excellent, as always, though her character is not analyzed in depth, nor is her running time of star length. Murray Hamilton and the dogs seem to come out best in the long run, though Tony Franciosa tries as the rascally cop and Coral Browne lends crisp incisiveness to her role (she gets murdered too early).

If Newman had hoped to duplicate the 1966 success of *Harper,* he was to be disappointed; critical reaction was luke warm, and the box office was only fair to middling.

REVIEWS

Archer Winsten in *The New York Post*

Throughout, the imperturbable Paul Newman at last triumphs in ways that are deeply soul-satisfying to his adoring public, which is the QED of this highly professional detective story movie. The suspense is constant.

A. H. Weiler in *The New York Times*

This second time around for "Harper" is a lackluster workout despite its colorful settings, occasional tension and a cast that includes Joanne Woodward (Mrs. Newman). As a convoluted caper it generates action rather than character and surface mystery rather than meaning. If [Newman's] performance is not outstanding, it is a shade more convincing than the characterizations of the other principals, who emerge as odd types and not as fully fleshed, persuasive individuals.

William Wolf in *Cue*

Even the presence of [Newman and Woodward] can't overcome the listlessness of this private-eye yarn based on the Ross MacDonald novel. . . . The script meanders from one crisis to another.

With Tony Franciosa

The direction by Stuart Rosenberg is equally perfunctory, and the stars generate few sparks. . . . The aura is one of a long, routine TV mystery melodrama. . . . The film is mostly a tepid collection of clichés.

Jay Cocks in *Time*

Newman is generally amusing and attractive to watch, even when he is chomping gum rather than establishing any stronger character points. His role demands only that he ask questions and piece together one of those traditional MacDonald puzzles about sudden death and damaged children. The dialogue is also obligatory, right down to the girl's wistful line, "You're not such a tough guy, Harper."

New York

The Newmans, of course, could get away with reading the telephone book; Rosenberg might just be up to capturing some of the nuances of that opus . . . a dull, dreary, and hackneyed pseudo-thriller clunkily directed.

Silent Movie

1976   20th Century-Fox

CREDITS
Produced by Michael Hertzberg. Directed by Mel Brooks. Screenplay by Mel Brooks, Ron Clark, Rudy De Luca, Barry Levinson. From a story by Ron Clark. Music by John Morris. Photographed by Paul Lohmann. Edited by John C. Howard and Stanford C. Allen. Production designed by Al Brenner. Orchestrations by Bill Byers and John Morris. Color by DeLuxe. Technicolor. Running time, 88 minutes.

CAST
Mel Brooks, Marty Feldman, Dom De Luise, Bernadette Peters, Sid Caesar, Harold Gould, Ron Carey, Carol Arthur, Liam Dunn, Fritz Feld, Chuck McCann, Valerie Curtin, Yvonne Wilder, Arnold Soboloff, Patrick Campbell, Henny Youngman, Barry Levinson and guest stars Paul Newman, Anne Bancroft, James Caan, Liza Minnelli and Burt Reynolds.

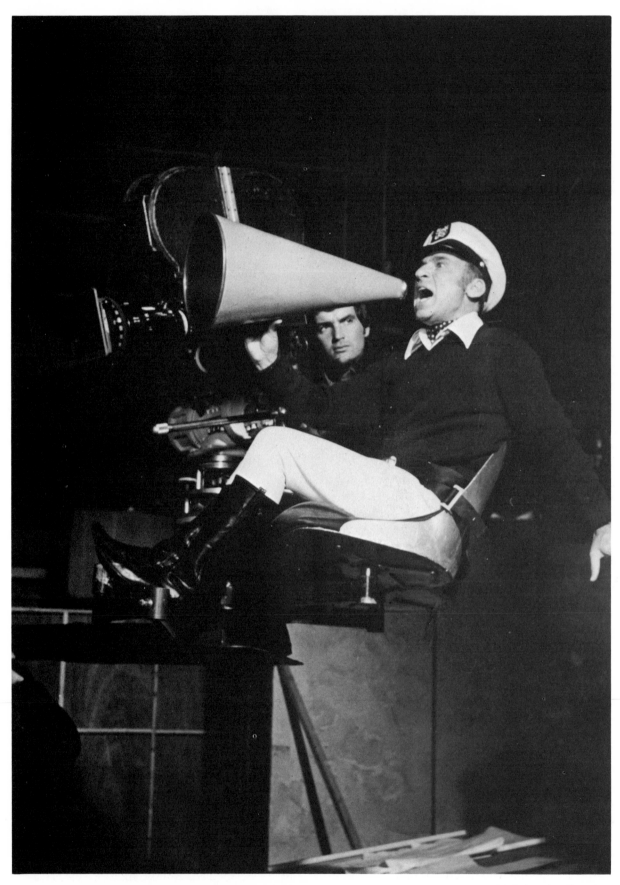

Mel Brooks directing

THE FILM

Paul Newman was strictly peripheral, in what is politely called (since its inception in the 1950s) a cameo role in comedian Mel Brooks's *Silent Movie*. He plays one of the stars to whom Brooks appeals in his attempts to bring back old cinematic times by making a silent film in the Hollywood of 1976.

Brooks is less his rambunctious self here, being, according to the script, quiet, sweet and vulnerable as he goes about pestering stars and executives to help him with what seems to be his highly untimely project. While rounding up talent for the film, Brooks and his two associates, Marty Feldman and Dom De Luise, rush about in a tiny sports car, and shore up the morale of studio head Sid Caesar, who has a variety of complaints including the project they contemplate. Then there are the nefarious machinations of the conglomerate, Engulf and Devour, which wants to take over Sid Caesar's besieged studio. And so forth and so on.

There is some added nonsense about the Engulf and Devour elements hiring a sex-pot (Bernadette Peters) to lure ex-alcoholic Brooks back to the bottle to frustrate plans the conglomerate doesn't care for. There is much slapstick of the usual Brooks kind, some of it deft, some of it leaden. Among the stars that the trio of Brooks, De Luise, and Feldman go about Hollywood signing up for the film within the film are Anne Bancroft (Mrs. Brooks in private life), James Caan, Burt Reynolds, Liza Minnelli, and of course, Newman.

In an interview with Ann Guarino of *The New York Daily News,* Brooks told how he signed up the box-office blockbusters for his film. He phoned them personally, told them he had a good comedy idea and asked them to trust his judgment, which they did. And he added that all five did their stints for minimum guild scale.

Newman is seen briefly rushing about in a wheelchair, his leg encased in a plaster cast. The next shot has *Daily Variety* announcing that Mr. Paul Newman has joined the venture. Liza Minnelli is persuaded while trying to eat her lunch, James Caan is lassoed while having problems with a trailer, and so forth.

All the guest stars give animated, amusing performances in the spirit of Brooks's intentions, though it is obvious that this is not Newman's natural métier, and some of his cameo colleagues fare better in the doings than he does.

REVIEWS

Jay Cocks in *Time*

[The film] is very much like a revue, laughs hung out on a thin line. It is a line that Brooks walks with zany skill, however. He is a tightrope artist who makes it from one side to the other with just a couple of false steps, and he has the inspired, reckless lunacy to turn a couple of handstands along the precarious route. All without a net, too.

Penelope Gilliatt in *The New Yorker*

We watch Paul Newman haring about cheerfully in a wheelchair with a leg stuck out in a plaster cast, in spite of which he looks very handsome. [In the movie] *Daily Variety* then carries a headline announcing that he has joined the cheerfully hapless endeavor. . . . The trouble is that though the jokes are for children, the references are very much grownups': *Daily Variety* headlines, showbiz financing, word-of-silent-mouth about success. There is nothing delicate or poignant here. . . . The difference between Mel Brooks and Woody Allen is perhaps that Brooks' humor rests on bulky rudeness but Allen's imparts fragility, solemnity and worry.

Vincent Canby in *The New York Times*

The lack of spoken dialogue doesn't disable the character. It's the concept. When you have a Mel Brooks who doesn't allow himself to be rude, testy and master of the low leer, you don't have a funny man. You have an affable floorwalker. [This] is not the greatest movie Mr. Brooks has made, but if you adjust your expectations, it could be one of the nicest things you'll see all summer.

Robert Asahina in *The New Leader*

[Brooks's films] do not work as cinematic comedies because they are essentially extended strings of raucous and vulgar one-liners, better suited to the nightclub floor than to the moviehouse. The only thing we are spared is the nervous sweating of the comedians at all those misses.

Paul Newman

Buffalo Bill and the Indians

1976   United Artists

CREDITS

Produced and Directed by Robert Altman. Story and Screenplay by Alan Rudolph and Robert Altman. Based on the play *Indians* by Arthur Kopit. Executive Producer, David Susskind. Tommy Thompson, Production Executive. Music by Richard Baskin. Production Design by Tony Masters. Photography by Paul Lohmann, A.S.C. Costumes by Anthony Powell. Edited by Peter Appleton and Dennis Hill. Running time, 123 minutes.

CAST

Paul Newman, Joel Grey, Kevin McCarthy, Harvey Keitel, Allan Nicholls, Geraldine Chaplin, John Considine, Robert Doqui, Mike Kaplan, Bert Remsen, Bonnie Leaders, Noelle Rogers, Pat McCormick, Shelley Duvall, and Burt Lancaster and Frank Kaquitts.

THE FILM

Newman did not seem to learn anything from experience, at least in some areas, and having debunked one legendary figure when the nation was 196 years old in 1972 (Roy Bean, courtesy of John Huston) and turned out a hopelessly bad picture in the bargain, he repeated the offense on the nation's 200th anniversary, 1976, by taking off after another Legend of the West, Buffalo Bill Cody. This time he had the pretentious and artificial director Robert Altman to guide him, and the result was roughly the same.

With Fran Kaquitts and Will Sampson

This does not seem to have occurred to the Altman-Newman forces, and the disaster of 1972 was compounded several times over with a mean-spirited, negativistic depiction of the rascalities and imperfections of yet another western legend.

Ironically, the television companies in the 1970s were putting out items of not merely historical but inspirational interest, such as the *Adams Chronicles*. In this respect, the television companies had progressed, while the movie companies had regressed, and Newman-Altman and Company led the pack.

Buffalo Bill is shown to be a topnotch carnival showman, an egomaniac with bad taste in singers and music in general, his legend "invented" by Ned Buntline (played by Burt Lancaster). Though he could ride a horse well, his long golden hair

Paul Newman

The script, by Altman and Alan Rudolph, based on the Arthur Kopit play *Indians,* which had achieved a fair notoriety, posed the theses that the white man mistreated the red man in monumental style and that the Wild West was a fantasy created to disguise the nefarious methods by which that same West was won. No one questioned that the whites were not of the morally pure variety, but some critics wondered just why Newman, Altman, Huston and others found it necessary to debunk, when there were fine historical subjects (the Adamses, Lincoln, Teddy Roosevelt, Andrew Jackson, even Washington) who might have been presented realistically (as befit the 1970s mode) but with some aspects of larger-than-life achievement and grandeur of vision.

Putting on a show

was a wig. The legendary fierce Sitting Bull (Frank Kaquitts) is shown to be quiet and civil, while Newman's Buffalo Bill is depicted as a boor, a lecher, a non-gentleman, and so forth.

"Puerile satire," said most critics. And they were right.

REVIEWS

Murf. in *Variety*

Robert Altman has already gone public with statements suggesting that [the film] is a disappointment. Well, he ought to know, but more to the point, he is totally correct. This presentation emerges as a puerile satire on the legends of the Buffalo Bill era. Silly when it's not cynical, distasteful throughout its 123 minutes. Paul New-man has rarely been seen so badly . . . rarely has so much manpower produced such cheap effluvium. Coming down hard on this film is like using nuclear devices to blow up an outhouse. Suffice it to say that technical production competence is wasted on self-destructive pretentiousness.

Kathleen Carroll in *The New York Daily News*

There is a danger in trying to structure and control Altman. His films depend so much on the natural exuberance of his actors that the editing, in this case, seems to have killed much of the original excitement. Paul Newman gives a marvelously loose, often very funny performance as Buffalo Bill, even though the character still lacks definition and Newman is stuck with an impossibly dreary monologue that drags the whole picture down.

With Joel Grey and Kevin McCarthy

Robert Hatch in *The Nation*

With Altman, you know yourself to be in the hands of a man of exciting visual imagination and almost alarming energy, who slams out pictures in a comic-strip *dell arte* style because that's the way he likes to express himself. In a time when salesmanship has succeeded steam as the prevailing mode of energy, Altman shows damned little solicitude for the sensibilities, prejudices, or even the comprehension of his audience. People walk out on him—five or six, I would guess, at every performance, and in the world of theatre that is usually a good sign: a few ostentatious departures signal that something at least unusual is going on.

Stanley Kauffmann in *The New Republic*

[Newman] tries hard, but is doomed. The Altman-Rudolph Buffalo Bill is two-dimensional, possibly biographically accurate but dramatically dull. . . . Nothing Newman does can make him a satirical epitome, as was evidently hoped, of the American ability to transform harsh experience into emollient entertainment.

With Burt Lancaster

Slap Shot

1977   Universal

CREDITS

A Friedman/Wunsch Production for Universal Pictures. A Pan Arts Presentation. A George Roy Hill Film. Produced by Robert J. Wunsch and Stephen Friedman. Directed by George Roy Hill. Original Screenplay by Nancy Dowd. Photographed by Victor Kemper. Music supervised by Elmer Bernstein. Edited by Dede Allen. Art Direction by Henry Bumstead. Ned Dowd, Stunt Coordinator and Technical Advisor. Technicolor. Running time, 123 minutes.

CAST

Paul Newman, Strother Martin, Michael Ontkean, Jennifer Warren, Lindsay Crouse, Jerry Houser, Andrew Duncan, Jeff Carlson, Steve Carlson, David Hanson, Brad Sullivan.

THE FILM

Many objective observers felt that Paul Newman, in his desire for sure-fire box-office success, catered to the lowest elements in the American population with *Slap Shot*, which the critics castigated for its filthy language. A few Newman defenders insisted that the objective of thirty-one-year-old scriptwriter Nancy Dowd's locker-room

Paul Newman

dialogue was to bring the humanity and gritti-ness of sports life more vividly to the fore—but just as twenty-six-year-old John Milius had badly botched Newman's *Roy Bean* opus, so Dowd now brought down a hail of criticism on Newman and Company for tastelessness.

Certainly the film in general, which deals with an aging player-coach (Newman) of a rundown Pennsylvania hockey team and his efforts to get it back into the big time via questionable meth-ods, came across as an amoral mishmash, filled with violence and strong language and anti-homo-sexual smears and subtle and not-so-subtle deni-grations of women. A number of rationalizations, of course, were posed by Newman apologists (*and* those critics who were puppeteered by the advertising departments of their papers to praise

any variety of slop if the ad setup were right), and as a result a variety of puff notices got into the national press, with the highlighting by the producers of the film's R rating praised lavishly when the truth was that the R brought in more four-dollar payments at the box office.

Newman parlays his team into major success by—it says here—"psyching-out the opposition with insults and converting his normally mild-mannered players into murderous goons." When the woman owner of the team tries to sell out for tax purposes, Newman rains harsh and abusive language on her. Newman plants phony news stories, alienates the more decent members of the team, like Michael Ontkean, whom he is for-ever trying to lure back into the action, beds down various females in sordid milieus and circumstances, and in general behaves like a cretin. As some critics noted, his was not a performance but a crude exhibition of visceral human impulses.

Why did he do it? Why did the director of sensitive human dramas starring his wife, Joanne Woodward, stoop to such debasing fare? The answer was and is simple. He wanted box-office winners; he had expenses to pay, a standard of living to sustain, retainers to shore up. Some of his failures in the 1970s had rankled, and in the view of some observers, Newman was out to bring them into theatres no matter what. None of the ads and puffs about "gutsy human drama" and "dazzling photographic versatility" and "frank, raw, adult situations" could disguise that.

REVIEWS

Arthur Knight in *The Hollywood Reporter*

Not even in my Army days did I hear such an incessant flow of four-letter profanities or coarse-grained obscenities.

With Michael Ontkean, Ronald L. Docken, Jerry Houser and Guido Tenesi

With Strother Martin

Pauline Kael in *The New Yorker*

[Newman] gives the performance of his life, to date. . . . What he does isn't very different from what he's done before: it's that the control, the awareness, the power all seem to have become clarified. . . . No other star in screen history has gone into middle age the way Newman has—at fifty-two, he's earned the right to be proud of how he looks.

Stanley Kauffmann in *The New Republic*

Newman is attractive, but it's all just one more lazy part for the good actor still lying dormant in him.

John L. Wasserman in *The San Francisco Chronicle*

The undeniably foul-mouthed language [helped] the major characters develop depth of personality and relationships. . . . A marvelous and funny film.

Richard Schickel in *Time*

There is nothing in the history of movies to com-

pare with [this film] for consistent, low-level obscenity of expression. Its producers, besides featuring an R rating more prominently than is customary, are also warning parents that its language is probably too rough for most kids. That's all to the good. Better to be up front about the matter than to apply a censorial pencil to a script that derives considerable power not only from what its characters say but from how they say it—i.e., *grossly*.

Roger Ebert in *The Chicago Sun-Times*

[The film] is going to make a lot of people happy, and a lot of people angry. It's filled with violence, obscenity and hilarity in about equal measures, and you wouldn't believe the words Paul Newman has learned since *The Silver Chalice* (his first, in 1954). Parts of the plot don't stand up to very close examination, but who's watching? Most of the audience is laughing and cheering for Newman's third-rate hockey team, and the rest of the audience is walking out and demanding refunds. There hasn't been a movie this divisive since the campfire scene in *Blazing Saddles*.

With Michael Ontkean

Quintet

1979   20th Century-Fox

CREDITS

Produced and directed by Robert Altman. Screenplay by Frank Barhydt, Robert Altman and Patricia Resnick. Photographed by Jean Boffety. Music composed and conducted by Tom Pierson. Edited by Dennis M. Hill. A Lion's Gate Film. Original Story by Robert Altman, Lionel Chetwynd and Patricia Resnick. Color by DeLuxe. Running time, 117 minutes.

CAST

Paul Newman, Vittorio Gassman, Fernando Rey, Bibi Andersson, Brigitte Fossey, Nina Van Pallandt, David Langton, Tom Hill, Monique Mercure, Craig Richard Nelson, Maruska Stankova, Anne Gerety, Michel Maillot, Max Fleck, Francoise Berd.

THE FILM

Quintet is just one more meretricious example of Robert Altman's self-indulgent and anarchistically meaningless films. It would be bad enough if Altman had pulled himself alone through the mire of pointless and often misdirected plumbings of his unconscious, but he has involved a lot of truly talented people in his negations, Paul Newman being the most outstanding of them.

Newman has an unfortunate tendency to put his trust in directors and writers who, throughout the 1970s, misused and distorted his image and acting abilities in half-baked, sophomoric trash that clever hype succeeded in passing off as some variety of "modern art" but that in reality was undisciplined, foolish effluvium that minimally talented directors like Altman pass off on a current audience that lacks the education and esthetic grounding to separate creative wheat from self-indulgent chaff.

Quintet is unmitigated nonsense about the end of the world, an ice age due to the world's being thrown off its axis by one war too many. Frozen landscapes, women who cannot conceive, dogs gnawing on those who die of cold, people wandering an alien, barren environment in passionless zombie style—these are fixtures of a scene that only an art director could love. Love it got,

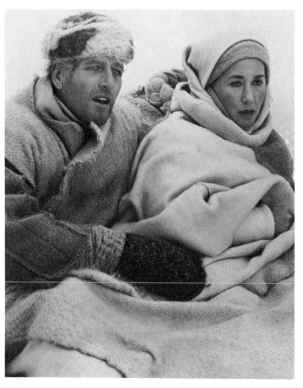

With Brigitte Fossey

at least in that department, with escalators that don't move, buildings steeped in snow at what might once have been airports, rooms chill and characterless, and all the rest. And that game called Quintet, a sort of backgammon in which the stake is death at the hands of one of the other four players, with referee Fernando Rey calling it the Game of Life.

Newman wanders in, gray and bleak, drably dressed in a furry outfit of no particular style, and finds that his woman and his family have been murdered. In tracking down the killer, he encounters the Quintet players (depicted at their lethal sport in one of many scenes of monumental dullness). Understandably, Newman gives up on it all (more, we suspect, out of boredom than out of fear for his life), and the last we see of him he is setting off across the tundra alone, for Divine Providence knows where—a place more exciting with people in it more rational, one would hope.

REVIEWS

Vincent Canby in *The New York Times*

Robert Altman directing Newman in a scene

235

At its least boring, [the film] has a dream-like quality that is very soothing even when the movie means to be stern and scarifying, if only because nothing seems to be very important. Like its characters, [the film] is passionless, to such a degree that when one person stalks another with murder in mind, there is absolutely no suspense. Such total apathy is not easily attained without the help of chemicals. At its worst, which is most of the time, [the film] discovers a lot of small ideas that sound as if they'd been borrowed from "Tomorrow," the shrilly dreadful song from "Annie" that reveals there's always another day. Some excellent actors move through the movie looking chilled to the bone, like guests at the end of a costume ball when the heat has been turned off. . . . It's not a movie for [Altman's] admirers but for members of his entourage.

Kathleen Carroll in *The New York Daily News*

Director Robert Altman was not only able to persuade an impressive array of international stars to appear in his latest project, he also con-

vinced them not to reveal anything about the movie to the press. Now it is clear why [the leading cast members] had to be sworn to secrecy. Had they so much as attempted to describe this bizarre, absurdly pretentious movie, they would have been laughed right out of town. In the movie business, as in gambling, it's how one plays the game that counts. This time, I'm afraid, Altman has played the game badly.

Andrew Sarris in *The Village Voice*

What redeems this film is its immense physical authority and Altman's mesmerizing camera style. Newman plays a straight heroic lead, with none of the distancing irony of Buffalo Bill. The result is an engrossing entertainment, almost in spite of its bleak spirit. . . . Altman's characters endure, as Altman himself endures, not by any shafts of wit but by sudden flashes of intuition and by a visual grasp of the immensity of the unknown.

With Bibi Andersson

When Time Ran Out

1980   Warner Bros.-Irwin Allen

CREDITS

An Irwin Allen Production. Directed by James Goldstone. Screenplay by Carl Foreman and Stirling Silliphant based on the novel *The Day the World Ended* by Gordon Thomas and Max Morgan Witts. Photographed in Technicolor by Fred J. Koenekamp. Music by Lalo Schifrin. Edited by Edward Biery and Freeman A. Davies. Production designed by Philip M. Jeffries. Special Photographic Effects by L. B. Abbott. Art Direction by Russell C. Menzer. Running time, 121 minutes.

CAST

Paul Newman, Jacqueline Bisset, William Holden, Edward Albert, Red Buttons, Barbara Carrera, Valentina Cortesa, Veronica Hamel, Alex Karras, Burgess Meredith and Ernest Borgnine, and James Franciscus as Bob Spangler.

THE FILM

Poor Irwin Allen. No matter how hard he tries to please, he pleases not—at least, not in the early 1980s and not in quarters where the film intelligentsia, snob-didactics and fussbudgety metropolitan critics thrive. The man who is identified with that genre known as the disaster film—the man who brought us *Towering Inferno, Poseidon Adventure, The Swarm* and yes, *Beyond the Poseidon Adventure*—has committed what early-eighties critics seem to regard as the highest crime and misdemeanor: you see, he simply wants to entertain.

I know good and bad stuff when I see it, and *When Time Ran Out* is no Oscar contender, but it is unpretentiously direct, moves along quickly and crisply, makes its points, provides more than its fair share of thrills and tensions, and the allegedly great unwashed audience with whom I saw it in a Times Square movie house seemed to be enjoying it mightily. Of course, it has a beginning, middle and an end and moves from point to point and place to place with dispatch; its cast give clear, economical, no-nonsense accounts of themselves, and—crime of crimes as far as the critics are concerned—it is free of obscurantisms, obfuscations, Altman-style nihilisms and nonsense masquerading as profundity. (No self-indulgent fusspot is director James Goldstone.)

In fact, it is in the good old-fashioned tradition of entertainment for entertainment's sake—a tradition that precedes even the Allen disaster genre, by many decades.

The plot is sweet and simple. A luxury resort island's volcano erupts after lying long dormant. Some people at the posh hotel want to run for safety; others want to stay around, gambling that the volcano is only making threatening gestures that will come to nothing. Oil driller Paul Newman (in a quiet, no-nonsense performance that is far from his worst) leads a gang to safety—but only after maneuvering passage on a frail bridge over the wildest lava flow I have ever seen. Jim Franciscus is the foolhardy egoist who keeps the others back at the hotel, where all promptly meet their doom. Going along with Newman are his love interest Jacqueline Bisset, hotel owner William Holden, elderly couple Burgess Meredith and Valentina Cortesa, Red Buttons and the ubiquitous (in such fare as this) Ernest Borgnine.

The action is all and the character development less than nothing, but then who wants to analyze Freudian or Jungian motivations when so much is happening all the time? A nice little item, this, perhaps deserving of no more than two and one-half stars, but its intentions are of the best. It did *not* deserve its relatively brief run and its cavalier press dismissal. *When Time Ran Out* got an unfairly rough deal, I say.

With James Franciscus

REVIEWS

Lawrence J. Quirk in *Quirk's Reviews*

Paul Newman's *When Time Ran Out* was barely reviewed in New York and the critics sneered at it no end, but I found its tale of an erupting volcano and its victims engrossing, entertaining, slickly made, without pretensions, and designed frankly to *entertain*—which, Heaven knows, few films really do in 1980.

Janet Maslin in *The New York Times*

The latest Irwin Allen disaster movie is *When Time Ran Out,* which is waxen even by Mr. Allen's standards. A volcano erupts in Hawaii, killing off an all-star cast in something like reverse-billing order. So those who die before Valentina Cortese does are mostly extras. And Paul Newman doesn't die at all. The ever-delightful Ernest Borgnine, without whom it is evidently not possible to make one of these things, is singed in a fire halfway through the story and wanders around with a bandage over his eyes the rest of

William Holden and Jacqueline Bisset

With Jacqueline Bisset

the time. But because the only other really big names on the bill (of Mr. Newman's starrer) are Jacqueline Bisset, William Holden, James Franciscus and Burgess Meredith, Mr. Borgnine automatically makes it through. The dialogue tends to be crisp. "It's rough country, so dress for it," orders Mr. Newman, giving everyone five minutes to evacuate a resort hotel. (They're all extras. They all die.) And a sample scene: "What happened?" "I don't know." "Get him to a hospital." "How 'bout you?" "I'm all right." No, he isn't, or he wouldn't be here.

Berg. in *Variety*

[Irwin Allen] has once again gathered some heavy boxoffice names, thrown them into seemingly hopeless peril and dared them to get out alive. Given the public's everincreasing resistance to these kinds of offerings, pic's stay at theatres should be relatively brief. [The film] has several of the unintentional jokes characteristic of most disaster pix and a handful of semi-scary scenes. But it basically stands as a poor imitation of a type of picture that Allen was much more astute at producing years ago.

With Ken Wahl

Fort Apache, the Bronx

1981   20th Century-Fox

CREDITS

A 20th Century-Fox release. Produced by Martin Richards and Tom Fiorello. Directed by Daniel Petrie. Executive Producer, David Susskind. Screenplay by Heywood Gould. Photographed in DeLuxe Color by John Alcott. Edited by Rita Roland. Production designed by Ben Edwards. Co-produced by Mary Lea Johnson and Gill Champion. Assistant Director, Alex Hapsas. Art Direction by Christopher Nowak. Music by Jonathan Tunick. Suggested by the experiences of Thomas Mulhearn and Pete Tessitore. Produced in Association with The Producer Circle Company. Running time, 125 minutes.

CAST

Paul Newman, Edward Asner, Ken Wahl, Danny Aiello, Rachel Ticotin, Pam Grier, Kathleen Beller, Miguel Pinero, Tito Goya, Jaime Tirelli,

Lance William Guecia, Ronnie Clanton, Clifford David, Sully Boyar, Michael Higgins, Rik Colitti, Irving Metzman, Frank Adu, John Aquino, Norman Matlock, John Ring, Tony DiBenedetto, Terence Brady, Randy Jurgenson, Marvin Cohen, Paul Gleason.

THE FILM

I joined a long line for a late showing of *Fort Apache, the Bronx* at a neighborhood theatre in Manhattan and found myself later in the midst of an audience, mostly below thirty-five, that seemed to me to represent all races and nationalities.

Amidst the smoke—grass smoke, that is—that at times threatened to obscure the goings-on in the film, and raucous and colorfully variegated obscenities hurled at the love scenes, the murders, the chases and the hostile confrontations, I got the distinct impression that this audience, which included many blacks, Puerto Ricans, Irishmen, orientals, Jews, Italians and just about everyone else, from what I could see, was enjoying itself mightily. There was some wild and protracted

With Edward Asner and Ken Wahl

With Rachel Ticotin

applause at the end from all sections of the auditorium. But their collective glee was mixed with some not-inconsiderable contempt, and one got the feeling that the typical movie audience lured into a showing of *Fort Apache, the Bronx* was there primarily to partake in all the excitement that the controversy over the film's "racism" and "distorted portrayals of blacks and Puerto Ricans" had generated and that their reaction was more curious than friendly.

I had a mixed reaction to what I saw. The sordid and sensationalized adventures of two New York policemen (Paul Newman and Ken Wahl) at the South Bronx station, known as Fort Apache because it found itself in a constant state of siege from all the wild goings-on around it, smacked more of the superficialities of TV cop-chase stuff than of a serious depiction of a deplorable social and environmental blight.

Newman never seemed to come truly to grips with his role; his performance is glib, surfacy, pedestrian in intent and execution, and he made no attempt to characterize in depth. There seems to have been some attempt to show that *all* are victims of this kind of blight: a young black cop is callously murdered, along with his white partner, by a crazed hooker (well played by Pam Grier); a white cop (Danny Aiello) unconcernedly throws a Puerto Rican youth (an innocent bystander) off a roof during a riot; a Puerto Rican nurse (Rachel Ticotin) falls victim to a heroin OD (she also doubles as Newman's love interest) and an oddly old-fashioned, indeed quite-1930s brand of sentiment is dragged in when Newman delivers the baby of a Puerto Rican teenager.

But I must side with those who declare that this film gives a biased impression of the unfortunate blacks and Puerto Ricans who inhabit the sadly blighted South Bronx; we are inundated with hookers, drug freaks, wild-eyed rioters, mayhem-perpetrators of all kinds; yet the law-abiding, constructive people of the area, though tendered perfunctory acknowledgment in a foreword, are given no chance to *balance* things via positive portrayals.

The argument is set forth that this picture shows the South Bronx from a cop's perspective and that cops deal primarily with negations. But why should this have precluded *some* sympathetic black and Puerto Rican images? The picture's overall conception is rampantly commercial; action is deified over analysis; humanity is shortchanged in favor of overdrawn sensationalism; there is no sense of the tragic, no compassion, no attempt to penetrate the dark, contradictory beauties of the human condition, which exist in all races, all nationalities.

I strongly suspect that some clever public-relations people undertook deliberately, on the producers' behalf, to drum up a lot of controversy over the film's alleged bigotry, one-sidedness, etc., with box office the motivation. If this be so, the purpose was certainly achieved. But if you are looking for a serious drama about the tragedies and contradictory subtleties implicit in the human condition; if you are looking for a sincere, deeply humanistic depiction of human blight and all who fall victim to it; if you are seeking a many-sided human panorama of struggle, hope, victories, defeats—you had better look

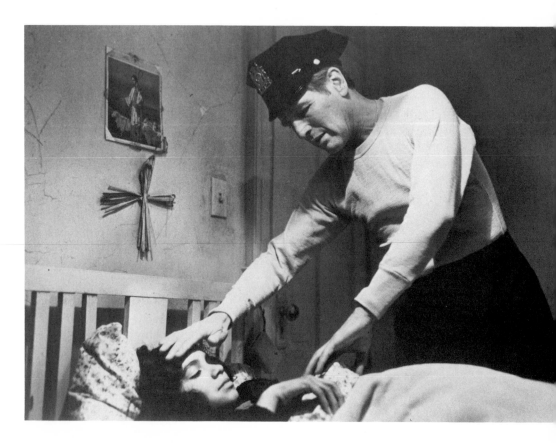

Newman helps
a Puerto Rican
teenager in labor

242

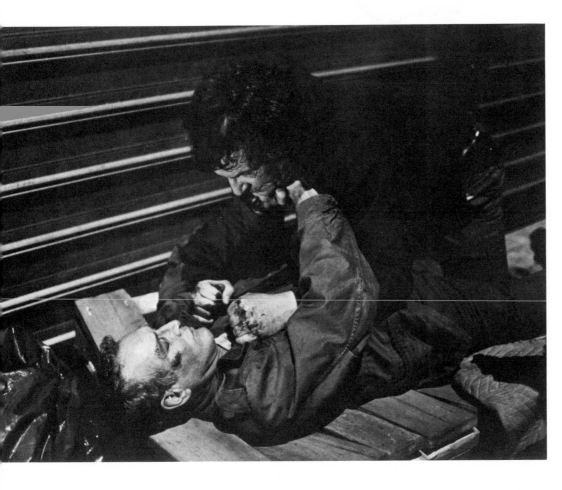

With Danny Aiello

to the future, to some artist who will take these same raw materials and forge from them a fiercely sensitive drama that *purges* while it *illuminates*.

Fort Apache, the Bronx at times entertains, in a cheap, vulgar, sensational way. The acting, especially by Ken Wahl and Rachel Ticotin, is fine. The conception is cheap, however, and the realization tawdry. But all that controversy, be it accidental or, as I suspect, cynically engineered, certainly brought in the curious for box-office results.

REVIEWS

David Denby in *New York*

Unfortunately, the people who've made *Fort Apache* don't seem to realize that a social situation of unparalleled chaos requires more than stock characters and TV-style filmmaking. Too many skeletons are stood on their feet and made to walk. . . . Newman's performance has greater warmth than anything on TV, but it's not one of his best. Playing a man who approaches the day's nightmares with good sense and even a kind of triumphant gaiety, he tries too hard for charm and all-around good-guyism; the performance lacks the darker shades that would have made it exciting. Daniel Petrie, working with one of the most frightening urban landscapes in the world, fails to produce a single memorable image.

Archer Winsten in *The New York Post*

Perhaps realizing they were treading on delicate issues, the makers of the film seem to have buttressed their events with factual material that's been frequently placed on the public record. Producer David Susskind, a veteran of publicity and controversy, is not likely to miss any bets favoring his side of a potential argument. Essentially, though, it's a drama of that police station in the Bronx, the men who man it, for better or worse, and the area's poverty-stricken, drug-dealing inhabitants. Those who object to the view should take into consideration that what a policeman sees and experiences is by definition on the seamy side. [The makers] have added another tense slice of realism to moviedom's long list of cop-and-crime pictures. It is not without pathos. Of course, the thoughtful center of the film is found in Newman's remarkably controlled performance.

Kathleen Carroll in *The New York Daily News*

This controversial movie, which has already aroused the wrath of Black and Puerto Rican organizations, rarely makes sense. Unlike *Serpico,* a gritty, no-nonsense cop movie that treated its subject with appropriate seriousness, *Fort Apache* seems to be reaching for laughs all the time, instead of trying to present the grave social problems of this urban disaster area as they really are. Paul Newman gives his most relaxed performance in years and he is admittedly appealing as he disarms a knife-wielding nut by pretending to be a nut himself or stops dead from exhaustion in the middle of a frantic chase. But [he] remains a half-baked, paper-thin character. [The film] deserves to be greeted with hostility,

but not necessarily by Blacks and Puerto Ricans. If anyone should be outraged by their treatment in this glib, superficial movie, it is New York's hard-working policemen. The two most arresting performances are given by Ken Wahl, as [Newman's] clothes-conscious Italian partner, and Pam Grier, as the demented hooker.

Har. in *Variety*

Driving relentlessly to make points that are almost pointless, [the film] is a very patchy picture, strong on dialog and acting and exceedingly weak in story. . . . Similar story fragments clutter the picture throughout and when the final corny freeze frame comes up, it seems like the picture still hasn't started. But Newman plays his character beautifully, as does Wahl as his protege. . . . Unfortunately the excellent talents of Edward Asner are wasted. Gould's dialog, however, is snappy and straight from the streets, creating one good scene after another. It's too bad the scenes never connect into a complete film.

With Ken Wahl

244

With Edward Asner

Absence of Malice

1981   Mirage Productions-Columbia

CREDITS

A Mirage Production for Columbia release. Produced and Directed by Sydney Pollack. Executive Producer and Production Manager, Ronald L. Schwary. Screenplay by Kurt Luedtke. Photographed by Owen Roizman. Production Designed by Terence Marsh. Edited by Shelly Kahn. Costumes by Bernie Pollack. Location Manager, Ned McLeod. Production Coordinator, Pat Matzdorf.

CAST

Paul Newman, Sally Field, Melinda Dillon, Bob Balaban, Don Hood, Barry Primus, Annie Ross, Josef Sommer, Luther Adler, John Harkins, Joe Petrullo, Sean McAllister, Rooney Kerwin, Oswaldo Calvo, Clardi Malugen, Frank Schuller, Pat Sullivan, Sharon Anderson, Jodi Wilson, Kim Nicholas.

THE FILM

Newman sought to vary his subject matter with *Absence of Malice,* which he completed in early 1981 in Miami. Sally Field, recent Oscar winner for *Norma Rae,* was enlisted as his co-star. A newspaper story, it deals with the complicated relationship of what has been called "those two natural adversaries: journalist and subject."

The fast-paced melodrama, directed by Sydney Pollack, showcases Newman as Michael Gallagher, a warehouse owner who has stayed "legit" but must live with the memory of his father's past associations with the underworld. Field plays Megan Carter, a dedicated newspaperwoman who is tenacious, often ruthless, in getting her story.

The two stars generate considerable dramatic tension under Pollack's guidance. Melinda Dillon gives a strong performance as a teacher who wants to help clear Newman from an associational smear she considers unwarranted. She makes the mistake of confiding in Field, whose "get the story" instincts overrule her humanity and compassion, and as a result Dillon finds her life ruined.

Pollack, in discussing the film with journalists, has cited Justice Oliver Wendell Holmes's dictum "There can be no higher law in journalism than to tell the truth and shame the devil." As a director who has always enjoyed pitting strong characters against other strong characters or against nature, Pollack has on his credit list *They Shoot Horses, Don't They? Bobby Deerfield, Jeremiah Johnson, The Electric Horseman* and *Three Days of the Condor.* During production he said of the Newman-Field combine: "Their chemistry is perfect; *Norma Rae* proved the strength of Sally's cinematic personality, and Newman's many strong performances leave no doubt as to his own continuing incandescence. Here we have a strong story, genuine conflict, two exciting stars whose characters are colorfully at odds, and I feel it will all spell Magic on the screen."

A well-known union leader disappears under mysterious circumstances (shades of Jimmy Hoffa), and there is pressure locally to break the case, with everyone trying to get into the act. An overzealous investigator tries to get at the true culprit by falsely implicating Newman. When Field gets wind of it, she goes after Newman, and the irresistible force of journalistic investigation meets the immovable object of a lone individual fighting for his good name.

Four
NEWMAN PLAYS

With Ralph Meeker and Janis Rule

Picnic

1953

CREDITS

Produced by the Theatre Guild. A play by William Inge. Staged by Joshua Logan. Setting by Jo Mielziner. Costumes by Mildred Trebor. Presented by the Theatre Guild and Mr. Logan at the Music Box Theatre, New York, February 19, 1953.

CAST

Ralph Meeker, Janice Rule, Kim Stanley, Eileen Heckart, Paul Newman, Arthur O'Connell, Ruth McDevitt, Maurice Miller, Peggy Conklin, Reta Shaw, Elizabeth Wilson.

THE PLAY

Paul Newman made his Broadway debut in William Inge's *Picnic* at the Music Box Theatre in New York on February 19, 1953. He played Alan Seymour, the rich boy who loses Madge, the prettiest girl in a Kansas town, to Hal Carter, his roustabout ex-college mate. Newman garnered excellent reviews for his performance, with such adjectives thrown his way as "well-played," "excellent," and "well-done."

Age twenty-eight at this time, Newman was a handsome and self-assured young man who caught the aristocratic nuances of Alan along with his insecurities. Alan is well-meaning, and, within limits, wishes to help his friend Hal, but he has no illusions about him, and realizes that he is unambitious and ill-educated and has traded on his good looks and masculine charm for much too long.

Hal, who was played by the star, Ralph Meeker, has wandered into a Kansas town offering to do odd jobs and he has a devastating effect upon the lives of Madge Owens (Janice Rule) with whom Alan is in love; her unattractive but intelligent sister Millie (Kim Stanley), their mother Flo (Peggy Conklin) and, above all, Rosemary Sidney (Eileen Heckart), a frustrated old-maid schoolteacher who is embarked on a campaign to get her middle-aged beau Howard Bevans (Arthur O'Connell) to marry her. At a picnic the hidden needs and neuroses emerge from the woodwork. Madge and Hal are attracted to each other; she is tired of being thought merely pretty and he treats her like a person. Millie develops a crush on Hal and is devastated when she realizes he prefers Madge. Rosemary gets high and makes a crude pass at Hal which causes general embarrassment. Later that night she begs Howard to marry her. Hal and Madge disappear, to Alan's chagrin and Flo's concern.

Later Alan has Hal accused of car stealing and gets him run out of town. Before he leaves he begs Madge to come with him. Flo urges her to stay at home, insists that Hal will only make her unhappy, will drink and be faithless later, etc., but when called to make a choice between love and the security Alan offers her, Madge elects for love with all its uncertainties.

REVIEWS

Richard Watts, Jr. in the *New York Post*
Here is a dramatist (William Inge) who knows how to set down how people behave and think and talk, who can create the feeling of a small Kansas town, and is able to write dramatic scenes that have vitality, emotional power and heart-break. There is a true sense of the power and wonder of life in this new dramatist. . . . There isn't a performance in the play that doesn't seem to me just right. . . . There is excellent work by Paul Newman as the young man who loses his girl.

John Chapman in the *New York Daily News*
The rich lad is well-played by Paul Newman. . . . Logan has staged *Picnic* with thorough professionalism. When an intelligently observant play is written, is acted by real actors and is directed by a man who knows his stage business, it means good theatre.

Robert Coleman in the *New York Daily Mirror*
Paul Newman is excellent as the boy who tries to help a pal, only to lose his girl to him . . . as we left the Music Box, the first-nighters had risen to their feet to cheer *Picnic* and its superlative company. Their applause was ear-shattering, spontaneous and heartfelt. We shared their enthusiasm for a stirring, tender, hilarious click. It has everything.

William Hawkins in the *New York World-Telegram & Sun*
It is a fascinating play, a jigsaw of action that usually conveys more than is literally said. Joshua Logan's direction illuminates the characters with his fantastically sure sense of what is effective theatre. . . . Paul Newman does well with the lovely sister's rich suitor.

Brooks Atkinson in *The New York Times*
Paul Newman as a college lad infatuated with pretty faces . . . [helps] to bring to life all the cross-currents of Mr. Inge's sensitive writing. . . . Mr. Inge knows his characters so well that you cannot distinguish them from the drama. Everything seems to progress under its own momentum once the characters are defined and the situation created. For Mr. Inge seems to have no personal point of view but only a knowledge of people and an instinct for the truth of the world they live in. . . . *Picnic* is an original, honest play with an awareness of people. Most of the characters in *Picnic* do not know what is happening to them. But Mr. Inge knows, for he is an artist.

With Karl Malden and
Nancy Coleman

The Desperate Hours

1955

CREDITS

A play by Joseph Hayes, based on his novel of the same name. Staged by Robert Montgomery. Setting and lighting by Howard Bay. Costumes by Robert Randolph. Presented by Howard Erskine and Mr. Hayes at the Ethel Barrymore Theatre, February 10, 1955.

CAST

Karl Malden, Nancy Coleman, Paul Newman, James Gregory, George Grizzard, George Mathews, Fred Eisley, Judson Pratt, Kendall Clark, Malcolm Broderick, Patricia Peardon, Wyrley Birch, Rusty Lane, Mary Orr.

THE PLAY

Newman returned from Hollywood, where he had made his first picture, in late 1954 to accept the role of Glenn Griffin in Joseph Hayes' exciting play, *The Desperate Hours*. In this he had the benefit of Robert Montgomery's able coaching, and he more than made up for whatever ego-wounds the abortive *Silver Chalice* film may have inflicted with a performance the critics hailed for its fiercely manic vitality. "Fascinating" was among the adjectives thrown his way. The play itself was hailed for its superb suspense elements, which at times amounted to the excruciating and kept the audience on the edge of their seats.

The story deals with three criminals who escape from a penitentiary and invade the home of an Indianapolis family composed of Dan Hilliard (Karl Malden), his wife Eleanor (Nancy Coleman), their daughter Cindy (Patricia Peardon), and their young son Ralphie (Malcolm Broderick). Here the criminals, Glenn Griffin (Newman), his brother Hank (George Grizzard), and Robish (George Mathews) terrorize the household while awaiting a package of get-away money from a confederate. The criminals play upon the older folks' fears of harm to their children. Glenn, who hated his father, transfers his feelings to Dan Hilliard and in general makes him and his family miserable. The young son repeatedly puts the family's life in jeopardy by devising means to get rid of the thugs, and at one point even maneuvers them out of the house, only to have them get back in via a fluke. Father and daughter are told to go to work and an appearance of a normal life is maintained; the boy is held as a hostage to assurance their compliance. The police, alerted, must stand by helplessly lest lives be lost. Eventually one criminal deserts, another murders a trashman and Glenn is eventually outwitted by the resourceful family.

REVIEWS

William Hawkins in the *New York World Telegram & Sun*

. . . a melodrama that frankly sets out to pulverize your nerves. Before it is over, it does just that. . . . And it also does the same thing to the nerves of most of its characters . . . the play is the closest thing ever attempted to putting a movie on the stage. . . . The setting shows a four-room house, an exterior and rooms in two other buildings. Curtains and lights block off the view and the action moves at a wild rate around the set . . . the most flamboyant of the criminals is a complex role played by Paul Newman. This is a real mental case, taking his hatred of his own father out on the world. Newman has exciting passages despite the fact that he tips the character's derangement much too early. . . . Robert Montgomery has staged the show at a sprint . . . a whirlwind

With George Mathews, Karl Malden, Patricia Peardon and George Grizzard

melodrama with no time for breath or wonder.

Robert Coleman in the *New York Daily Mirror*
. . . Hayes wrote a best-seller called *The Desperate Hours*. Then he dramatized it and decided to produce it . . . [the play] pulled the firstnighters forward to the edge of their seats . . . a terrific psychological thriller . . . the most absorbing chiller-diller of its kind to hit Broadway since *Blind Alley*. . . . Under Robert Montgomery's vigorous direction, it is played to the hilt. . . . Paul Newman, with but one previous Main Stem appearance, is fascinating as the mastermind of the escapees who wilts under pressure.

Brooks Atkinson in *The New York Times*
A graphic crime play that makes sense. [The play] does show more interest in the characters than most thrillers do . . . like a genuine writer, Mr. Hayes is interested in the inner life of his people . . . Paul Newman plays the boss thug with a wildness that one is inclined to respect. [The play] shatters the nerves.

Richard Watts, Jr. in the *New York Post*
[The play] is something a little more than a play to be enjoyed for its thrills and its atmosphere of

menace. In a fortunately unostentatious manner, wisely without pretensions, it manages to be a cheering and credible little tribute to the potential courage of decent, average people pushed too far . . . the three intruders are ably played by Paul Newman, George Mathews and George Grizzard.

Walter Kerr in the *New York Herald Tribune*
Paul Newman's grinning gunman, with close-cropped skull and a firm assurance that there's something in it—may start off with the throttle too far open, but it is finally an effective performance on a fairly splashy level.

John Chapman in the *New York Daily News*
There could be no more stir-crazy and animal-crafty desperado than Newman. . . . Newman's is a splendid, tensely maniacal performance . . . Robert Montgomery has directed the play to perfection. My hat is off to every actor in the cast, and I doff it twice to Newman, Malden, Gregory and Miss Coleman.

John McClain in the *New York Journal-American*
Paul Newman, the top gangster, registers strenuously as the swaggering neurotic who masterminds the festivities.

With George Grizzard, Karl Malden, Nancy Coleman, Malcolm Broderick and Patricia Peardon

With Geraldine Page and
Sidney Blackmer

Sweet Bird of Youth

1959

CREDITS

A play in three acts and five scenes by Tennessee Williams. Staged by Elia Kazan. Settings and lighting by Jo Mielziner. Costumes by Anna Hill Johnstone. Presented by Cheryl Crawford at the Martin Beck Theatre, New York, March 10, 1959.

CAST

Geraldine Page, Paul Newman, Sidney Blackmer, Madeleine Sherwood, Rip Torn, Diana Hyland, Logan Ramsey, John Napier, Patricia Ripley, Milton J. Williams, Martine Bartlett, Earl Snyder, Bruce Dern, Charles Tyner, Monica May, Hilda Browner, Charles McDaniel, James Jeter.

THE PLAY

Paul Newman returned to Broadway on March 10, 1959, after several years of continuous film-making, as the co-star (with Geraldine Page) of Tennessee Williams' powerful new play, *Sweet Bird of Youth*. As Chance Wayne, the beach boy who is the consort of a has-been movie actress, he

253

garnered the best reviews of his career to date. The play was far superior to the movie version which he and Miss Page did for Metro-Goldwyn-Mayer a couple of years later; in fact there is no comparison between the sensitive, able direction of Elia Kazan, who is in his métier a genuine artist, and the mere craftsmanship of Richard Brooks who did the film version in slick, pat style—and, worse, retooled the play's story to satisfy the Production Code requirements, thus draining all the bite and originality and fierceness out of it. The Broadway critics heaped such encomiums on Newman's performance as "perfect," "frightening," "moving" and "memorable."

Hoping for a film contract through the good offices of his jaded inamorata, film star Alexandra Del Lago (Miss Page), Chance Wayne (Newman) has come back with her to his Florida hometown to seek out his former love Heavenly Finley (Diana Hyland), daughter of corrupt politician Tom Finley (Sidney Blackmer). In her hotel room, Alexandra gives herself up to her favorite recreations, booze, hashish and brooding over her lost career. Chance had infected Heavenly with a venereal disease, and gotten her pregnant, and she is told by her family never to see him again. Walter Winchell tells Alexandra that her comeback picture has been a success, and she plans to leave for Hollywood, disdaining Chance. Chance's efforts to pursue Heavenly are frustrated by Tim Finley, Jr., her brother (Rip Torn) and as they prepare to come after Chance and castrate him, he sits in a solemn soliloquy mourning "time—the enemy in us all." (See the section devoted to an analysis of the movie version for a thorough comparison of play and film).

REVIEWS

Frank Aston in the *New York World-Telegram & Sun*
Mr. Newman is superb in a role that requires him to be almost constantly repugnant.

Brooks Atkinson in *The New York Times*
Sweet Bird of Youth is hardly a noble play. But it has overtones of pity for those who are damned. Although the old harridan from Hollywood is a monster, she is no fiend; she knows what she is doing and why. Although the young man is a monster, he represents the seamy side of the American dream. He means to take whatever he can snatch; he is the perpetual adolescent, steeped in gaudy illusions of success and grandeur. . . . Knowing his subject with chilling intimacy, Mr. Williams daintily peels off layer after layer of the skin, body and spirit of his characters and leaves their nature exposed in the hideous humor and pathos of the truth. As a writer of prose drama, Mr. Williams has the genius of a poet. . . . In the central roles, the acting is magnificent. . . . Miss Page is at the peak of form . . . and Paul Newman's young man is the perfect centerpiece. Although he has a braggart, calculating exterior, he is as immature as an adolescent; brassy outside, terrified and remorseful when he stops strutting.

John McClain in the *New York Journal-American*
It will be a very long time until we see a more moving portrayal than that of Paul Newman.

Robert Coleman in the *New York Daily Mirror*
Paul Newman etches a frightening portrait of a small-town hotshot who hasn't the stuff to be a big-shot. His disintegration, when he finally faces up to reality, has genuine emotional impact. Newman, as well as the audience, was moved by the concluding passages of the play. There were tears in his eyes as well as in those of many outside.

Richard Watts, Jr. in the *New York Post*
. . . whatever the sensationalism and the preoccupation with evil may be, there is the impression that they are being used to make a point in respect to Mr. Williams' dark vision of a tormented world. Here he is concerned with a doom of lost youth, when that youth has been wasted and spoiled, and the shocking episodes are his terrible symbols of destruction . . . the acting is nothing short of superb. Paul Newman, as the ill-fated young man, and Geraldine Page, as the movie star, offer memorable performances.

Walter Kerr in the *New York Herald Tribune*
Paul Newman plays [Chance Wayne] for all the greedy urgency and small-boy insecurity he is worth. [The play] is the noise of passion, of creative energy, of exploration and adventure. Even in excess, it is enormously exciting.

Baby Wants a Kiss

1964

CREDITS

A comedy in two acts by James Costigan. Staged by Frank Corsaro. Settings and costumes by Peter Harvey. Lighting by David Hays. Presented by the Actors Studio, Inc. at the Little Theatre, New York, April 19, 1964.

CAST

Paul Newman, Joanne Woodward, James Costigan, Patrick (a dog).

THE PLAY

In 1964 the Newmans took a sabbatical from film-making to appear for The Actors Studio in James Costigan's play, *Baby Want a Kiss* at a New York off-Broadway theatre—and garnered the best comedy reviews of their careers. Miss Woodward had always demonstrated a certain aptitude for comedy, but it was generally believed by critics and public alike that this was not among Newman's gifts. Surprisingly, he proved them wrong in this play, and the critics hailed him as "admirable and stylish," and commented on his "flair" and "attractiveness." Possibly it was the novelty and exhilaration of doing comedy on the stage; or he was glad to be back on the boards, or (this is the most frequently advanced explanation for his comic accomplishment in this play) Frank Corsaro gave him excellent coaching in his capacity as director. The play itself did not do as well as its stars with critics and public, and they were soon back in Hollywood. Playwright James Costigan co-starred with the Newmans and the only other character was a dog.

The plot concerned two glamorous and successful Hollywood stars, Mavis and Emil (Miss Woodward and Newman), whose domestic felicity as husband and wife is the popular subject matter of fan magazine lore, though actually they can't stand each other. These two frauds descend on an old friend, Charlie (Costigan), a writer who is far less successful. One reason for their visit is that they wish to assure him that success has not gone to their heads, and that they are still "just folks," but they only succeed in exposing themselves as thorough phonies and gilded monsters of rampant sexuality and self-centeredness. Mavis tries to find out if the hapless Charlie still has a crush on her; the narcissistic Emil makes homosexual advances in the course of a confidential talk—and after these two whirlwinds have thoroughly exhausted him, they leave him sitting alone and bewildered, pondering the complexities of human nature.

REVIEWS

John Chapman in the *New York Daily News*
The players, Paul Newman, Joanne Woodward and James Costigan, are admirable, stylish comedians, and they have time and room in which to exercise their undoubted gifts. And Costigan, the author, has a delightfully whimsical imagination and a sardonic viewpoint as he rummages among various human frailties. The director, Frank Corsaro, has staged this exercise most skillfully, making one hope that something may happen—but *Baby Want a Kiss* is eventless . . . an offbeat theatrical exercise [but] more fun for those who are in it than those who were at it.

Howard Taubman in *The New York Times*
Mr. Newman manages the rich Hollywood husband with a certain flair. When he fuels a fire with cognac or douses it with carbonated water, he has the casual manner of a man accustomed to living grandly. But in the scene where he proposes at great length to the author, he is like an actor who has wandered into the wrong theatre. And you wish you had, too.

Walter Kerr in the *New York Herald Tribune*
The author is not entirely without wit, any more than performers Paul Newman and Joanne Woodward are without personal style. In putting together a Costigan stew concerning the kind of plastic people who are now being produced by the American cults of success, beauty, virility and socially acceptable neuroses, our playwright has now and again put his finger on an obviously twitching nerve . . . [but] while Mr. Costigan is busy pushing his luck to the point where it turns on him, Mr. Newman and Miss Woodward are working quietly and intelligently to establish an atmosphere which will be possible for them, if not for the rest of us.

Richard Watts, Jr. in the *New York Post*
Perhaps it is good for the souls of Paul Newman and Joanne Woodward to absent themselves from Hollywood felicity a while to tell James Costigan's story. It is nice to have them back, too, because they are attractive players. But their appearance in Mr. Costigan's [play] is unlikely to contribute anything else of value to the battered cause of noteworthy dramatic entertainment in our harried season . . . the Newmans play . . . with not only skill and humor but high relish. . . . Mr. Newman and Miss Woodward prove they are game, have a courageous sense of humor and retain their acting talent but there is little other visible justification for [the play].